Let Me Be Frank

Let Me Be Frank
My Life at Virginia Tech

Frank Beamer

with Jeff Snook

TRIUMPH
BOOKS

Library of Congress Cataloging-in-Publication Data
Beamer, Frank.
  Let me be Frank : my life at Virginia Tech / Frank Beamer with Jeff Snook.
    pages cm
  ISBN 978-1-60078-846-8 (hardback)
  1. Beamer, Frank. 2. Football coaches—United States—Biography.
  3. Virginia Tech Hokies (Football team)—History. 4. Virginia Polytechnic
Institute and State University—Football—History. I. Snook, Jeff, 1960– II. Title.
  GV939.B423A3 2013
  796.332092--dc23
  [B]
                                                          2013019897

This book is available in quantity at special discounts for your group or organization. For further information, contact:
    Triumph Books LLC
    814 North Franklin Street
    Chicago, Illinois 60610
    (312) 939-3330
    www.triumphbooks.com

Printed in U.S.A.

ISBN: 978-1-60078-846-8

Design by Amy Carter

Photos courtesy of the author except where otherwise noted.

To Hokie fans everywhere, you've made coaching for my alma mater a pleasure.

To all of the assistants who have worked for me since 1981, my success is your success.

To the hundreds of players who have played for me, I can honestly say it was an honor to be your coach.

To John Ballein, our director of football operations at Virginia Tech, I have always trusted your guidance and treasured your friendship.

And to Cheryl, the head coach of our family, your support was always there for me when I needed it most.

—Frank Beamer

To the memories of the 27 Virginia Tech University students and five professors who needlessly died on one of the darkest days in U.S. history, April 16, 2007; and to the survivors and first responders whose lives will never be the same.

—Jeff Snook

Contents

	Foreword by *Bob Knight*	viii
	Introduction	xi
CHAPTER 1:	Go Out of Your Way to Make Good Memories	1
CHAPTER 2:	Humble Beginnings	6
CHAPTER 3:	Playing Days	18
CHAPTER 4:	To Teach or to Coach?	32
CHAPTER 5:	Coming Home	54
CHAPTER 6:	Turning It Around	68
CHAPTER 7:	A Special Player, a Special Season	90
CHAPTER 8:	One Night in New Orleans	101
CHAPTER 9:	Two Years and Out	115
CHAPTER 10:	My Loyalty Is Tested	125
CHAPTER 11:	The Quarterback Closest to Michael Vick	132
CHAPTER 12:	Winning off the Field	140
CHAPTER 13:	Darkest Day in Virginia Tech History	158
CHAPTER 14:	Did We Make a Difference?	174
CHAPTER 15:	Recruiting: How Many Stars? Who Cares?	182
CHAPTER 16:	They Call It "Beamer Ball"	197
CHAPTER 17:	Don't Get Too High and Don't Get Too Low	205
CHAPTER 18:	Surround Yourself with Good People	224
CHAPTER 19:	Hitting the Links	237
CHAPTER 20:	College Football: The Game I Love	262
CHAPTER 21:	What's Next?	278
	Acknowledgments	291

Foreword

When I first started my coaching career, I always took the time to study other coaches, such as Henry Iba, who coached for 36 years at Oklahoma State; the legendary Pete Newell; Joe Lapchick; and my old coach at Ohio State, Fred Taylor, who took us to three consecutive Final Fours while I was in college.

I wanted to learn what things were important to their coaching philosophies and what approaches brought about winning records and championship teams. Later on, I was fortunate to get to know all of these wonderful coaches.

I didn't just limit this to basketball—I did the same with football. I spent probably as much time looking at the older football coaches and how they did their jobs as I did the basketball coaching legends. I studied Vince Lombardi even though he is the one coach I never had the opportunity to meet. I studied Paul Brown and Woody Hayes. As a student at Ohio State, I once took a class from Coach Hayes and later had him speak to my Indiana basketball teams.

Later, Bo Schembechler and I became very good friends. He had been an assistant coach at Ohio State while I was a student there.

When he became the head coach at Michigan, we had a lot in common over the years and got to know each other well. Bo once told me I was his closest friend within the Big Ten and that meant the world to me.

One day, Bo and I were having a conversation about football coaches and he mentioned Frank Beamer's name. He had a very high regard for what Coach Beamer was doing at Virginia Tech.

I already was interested in Frank's program, because he was winning, and yet I knew he wasn't in one of the best recruiting areas in the country. Southwest Virginia is beautiful, but he had to go a ways to find the necessary numbers of top football players to compete at that level. There wasn't the population base there to provide a fertile recruiting ground as some other top programs had. Most really good programs like Ohio State or Michigan or Texas or Oklahoma have one thing in common—great recruiting areas. It was much easier for kids in the East to get to all those schools on the Eastern seaboard than it was to get to Blacksburg, Virginia.

As the years went on, I continued to pay attention to Virginia Tech. Nobody did a greater job of consistently putting together good teams that could compete with anybody in the country. The consistency—20 consecutive seasons of winning records and bowl games—speaks for itself. Frank's teams have been good year after year.

He has established a program and a situation where kids want to come to Virginia Tech, because they would be playing for Frank Beamer.

Another thing I noticed is what he did defensively over the years coincided with my philosophy in basketball. You have to be able to keep the other guy in reach and keep him from scoring a bundle of points on you. Rarely did Virginia Tech have poor defenses, and I know that is a credit to his defensive coordinator, Bud Foster, as well.

During one of my trips to Blacksburg to call a college game a few years ago, I sat down with Frank and we discussed offense and defense and how to attack the other team. I listened to him for a while and I was very impressed with everything he had to say.

On January 3, 2012, I was watching the Sugar Bowl on television. I couldn't help but think Virginia Tech got screwed that night by the replay official who overturned a touchdown that would have beaten Michigan. Frank went about his business and continued to coach the game and really handled himself very well.

That next week, I called him in his office to tell him I admired the way he handled himself and how he coached his kids to play hard and to play the game the right way. You rarely ever see Virginia Tech kids acting up or taunting or celebrating. I could tell that his kids always behaved the right way on the football field.

The other thing that has impressed me has been Virginia Tech's graduation rates. I can tell that having his kids get a college education means so much to him. And I would bet you this: they may not realize what Coach Beamer has done for them or what he means to them until they finish football and are gone from Virginia Tech. But I guarantee you they will all realize it at some point in their lives.

Frank Beamer's at the top of his field in wins and graduation rates and in developing his players as good people. You can't ask any more from a coach than that. He's a great example for any of us in the coaching business.

I want to say one final thing here: I wouldn't write the foreword for a book for just anyone, but I am pleased—in fact, I am very tickled—to do this. I consider it an honor to write the foreword for Coach Beamer's book.

I am sure you will find it worth reading.

—Bob Knight

Introduction

Frank Beamer eased his car into a parking spot at the head of the famed Drillfield at Virginia Tech. He waved to one of his football players sitting on a nearby bench and walked slowly over to the 32 stone memorials representing the students and professors who died on April 16, 2007.

Flowers were laid at the base of a few monuments and one was covered with happy birthday notes. Beamer stared down and shook his head. It was May 24, 2012—more than five years since the deadliest mass shooting in U.S. history.

The head football coach of the university sees these monuments during his daily walk while he is in Blacksburg, but their significance never diminishes with time.

"I walk by them every day and I think about it every day," he said. "It's not something anybody around here will ever forget."

He turned and walked away, heading up to the steps toward Norris Hall, the site of the shooting.

A groundskeeper recognized him and instantly put down his shovel and smiled.

"How you doing today?" Beamer asked.

"Good, Coach, thanks for asking," the man answered, grabbing his shovel to resume his work.

Beamer, a 1969 Virginia Tech graduate, grabbed the door handle and entered Norris Hall.

"I am pretty sure this is the first time I have ever been in this building…I don't think I ever had a class in here," he told a visitor. "Look at the doors. The handles have been re-designed so you cannot chain them shut. Everything smells new…new linoleum…new paint."

As he reached the second floor, he stopped and looked down the hallway. Odd-numbered rooms were to his left and even-numbered rooms to his right.

"Which side did the shootings take place?" he asked.

"Both sides," he was told. "People were killed in every room."

He shook his head again and peered inside Room 204 and noticed a framed picture of Liviu Librescu, the 76-year-old professor of engineering and Holocaust survivor. Librescu's students later said he blocked the door to prevent the gunman from entering while some students took cover underneath desks and others leaped out windows. The professor then was killed in the doorway.

"You know, he really looks familiar to me, like I had met him before, but I can't be sure," he said. "I know one thing: he died a hero."

He closed the door and walked toward the steps, turning for one more glance down the hallway, as if to commit the scene to memory.

"Hard to imagine," he said. "It's just hard to imagine. So many lives lost here…all needlessly lost because of one disturbed man. This place has come back strong though. I think students and teachers and everyone at Virginia Tech have grown closer because of this tragedy. You just have to hope it never happens again."

Less than six months later, on November 1, Beamer stood on a small stepladder as his team gathered around him in the bowels of Sun Life Stadium in Miami. His players were covered in grass stains, sweat and disappointment, having lost 30–12 to the Miami Hurricanes moments earlier. The Hokies had a 4–5 record—the school's first losing record this deep into the season in 20 years.

"Look at me! I want your attention!" he shouted. "You are better than this! We need to start playing our asses off! Y'all are standing around feeling sorry for yourselves. Just keep fighting! Keep fighting!"

He paused for a moment and lowered his voice a little.

"I do know this: something good will come out of this," he said. "Next Thursday night, the best team in the ACC is coming to our place, and if we do what we are supposed to do over the next week, we will be celebrating a week from right now. Now…show some class when talking to the media. Give credit to the other team for beating us."

The Hokies didn't celebrate a week later either, but they did fight eighth-ranked Florida State to the end before losing 28–22, as the Seminoles scored the winning touchdown with only 40 seconds remaining. In a season of tough losses, this was the toughest. Virginia Tech would have to win its final two games to extend its consecutive bowl streak to 20 years. Then they would have to win the bowl to avoid the first losing season since 1992.

"We've experienced some things this year that guys haven't experienced around here in a long time," Beamer admitted. "It's tough, but you can never feel sorry for yourself."

Eight weeks later, on a warm, sunny day in Orlando, Florida, the longest-tenured and winningest coach in major college football stood at midfield of the Citrus Bowl.

It was December 26 and his team had just concluded practice preparing to face Rutgers in a bowl game, which would kick off two days later. Just as he had hoped, his team had beaten Boston College in overtime and rival Virginia with a late field goal in the season's final two games to qualify for the bowl. They showed the fight he was looking for in winning those two games amidst mounting pressure.

On this day, their maroon helmets were adorned with a green and orange ribbon with the No. 58 underneath the word "PREVAIL."

Because, 12 days earlier, *it* had happened again.

A shooting at Sandy Hook Elementary School in Newtown, Connecticut, had left 26 students and teachers dead. The "58" on the Virginia Tech helmets represented the total number of victims from the two mass killings. The team mapped out its plans for the week: beat Rutgers and then send the banner, adorned with the giant "58" ribbon, which they would carry onto the field, to the Sandy Hook school, along with a signed helmet.

At this moment, however, Beamer just wanted to compliment his players.

"I am proud of the way you handled yourselves yesterday at the 'Give Kids the World Village.' You see those kids who have illnesses and it puts it all into perspective, doesn't it? The people who work there told us that you were the best group that they've ever hosted, and they do this every year with both bowl teams," he told his players. "I am happy to hear that. It's one of the things which make me proud of you. You never know when you meet somebody if they can help you down the road. Anyway, it's always good to be nice to people.

"Now, curfew is at what time?"

"*Eleven!*" came the reply in unison.

"And no what?"

"*Drinking!*" came a second reply.

"Now we all know we didn't have a great year. We had some rough times, long days, and tough losses. But you didn't get down on yourself and you fought your way through it. You fought your way to get here and kept our bowl streak alive and I am proud of you for that. I really am. We have a lot to play for in this game. Rutgers is a good football team and they will be ready to play, because they say this is the biggest bowl they've ever been to. One thing about these bowls… the underdog wins a lot of them because they are ready to play. They *want* it more. We need to be ready to play. We have a streak of having a winning record on the line. Now what will we do?"

"Play for each other!"

The next morning, Rutgers coach Kyle Flood sat at a podium during a press conference to promote the bowl. He said one of the highlights of the week was having his 10-year-old son meet the Virginia Tech head coach.

"He doesn't realize it yet, but he got to shake the hand of a legend," Flood said. "Someday he will know how big it was."

When Flood finished, Beamer entered the room and took his turn with the media.

"Coach, how has your demeanor been this season given it didn't go the way you wanted?" a reporter asked. "Have you been a little grumpy?"

"What do you mean GRUMPY?" Beamer yelled, feigning anger.

Everyone in the room laughed.

Two hours before kickoff the next night, Beamer sat quietly in the coaches' locker room. He bounced his eyes from his play-sheet to the television showing another bowl game, then back to his play-sheet.

He sighed and whispered, "We've got to get this one. Nobody in here wants to finish with a losing record. I know I sure don't."

For much of the night, it appeared the Hokies would indeed be saddled with a losing record. The offense committed a turnover on its second play of the game, leading to a 7–0 deficit. After three quarters, Rutgers led 10–0 and Virginia Tech was going nowhere fast with 85 penalty yards and only 79 yards of offense.

Then the rain started to fall and somehow the Hokies' offense came to life, scraping together 10 points to send the game into overtime.

After Virginia Tech kicked a field goal to take a 13–10 lead, Rutgers lined up to kick a game-tying 42-yard field goal of its own. The football sailed just right of the uprights as Virginia Tech players stormed the field in celebration.

It was the 258th victory of his 32-year head-coaching career, surpassing retired coach LaVell Edwards of Brigham Young, and placing him behind only Bobby Bowden, Glenn "Pop" Warner, Bear Bryant, and Joe Paterno among major college coaches.

After he had dried off and congratulated his players and assistant coaches and thanked the seniors who had just played their final game, Beamer retreated to a hallway.

"Whew!' he said, smiling. "Ugly game huh? But a win is a win. An ugly win is better than a pretty loss. And I'll take it."

He then headed to the postgame press conference, which he started by announcing, "Our thoughts and prayers are with those in Sandy Hook. We know what they are going through up there and we want to let them know people are thinking about them. We prevailed in Blacksburg and I think, if anything, it brought us closer together and more determined. And I think the same thing is going to happen up there."

An hour later, Beamer walked into the lobby lounge of the Orlando Hilton. His daughter, Casey, hugged him as he settled into a seat between her and his longtime friend Wayland Overstreet, as a few prominent Virginia Tech boosters pulled their chairs closer.

"We needed that win...we really did," he said. "It will be so much nicer to go through the next few months and the entire off-season coming off a win...I was sitting here a year ago, about as miserable as you can be, because we had lost to Michigan in the Sugar Bowl. That game still bothers me. That game will always bother me. We were so much better than them, and faster, too, and we somehow lost.

"Oh well, you can't dwell on it forever...."

For the next hour, the Virginia Tech head coach regaled the group with football stories from days gone by. In between, he shook hands and had his picture taken with anyone who approached his table.

Another season was in the books.

And this one, for the first time in three years, ended with him laughing and smiling.

Granted, the coaching profession has never attracted a group of Mr. Rogers-types who wear cardigans, who abhor swear words, and who take the time to treat others, no matter how low on the business totem pole, as they would wish to be treated.

Unless you are a five-star recruit, big-moneyed booster, or university president, head coaches usually don't have the time or patience to give you the time of day. There are head coaches today who earn more than $4 million per year and actually walk through a crowd of fans with a cell phone glued to their ear, although nobody is on the other end of the line, simply to avoid signing autographs or shaking hands. There are coaches who don't like to eat buffets on the booster circuit or pose for pictures with fans. It is a necessary inconvenience for them and they wear their displeasure on the sleeves of their monogrammed dress shirts.

"Can you imagine not wanting to treat your own fans with respect?" Beamer asked rhetorically. "I will stop and sign every autograph and take every picture. I remember what it was like those first six years here when we struggled to win games. Now, the wins and all that are nice, but in the end, I think we all are judged on how we treat other people."

Shane Beamer describes his father as naturally friendly. There is no pretense and no airs about him.

"I've been around other head coaches on the golf course and they don't want fans to bother them," Shane said. "They'll go as far as to say, 'Get the heck away from me, I'm putting!' Dad would never do that. He's great with people at all times. I have never once seen him get upset or annoyed with people approaching him. He never once has said anything under his breath, like, 'God, I get tired of that.' Never. It's just who he is; it's not an act."

Football coaches have issued many memorable quotations over the years.

"Winning isn't everything—it's the only thing."

"It's not whether you got knocked down; it's whether you get up that's important."

"Winners never quit and quitters never win."

They're all tried and true and inspirational, but when I think of Frank Beamer, I think of philanthropist John Templeton's favorite quote: "It's nice to be important, but it's *more important to be nice.*"

It is something Beamer has often told his players over the past 30 years. Another is, "Don't act special and people will treat you special."

A few years ago, the Virginia Tech team bus had pulled over to a rest area and Beamer got out of the bus to stretch. Four men wearing University of Virginia shirts noticed. It was an autumn Saturday and they may or may not have indulged in adult beverages.

"That's Coach Beamer!" one of them shouted.

They approached and requested a picture: four die-hard Cavaliers surrounding their rival's head coach. All were smiling in the photo.

"Do you think that will wind up on the Internet?" somebody asked.

"I figure that one will be hanging right on their bathroom wall!" the coach joked, before hopping back on the bus.

There are plenty of reasons a recent *Seattle Times* poll among college coaches pegged Beamer as the most respected among his peers. Of all the legends of the game, such as Paul "Bear" Bryant, Darrell Royal, Joe Paterno, Woody Hayes, Bo Schembechler, Tom Osborne, and Bobby Bowden, some were nice—like Osborne and Bowden—and others were, well…let's just say they could be unpleasant, even churlish, at times.

To that end, Beamer reminds me of one legend who coached the game during another era—Oklahoma's Bud Wilkinson—who was beloved by his players and admired and respected by his fiercest opponents. Anybody who knew Bud Wilkinson loved Bud Wilkinson. He was labeled "a true gentleman who just happened to be a football coach."

Most all of these coaching legends had much in common: they were intensely competitive, mentally tough, and driven to succeed—and they hated losing more than they enjoyed winning.

"That's probably true of me," Beamer told me. "I think I take the losses harder now than I ever did when I was younger. I absolutely *hate* to lose."

At anything, whether it be football, golf, racquetball, or just picking the time his flight will land.

"We were headed to the Dominican Republic a few years ago on a staff outing," said Bruce Garnes, deputy director of football operations, "and he and John Ballein and Greg Roberts were arguing about what time the wheels of the airplane will touch the ground. So Coach Beamer made them all set their watches together and they each picked a time. Coach Beamer won the contest, because he had figured out the time-zone change. He wants to win every time he competes in anything."

You also can't be an emotionally fragile person and survive the type of seasons Frank Beamer endured from 1987 to 1992 and then go on to construct one of the country's premier programs. Those were years that would break most football coaches, whose frustration and perhaps panic would naturally lead to their eventual demise.

"Two and nine, 3–8, 6–4–1, 6–5, 5–6, and 2–8–1," Cheryl Beamer rattled off her husband's string of miserable season records for those six years one night over dinner. "I have them memorized. I don't think we will ever forget those years. But Frank never let losing get to him or change him. He was the same person then as he is now.

"He continued to do the same things. He stayed, he persevered, and he found success. It was just a matter of time."

For the legends who have passed, such as Bryant, Royal, Hayes, Schembechler and Wilkinson, their obituaries were written based on their success, littered with statistics recounting their wins and championships. More importantly, however, each will be forever associated with a certain university, where they arrived young and remained to thrive as living legends. Just look at that prestigious list of coaches in this paragraph again and you realize their associations come to mind easily: Alabama, Texas, Ohio State, Michigan, and Oklahoma.

These coaches didn't just win games. Their years of dedication and success built things that will never fade—legacies, memories, huge stadiums that will be filled each autumn Saturday decades after they've been gone.

And so it will be for Frank Beamer and Virginia Tech, forever together in the college football history books as well. His name someday will be listed with these legends of the game—and deservedly so. Virginia Tech director of sports medicine Mike Goforth has grasped the perfect perspective of his legacy.

"You know, I just read Bo Schembechler's book," he said. "He's a true legend, right? Do you know how many years he coached at Michigan? Twenty-one. Do you know how many national championships he won? Zero. Do you know who passed Bo in 2011 in total career wins? That's right—Coach Beamer. I think we are so close to him, we don't realize we are working for a true legend of the game."

My favorite comedy in television history is and always will be *The Andy Griffith Show*, not only for Don Knotts' hilarious exploits but also for the underlying lesson Andy would convey in that half hour, usually leaving us feeling good about ourselves. He used the down-home wisdom that extended well beyond the town borders of Mayberry, a place where good people would want to live, driven by good values and forever aware of what's important in life—and what's not.

In one episode, Andy's high school sweetheart returns for a reunion and tells him, "This was a great place to grow up, but I have to get back to Chicago. You can't live up to your potential here. In a big city, you have room to grow, to expand, to lead a different kind of life."

Andy answers her by saying, "How can life be that much different, as long as you're happy? That's the main thing, ain't it?...To be happy? Isn't that the prize of the game?"

"Yes, but how can you find that here?" she asks. "I like to be a big fish in a big pond, not a big fish in a little pond."

"Well, what's wrong with that?" Andy asks. "I found what I want right here."

"How do you know," she wonders, "if you haven't tried anything else?"

"I don't have to, I don't have to," he says. "And even if I did try, I would find out I already found it."

See the parallels here?

Beamer knows what is important. Sure, he considered other jobs in so-called bigger markets over the years, as you will read in this book. He turned them all down to stay home, to build something special in his home state, near his hometown. To build something that will last beyond his career, even beyond his lifetime.

And any true Hokie fan knows where Beamer was born. That's right—in Mount Airy, North Carolina—the real Mayberry that Andy Griffith called home.

"He loves that show," Cheryl Beamer said of her husband. "He's seen them all a million times."

Beamer pulls his wife's car down a country road and struggles to get the seat just right. He turns on the radio. It was tuned to a sports talk station dedicated to Virginia Tech football and he cringes. He listens as two broadcasters describe how each of his recently hired assistant coaches should fare in recruiting and the outlook for the 2014 signing class.

It is just five days after Virginia Tech signed 19 prospects to a letter of intent for the incoming freshman class.

"They're already talking about next year's recruiting class and we're 11 months and three weeks away," he says to his wife of 41 years. "Honey, why do you listen to this stuff? How do I get off this station and find 94.9?"

He fiddles with the knobs, until the sweet sounds of Tim McGraw fill the car.

"That's more like it," he says with a smile.

"He's got to have his country station on!" Cheryl tells a passenger in the front seat. "I love listening to what the sports talk guys are saying, but Frank doesn't want to hear a bit of it."

"I am beyond that point," Beamer admits. "When you are a young coach starting out, you may worry about what people are saying about you, your team, or your program. After coaching for 40 years, why would I care about it now? I know what we've done and what we're doing."

What he has done can't be measured in wins and losses, or trophies, or coaching awards, or salary figures.

In compiling information to collaborate with him for this autobiography, I spent countless hours over two years with his assistants, Virginia Tech athletic personnel, and Beamer himself.

Throughout this book you will read quotes from those around him, helping tell his story. You see, Frank Beamer truly is a modest man. To talk about himself, he fears it would be conceived as bragging. If you know him, you know he would rather listen to anyone else speak but himself anyway.

He's the type of guy who could sing on stage with Brad Paisley on Monday night, play golf with Phil Mickelson and Donald Trump on Tuesday, swap racing stories with Jeff Gordon on Wednesday, then visit with the President of the United States in the Rose Garden on Thursday. And when somebody asked him on Friday, "Frank, what have you been up to this week?" he would answer, "Not much…our youngest granddaughter got her first tooth yesterday."

And by the way, he has done all those things I just listed.

Beamer never acts special, even though everyone working around him and every friend he has would agree unanimously that he's the most special man they've ever known.

"Through all his success, he has maintained an even keel about himself with absolutely no ego," said Bryan Stinespring, an assistant on Beamer's staff since 1993. "He's a great leader, a teacher, and a mentor. He has mentored me not just as a football coach, but to become a better person, better man, and better father.

"You know what he always reminds us? 'Our players aren't here for us to be successful; we are here for them to be successful—in football and in life. We have an awesome responsibility to do our best every day for them.'"

Billy Hite arrived at Virginia Tech in 1978 as running backs coach and was the only assistant retained by Beamer when he replaced Bill Dooley in 1987. One day, three months later, the new head coach drove to Hite's house.

"It was during March Madness and Carolina was playing on TV," Hite remembers. "Well, Coach Beamer is a big Carolina fan and he knew I went to Carolina. He showed up at my front door out of the blue and said, 'Look, Cheryl's out of town…I thought I would come watch the game with you, if that's okay?'

"Coach Dooley never knew where I lived, but Coach Beamer had been head coach for three months and he already had spent time in my house. I had told my wife when we got here all those years ago, 'Don't get to know anybody, we won't be here long.' Well, that was before I met Coach Beamer. He's the only coach I am aware of who is friends with everybody on his coaching staff. I've had three other job offers since Coach Beamer arrived and I turned them all down. Blacksburg became our home because of Frank Beamer."

One of the people I spoke with was Minnis Ridenour, Virginia Tech's executive vice president and chief operating officer from 1987 to 1994. He agreed with the decision by then athletic director Dave Braine to keep Beamer following a 2–8–1 season in 1992, undoubtedly the turning point in the football program.

Ridenour is retired and still living in Blacksburg.

"He has been a wonderful match for Virginia Tech," Ridenour said. "If I could wish for anything, it would be for Virginia Tech to win a national championship—for the university, sure, but more for Frank Beamer. He deserves it."

Then there are his players.

Perhaps Virginia Tech's most important recruit in the school's 121-year football history, who currently coaches the Hokies' outside linebackers and defensive ends, described his boss' influence best.

"I was recruited here in 1992 and from the time I met him, he told me he wanted me to study hard, go to class, get tutoring if I needed it, but always, always have a goal of getting my degree," Cornell Brown said. "He's an ex-school teacher, his mother was a teacher, and he knew the value of a college education long before I did. He told me that I couldn't play football forever. You know what? He pushed me in the classroom more than he ever did on the football field. I figured out why: he cared about me more as a person than he did as a football player.

"Here's another thing: some kids today get caught up in thinking that playing college football makes them special. Coach Beamer tells them constantly, 'Hey, it's sports…nothing more. Don't act special. Don't walk around this campus with an air about yourself, thinking you are better than the average student just because you play football.'"

Bill Roth has been Virginia Tech's radio play-by-play announcer since Beamer arrived as head coach. He knows him well.

"He has got this incredible heart and he's ego-less," Roth said. "He's the type of guy who will climb in the back seat of a car and be uncomfortable just so you can sit in the front seat. Who's like that in the coaching business these days? He has a unique ability to make the person with him the most important person in the world. It could be a booster, an ESPN guy, a janitor, or a student. He never looks at his watch or acts as if he's busy. Then when that person leaves, the next person to talk to him becomes the most important person in the world. I've never seen anybody like him."

Beamer is just the type of guy to make coffee for the office secretaries, move his car so an elderly person could have a better parking spot, take a campus visitor to lunch, buy a gift card for a staff member who became engaged a day earlier, drive 80 miles round-trip to spend an hour with a friend dying of cancer, stand up five times during dinner to have his picture taken with fans, smiling and laughing each time as if he had known those strangers for a lifetime, or tip a waitress 50 percent of the bill because he overheard her say she was struggling to pay off her student loans.

You know what makes the man special? I witnessed him do all of those things in *one* day—February 11, 2013, to be exact.

For most public figures so accomplished, so recognized, and so admired by so many, not to act special would truly be a formidable task.

But it just comes naturally to Franklin Mitchell Beamer.

I hope you enjoy reading his life story.

—Jeff Snook

1

Go Out of Your Way to Make Good Memories

"There is nothing stronger than gentleness."

—Abraham Lincoln

I always loved that quote from our nation's 16th president and I felt the same way. Throughout history, leaders like Lincoln usually exuded strength in a time when they needed it most. Finding the gentleness within oneself was the hard part for some. I somehow needed to find all my strength at this very moment. The gentleness was there.

It was April 18, 2007.

I was about to enter a room full of people who had just lost a son, a daughter, a brother, or a sister only two days earlier. Thirty-two lives. All but two were taken in an 11-minute rampage carried out by one lone madman, a killer who had turned his rage on innocent college students. They had awakened on a snowy Monday morning, wanting nothing more that day than to go to class, one small step toward graduating from college some day and leading happy, successful lives.

They were students and faculty at Virginia Polytechnic Institute and State University. My university. The school I have loved so much since I attended my first football game as a kid in the late 1950s. The school from which I received my degree in 1969. The school to which I returned to become head football coach in December 1986.

But they became victims of the worst mass shooting in U.S. history.

It happened in my town, Blacksburg, Virginia, one of the most peaceful and lovely college towns in the country.

It wasn't so peaceful now. The campus was overrun with reporters and satellite trucks and I took it upon myself to send a message to anyone who listened: "This was a lone act by a very disturbed man and it won't define Virginia Tech. We won't let it. We will react to this and we will become closer and stronger and we will treat people around us nicer. We will come together, using the pain of this horrible tragedy to become better people."

On this day, however, it was a time to grieve.

I'd just delivered that message to a few TV reporters outside the Inn at Virginia Tech, the university hotel where the victims' immediate families were grieving privately in a room secluded from the public.

I had walked back into the hotel following my interviews, when Larry Hincker, Virginia Tech's vice president for university relations, approached me.

"Coach Beamer, would you like to say a few words to the victims' families?" he asked.

Hundreds of times, I had spoken to our school's boosters about the prospects of a football team for the upcoming season. Exactly 106 times dating back to 1981, I stood before the media as the losing coach in a football game, answering questions about why I went for it on fourth down, or why didn't I play so-and-so at quarterback. I had spoken to business leaders in seminars, parents during recruiting trips and other coaches during national conventions.

But *this?*

This was different. This carried so much weight, so much importance. What could I possibly say to make any difference, to take away any of the pain? It was the worst kind. They say there is no greater pain than losing a child. I have two grown children and I could never imagine losing them.

I was a football coach, not a trained psychologist or a grief counselor.

This was bigger than any pregame speech I had ever given. This was so much bigger than any darned football game.

I just had a moment to think of what I would say; if there ever was a time I was speechless, this was it. I wondered, *What do I say? What can I say?*

How could my words begin to help ease so much heartache and so much suffering? I had never faced a situation like this, simply because it was impossible to prepare for. These poor people were grief-stricken and I wanted to help them. I'm sure many of them were angry, too.

I will never forget the next few moments as long as I live. I was sweating and my eyes were glassy with tears. I entered through the rear of the room and all of those heartbroken people were seated in front of me, facing the other way. As I walked around the side of the room, reaching the front, I turned to face them.

It was then...I can honestly say I never saw so much pain in my life. Their faces will never disappear from my memory. Particularly their eyes...I had never seen so much pain in people's eyes before. I could hear their muffled cries and sobbing as I started to speak.

"I can't imagine what you are going through," I told them. "Just know that there are people here who really, really care for you. I hope you can feel the caring and love that is coming from the people on this campus. I want you to know I will always be available for you if you want to come by my office and see me."

It lasted only a minute or two.

I walked out of the room, and by now tears streamed down my face. I didn't stop crying for a while that day.

Three days later, Lane Stadium, our campus football stadium, sat empty.

It should have hosted more than 40,000 fans on that sunny Saturday, as we played our annual spring football game. There were 11 funerals scheduled that day, many of them in Blacksburg. How in the world could we possibly play football at the exact time those families I had spoken to were burying their children?

One of the funerals, for Austin Michelle Cloyd, began that day at 2:00 PM. Austin was the daughter of Renee and Bryan Cloyd, an accounting professor at Virginia Tech. Their family had moved to Blacksburg from Illinois just two years earlier and attended Blacksburg United Methodist Church, which my family has attended since moving back to Blacksburg 20 years earlier.

Austin had curly red hair and was majoring in international studies and French. She had planned to start working for the Appalachian Service Project to renovate older homes in the Appalachian Mountains.

Just a few hours after he was notified that Austin was one of the 32 victims, Bryan sent an e-mail to all of his students. It read:

DEAR ACIS 3314 STUDENTS,

My family's worst fears were confirmed a few hours ago. My daughter, Austin Michelle Cloyd, was one of the victims in Norris Hall. She would have been 19 years old next Tuesday. My family hurts deeply for the loss of our precious baby. We ask that you pray for us and for the rest of the Virginia Tech community that has suffered so greatly.

At this point, I don't know how or where our class will continue. If we don't meet again, your final assignment from me is perhaps the most important lesson you will learn in life. Go to your mother, father, brothers and sisters and tell them with all your heart how much you love them. And tell them that you know how much they love you, too. Go out of your way to make good memories. At some point, these memories may be all you have left.

The contents of that e-mail really struck me.

"Go out of your way to make good memories."

I knew it as soon as I read it: there was no better advice by which to live our lives.

2

Humble Beginnings

Nobody can ever be prepared for something like what happened at Virginia Tech on April 16, 2007. It was beyond the scope of our worst nightmares. So we were all just feeling our way when it came to coping and dealing and speaking in public about the tragedy.

I had no road map or coaching manual to use so I just said what came from my heart, what I believed was the right thing to say.

That's not to say I did not have some experience dealing with—and trying to overcome—adversity.

And it didn't take me long in life to encounter it.

Our family already consisted of three kids by the time I came along on October 18, 1946, born just across the Virginia border in a hospital in Mount Airy, North Carolina. Billie Jean was born seven years earlier, Barnett five years earlier, and Betty a year and a half before me.

I was the baby of the family and I got the feeling as the years went on that I may have been one of those unplanned babies, although nobody ever told me that.

I guess my parents just ran out of B's by the time they got to me, because I probably should have been a Bob, a Benjamin, or a Bo if they had continued the pattern.

They named me for Franklin D. Roosevelt, who had died in April the year before during his fourth term in office. My parents were loyal Democrats who loved President Roosevelt, but they didn't give me his middle name. My full name is Franklin Mitchell Beamer. The Mitchell part is a family name.

We lived in a small house in Fancy Gap, Virginia, which was a wonderful place to grow up. As you can imagine, farm life was tough work. We had 70 acres and I had to do my chores in the morning before school, such as milking the cows. I baled hay in the summer and it was hard, hard work. We had pigs and cattle and one steer. It was hard enough work to make me realize I didn't want to be a farmer when I grew up.

I also hated it when they killed the pigs and cattle. I would have to go inside for the killings. I felt as if they were killing my buddies out there.

We were always a close family. Billie Jean was smart as heck and became the valedictorian of her class. Barnett was pretty much my best friend even though he was five years older. He was very tough on me despite our age difference, as far as not taking it easy when we played sports together. We slept in the same room upstairs while Billie Jean and Betty shared the other upstairs bedroom. We didn't have a shower in that house or an upstairs bathroom. When we had to get up in the middle of the night to go to the bathroom, we had to walk downstairs.

My dad, Raymond Harden Beamer, was of German descent and one of eight kids who were raised on a farm. He was a pretty good football player at Hillsville High in the 1930s and Dad absolutely loved sports—all sports. He would sit and watch whatever sports were on TV and he was a big Giants baseball fan. When the Giants moved from New York to San Francisco in 1958, it became harder for him to get their scores, but he would still listen to the radio and try to find out how the Giants did. In addition to farming, he was a highway engineer. He was what I call a "quiet" disciplinarian. You always knew when he didn't agree with you, but he was never loud or in your face about it.

Now my mother, on the other hand, would be right in your face.

Herma Allen Beamer was a wonderful lady. She was stern and very proud and she believed in education. Both of my sisters graduated from Radford while Barnett and I graduated from Virginia Tech. Having produced four college graduates—from a place in the country where not everybody goes to college—that says all you need to know about my mom. That was a result largely of her influence.

Mom and Dad went to a Methodist church, where one pastor served four churches. They brought us up to never miss a Sunday in church. It's tough to explain what a strong lady my mother was. She was a disciplinarian. Both of my parents were staunch Democrats and staunch Methodists. I know one thing: no matter how late we may have stayed out on a Saturday night, we had better get up to go to church on Sunday mornings. That was their rule.

Mom's family was well-known in Carroll County because her father—my grandfather—was an Allen. His first name was Barnett Allen, so I guess that is where they got the name for my brother. My grandfather was only 21 at the time, but his uncles were Floyd and Sidna Allen.

From what I had been told over the years, there were two political factions of Carroll County and on one side were the Allens, who were staunch Democrats. One of their rivals was a Republican who had just been elected to office in 1912.

They were involved in what some people in southwest Virginia referred to as "the Allen Tragedy" and you can find it in the history books. Other references call it the "Hillsville Massacre," but I can assure you nobody in my family ever did.

It all started when two of Sidna Allen's boys were playing outside of church one Sunday. I guess they were being loud during the services and the police charged them with disturbing a public worship. They fled across the border to North Carolina and the police tracked them down, chained them behind horses and made them walk about 16 miles back to the courthouse in Hillsville.

As they headed to Hillsville, they walked right by Sidna's store and Floyd's house in Fancy Gap. They saw the boys chained up and came running out of the store. Floyd told the police, "You can't make them walk another six miles. They've already walked 10 miles. Look, give them to me and I will bring them in tomorrow morning."

Apparently, one of the policemen pulled a gun and there was a scrape between the Allens and the police. The boys somehow got free.

Floyd brought them in the next day, just as he had promised, but the police then charged him with "interference of law enforcement" and arrested him on the spot. They had a trial at the Carroll County Courthouse and they convicted him of it. Just as they were handing down the sentence of one year in jail, on March 14, 1912, he stood up and said, "Gentlemen, I just ain't a goin'...."

That's the line I always remembered when I read about it.

"Gentlemen, I just ain't a goin'..."

Well, guns were pulled and the shooting began. A judge, the sheriff, an attorney, and two others were killed; but our side didn't have any killed. The Allens who escaped that day fled to the Midwest somewhere. From what I could gather, one of the nephews wrote a letter to his girlfriend back here in Virginia and that's how the police eventually found them.

The next year, Floyd and his son Claude went to the electric chair on the same day for the shoot-up.

I know one thing: Mom never wanted to talk about it. It was just something you didn't bring up, but I decided to write a paper on it for a speech course in college. As I started the project and my research, Mom asked me, "Are you sure you want to do this?"

"It was a good story," I told her. "And it will make a good speech."

I read a couple of different accounts of it and I talked to her about it—what little she would tell me—and then I gave the speech. I can't remember exactly, but I think I got an A on it.

As we grew up, everybody in the county knew the Allen name. They had been already labeled as "notorious" and violent mountain people, but the more I learned about them from my relatives the more complex the story became. When I talk to people who know that my family was involved, I just like to say, "There are two sides to that story."

My uncles told me that before all of this occurred they were well-respected landowners and business owners. He said they all worked hard and earned an honest living and weren't criminals at all, but they were being prosecuted because they were on the other side of the political fence in the county. And in all the accounts I read about it, nobody really knew who fired the first shot.

Everybody who knows me knows what happened to me when I was seven years old. It's kind of a blur all these years later, maybe because I want to forget it, but it probably helped shape who I am today.

It was early June in 1954 and the school year had just finished. It was about lunchtime and Dad was at work. Mom and my sisters were at my grandmother's house. We had a double-car garage without doors and a bunch of papers had blown in there, so one of the chores Dad gave Barnett and me was to clean out the garage. I guess we had done some painting earlier and we had used gasoline to clean the brushes, because there was a large can of gas there. Barnett and I had a fire going down by the creek next to the garage where we burned our trash. We were us-ing brooms to push the trash into the fire.

I had walked back toward the garage to get more trash, when I ac-cidentally knocked over the can of gasoline and it started to roll to-ward the garage. Barnett told me later I had kicked the can to keep it from reaching the garage, but I don't remember it. I was holding the broom, which still had some ashes smoldering in the fibers. The gaso-line must have splashed up on me, because suddenly, an explosion hit me right in the face. I screamed and ran outside to where Barnett got to me. He rolled me over in the grass several times and threw dirt and sand all over me to put out the fire.

I then went inside and filled the bathtub with water and sat down to clean off the dirt and try to ease the pain. I was burned on the right side of my face, my neck, my right arm, and my shoulders. Mom got home that day, took one look at me and took me to the doctor. He treated me but sent me home that night. I couldn't sleep at all. My body was covered in blisters and the pain was killing me.

The next day, Mom took me to the hospital, where the reality hit us that these burns were much worse than anyone thought that first day. I stayed in the hospital in Pulaski for three months, and over the next four years, I would undergo more than 30 surgeries.

A doctor by the name of James Martin performed those operations on me, trying to make the right part of my face better. The surgeries weren't any fun, either. Doctor Martin tried taking skin grafts from my knees and thighs, but they wouldn't grow on my face. Then he took grafts from my back and put them on my face and it worked. He would take some skin and feed it through a tube that was attached to my back, using healthy skin from my back to get it growing on my face.

He did all of the surgeries during the summer break from school. I would go into the hospital for a week and come home for a week. That is how I spent the next four summers.

After the 18th operation, I didn't wake up for a day and a half and they thought maybe I would never come out of it. That must have scared them pretty good, because for the next few operations, they just gave me a local shot for the pain, but I could still feel them cutting the skin out of my back.

They tell me I would walk room to room in the hospital with my little fake doctor's bag and I would check up on the patients. I was around the hospital so much as a kid, I really did think for a while that I wanted to be a doctor when I grew up. Then I realized that you had to be pretty smart and that ended that idea.

All those surgeries and the recovery weren't easy by any means, but Mom wouldn't let me feel sorry for myself.

I'd be lying there in the hospital, thinking about all my buddies out there playing baseball and I'd get to feeling sorry for myself. Mom, who always had that take-charge personality, had other ideas about how I should be feeling.

"Get up," she'd tell me. "Let's go down this hall right here."

We'd walk down the hallway, and it wouldn't be any time at all before we saw three people, five people, 10 people, who had it worse than me.

Mom would always tell me, "Concentrate on what you have and be thankful for it. Don't waste any time feeling sorry for what you don't have or for what happened to you in the past."

It taught me a lesson; something like, *Hey, take what you have, build on it, but it is what it is. Take the situation and ask, 'What can I do to make it better?'* That became a philosophy that has stayed with me for the rest of my life.

That was Mom's attitude. She always reminded me that somebody had it worse than I did and I would be okay, as long as I didn't feel sorry for myself about something that had already happened. She was a tough lady, a real trouper. She was the one who would carry me back and forth between hospital rooms or at the house.

Her attitude was, "Okay, this is what we have to do, so let's get it done."

Through the fire and my burns, I guess I found out a lot about myself, and I know that Mom's attitude had a big effect on my life.

When we had losing seasons later when I was a football coach, I looked at the problems and told myself, "Okay, this is what it is. How do we fix it? Now, let's go get it done."

By the time I was 11, I still had a couple of surgeries remaining. Dr. Martin had wanted to get some of the puffiness out of my face, but that is when he had a heart attack and died. I remember Mom searched for a new doctor, but by that time, people had accepted me for who I was and the puffiness there didn't bother me that much. We all decided I had had enough surgeries and that was that.

Betty and Billie Jean will tell you today that the entire family spoiled me after that, but I wouldn't have known it then. I just knew I had issues other people didn't have, so I probably was getting treated differently by people because of what had happened to me.

As I grew older, I don't even remember us talking much about it. My dad wasn't a big talker, anyway. It wasn't that he was cold. He just wasn't a guy to sit down and talk about your emotions. Ours was a very loving family, but most of my conversations went through my mom or my brother and sisters.

I do know one thing: if Barnett hadn't been there to put the fire out, I would have probably died that day. Even with that, he and I never talked much about it as we got older. I guess we knew, like Mom said, it was what it was. It became a part of who I am.

That was one of the thousands of lessons my mother taught me. And she literally *taught* me.

Through the third grade, I attended Sunnyside Elementary about three miles from the house, while my mom taught at Brookmoore. Then I went to another one-room schoolhouse, Mine Branch Elementary, before Fancy Gap Elementary opened. It was there that our paths merged and I was in Mom's class for the fifth grade.

Let me tell you, she was a lot harder on me than she was on all the other kids. I guess she was fair in grading me, but I sure didn't get any breaks, either. Let's just say there was a lot of discussion during our ride home from school every day.

If there was any trouble in the room, even if I was only near it, I was the one who got paddled later. Mom believed in paddling your rear end.

I know I never got into any real trouble, but on this one particular Sunday I was sitting in the back of church with my buddies when they got to goofing around, making noise and laughing. When I got home from church that day, my dad just busted my butt.

I said, "Dad, it wasn't me. It was those other guys."

He answered, "I don't care—you were in the vicinity!"

All these years later, I think that's a pretty funny line, but I sure wasn't laughing then.

Before I was in Mom's class, I went to a one-room elementary school that was right beside a cornfield. All the students in that district rode the school bus with us—even the high school kids. Somehow one day I had this bright idea to take a couple of ears of corn on the bus to take home. Well, these high school guys grabbed the corn from me and started throwing it around. Naturally, the principal wanted to know how the corn got on the bus in the first place. I think Barnett 'fessed up that his little brother Frankie did it.

My teacher, Mrs. Easter, got a paddle out and busted my butt that time.

But other than that, I never got into trouble. I guess we just didn't have the temptations kids have nowadays. But I like to think Mom and Dad raised us well, too.

I had another scare in addition to the fire. After I got my driver's license, I was talking to some friends at a service station. As I pulled out of the parking lot, I turned and waved to them and was not paying attention, because a car had stopped right in front of me. I swerved to avoid it and hit an oncoming car. I didn't have my seatbelt on and the impact slung me over to the right side of the car where I hit my head on the window. My head broke the window and there was blood everywhere. It took about 50 stitches to close that wound and we were picking glass out of my head for weeks after the accident.

I was very lucky I didn't die that day, too. I came back and played the final basketball game of that season with my head all bandaged up.

My uncle Sharrell Allen was the guy who introduced me to some things outside of Fancy Gap. He was my mom's brother and he would take Barnett and me to the VFW. He was a World War II veteran and that happened to be the spot in town where everything fun happened.

When I was about 15, he took us to Myrtle Beach; that was the first time either Barnett or I saw the ocean. Uncle Sharrell was also a scoutmaster and he sponsored the MYF: the Methodist Youth Fellowship. Both of us joined the Boy Scouts because of him. We got around by throwing hay in the back of a truck and all of us riding back there. He would drive into the mountains on Sunday mornings to offer people rides to and from church. He was a very kind, giving man.

Barnett always put it this way: Uncle Sharrell was "our outlet to the world."

He was a Virginia Tech grad and the best thing he ever did for me for me was introduce me to the school's football program. He would take us to games at the old Miles Stadium—that stadium seemed so big to me when I was a kid.

Carroll Dale was playing when I went to my first game, so I must have been no older than 12 or 13. Then I remember seeing Bob Schweickert and Sonny Utz play. All of those guys were larger than life to me. The game I remember most was the Florida State game in 1964 when I was a senior in high school. Virginia Tech dominated the game and won 20–11. They ran a tackle-eligible play, tricked Florida State, and hit it for a touchdown. But the play that really stands out in my memory is seeing the great receiver Fred Biletnikoff scoring a touchdown on the final play and throwing the ball into the stands in frustration. That image just stuck with me.

They were the VPI (many people outside of Virginia don't know the school is actually the Virginia Polytechnic Institute and State University) Gobblers back then, but they also were referred to as the "Techman" or the "Hokies." I guess the school had too many nicknames for everybody's liking, so the administration wanted only one. Since 1981, Tech has used only the Hokies.

Anyway, Uncle Sharrell never married or had kids, and I learned later, he was unhappy for whatever reasons. During my senior year, he took his own life. It was one of the saddest things to happen for us. That was a tough time on all of us, and I know it was very tough on Mom. He was only 47.

Mom made sure our family stuck together as the years went on. If it was Thanksgiving and I wasn't coming home because of football season, I would hear about it.

"Why aren't you coming home?" she would ask. "Listen, Betty and Barnett and Billie Jean are going to be here. You need to be here, too!"

And I never wanted to disappoint her.

I guess your heritage leads to who you are. Mom and Dad were wonderful parents to the four of us…just great, hard-working, loving people. Dad died in 1996 and Mom eight years later. They left us all something in their wills and what they willed me was Grandma

Mitchell's property. It's a nice house with some 50 acres right between the Fancy Gap exit and where you get on the Blue Ridge Parkway near Route 52 over by I-77.

My wife, Cheryl, asked me just the other day, "You want to sell it?"

"No, I want to keep it and will it to the kids," I told her. "It's been in the family that long. Let's keep it in the family."

I want our kids to have it someday. I guess it's my way of holding on to the memory of Mom and Dad and the memories from my childhood.

It was a heck of a childhood. I am probably lucky to be alive after the fire, all those operations, and the car crash. But all these years later, I can honestly say I don't think about that much anymore.

I guess that's just normal after about 60 years go by.

3

Playing Days

BARNETT BEAMER: *"Those first couple of years after the fire, if he ever got hit where that scar tissue was, he would go into a screaming rage, so I knew it must have been very painful for him. After all those surgeries, he couldn't throw very well at all. In fact, I liked to say he threw like a girl. Then as the years passed, he just kept getting better and better. To get as good as he eventually did, it was amazing to all of us. I really think because of what he went through that his goals and aspirations were a little bit higher than everybody else's. I always said Frank dreamed bigger dreams than the rest of us."*

Not only did my face get burned during the fire, but my right arm had been burned pretty badly, too. That made it difficult to throw a baseball or a football, until it finally healed completely.

You know how I told you Barnett was always tough on me? Well, he was. He didn't stand for me crying or whining when he ran over me while playing football or when one of his baseball pitches hit me in the face. After we finished all of our chores, just about every day, he would work with me and make me throw 10 strikes in a row before we could go into the house.

During his senior year in high school, he was assigned to write a paper about the happiest day of his life. He could have chosen anything, but he wrote about watching me throw a football without pain for the first time after the fire.

That says about all you need to know about my brother.

Not only did we share a bedroom, but Barnett and I bonded over our love of sports, too. I knew when I played sports with him there was no way he would ever take it easy just because I was his little brother. He was a running back and a better player than me and he had all the toughness he needed to be great. But he hurt his knee in high school and surgeries back then weren't like they are today. I am telling you, he would have made a fine football coach, too. He had a mind for the game.

We lived seven miles from Hillsville High, and after practice of whatever sport I played, I would walk a mile back through Hillsville to get to Route 52, where I hoped I could find someone to give me a ride home. Hitchhiking probably wasn't as dangerous back then as it is today, but I still would hope to see a familiar face whenever a car pulled over to the side of the road.

By the time I finished at Hillsville High, I had earned 11 varsity letters. I played quarterback and defensive back in football and passed for 43 touchdowns during my last two seasons. That was a pretty big number in those days when not every team was throwing the football much. I was a guard in basketball and played center field and pitched a little for the baseball team. I was just an average basketball and baseball player, but football was another story. I loved the game. And I could throw a football much better than I pitched a baseball for some reason.

Above all, the game of football always made sense to me.

Even back in high school, I could figure it out—the mental part of it anyway. I knew why certain players should be over here and not over there. I could sense what would happen next on the playing field. I knew why certain plays broke down and other plays worked. My head coach, Tommy Thompson, had a wide-open offense and he loved to throw it around the field. That was just fine with me, because I loved throwing the ball, too.

Coach Thompson had spent a year studying the passing game with the Baltimore Colts when Johnny Unitas was in his heyday. He even installed some shotgun formation during my senior season, because he was worried about protection. This was the 1960s, so that shows how ahead of the game he was.

His offensive philosophy helped me pass for those 43 touchdowns, which is the main reason I was being recruited to play football in college in the first place.

When it came time to think about college, or even playing football in college, the only schools which showed any interest in me were VMI, Tulane, Wake Forest, William & Mary, and Richmond.

Wake Forest was about the same distance from Hillsville as Blacksburg, so I knew I could get home often from there. I visited Tulane, but they probably thought I was too small. I really didn't think the military life would suit me so VMI was out. In the back of my mind, I always knew I wanted to play at Virginia Tech if they ever offered me a scholarship.

Finally, it was very late in the recruiting process when Virginia Tech came up with a scholarship offer over the telephone. One of the assistants called and told me, "I'll give you a couple of days to think about it."

I didn't want to take a couple of days, thinking they may have second thoughts, so I told him, "No, I will accept your offer right now."

It wasn't a tough decision for me.

They sent the baseball coach, Red Laird, to Hillsville to sign me, so that tells you how important I was to the football team.

My sister, Betty, was dating Dennis Semones at the time. He was a fullback and linebacker at Virginia Tech and a really good football player. He ended up hurting his knee, which cut his career short. I had an advantage when I came to campus early that summer before my freshman year, because he was there to show me around. I learned where all the buildings were and how to get around and it was one of the best things I ever did.

Then I went home for the second summer session to work. That part of the summer and memories of it would continue to make me a good student—it was my fear of being a farmer.

It wasn't anything against farmers; it's just that I wasn't cut out for that. There was way too much hard work involved.

I'd be out there hoeing the garden or baling hay in that hot sun and I'd get to scratching my forearms from the hay. Those thoughts were always running through my head, so I knew I had better study hard, get good grades, and get a college education. That motivated me in the classroom for four years, and I worked hard at being a good student.

When camp started, there were 60 freshmen on scholarship and six more freshmen walk-ons. Thirteen of us made it through by the time we became seniors, so that shows you how tough it was. Those were the days of unlimited scholarships and unlimited practice time. I tell you, if I ran practices like that today, there would be lawyers lined up at the gates to sue the university. We had bull in the ring about every day, where you would stand in the middle of a circle and just keep getting hit by other guys coming at you. It's mainly a drill used to toughen you up. We ran and ran and ran for conditioning. We didn't go lightly very many days, always working in full pads and blocking and tackling constantly. That was the way of the times back then and that fit Coach Jerry Claiborne's approach perfectly. It was just like *Junction Boys*, the movie about Bear Bryant's Texas A&M teams in the 1950s.

I was one of seven quarterbacks to come in that year, and I think it was the second day of practice when they moved me to defensive back. I thought, *Hey, don't they know I threw 43 touchdown passes during my last two seasons at Hillsville High?* I had played both ways in high school, so it wasn't like I didn't have experience as a defensive back. I just wanted to give it a shot at quarterback

Freshmen were ineligible to play back then (the NCAA changed the rule to allow freshmen to play in 1972), so getting on the field for those freshmen games was a big deal. In the first one in 1965, which actually was the first game ever played at the new Lane Stadium, we played Maryland's freshmen team on a Friday.

I would like to say I played in that first-ever game at Lane Stadium, but I didn't get into the game. Not for one play.

Let me tell you, I was embarrassed and devastated. That night, I didn't want to be around anyone so I went to see the Blacksburg High School team play and I just sat on a hill, watching the game with all these thoughts running through my head: *Am I good enough to play at this level? There are seven freshmen quarterbacks and I'm not good enough to be one of them? What do I do now?*

As I sat there, I became more and more determined that I had to prove myself. I just decided right then, that no matter what, I would go as hard as I could during every moment of practice. I didn't care how far I had to run, I would run 10 yards more.

My new philosophy worked for me that next spring. There was a pass near the goal line and I ran as hard as I could to get there. The ball got tipped up into the air, and I intercepted it—and the only reason was the fact that I ran as hard as I could to get there. I think that is exactly the point when the coaches began to notice me.

We opened my sophomore season at Tulane and I thought it would be very close whether I would make the travel squad. Thank goodness I did. We flew down to New Orleans and as we loaded onto

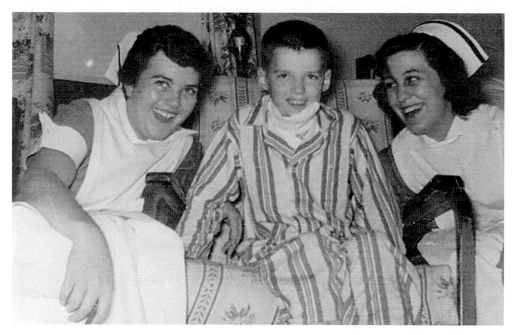

That's me as a seven-year-old, getting special attention from the nurses at the hospital, which became my second home for much of 1954. *(Photo courtesy of Ieta Blevins)*

Showing the form that resulted in 43 touchdown passes at Hillsville High.

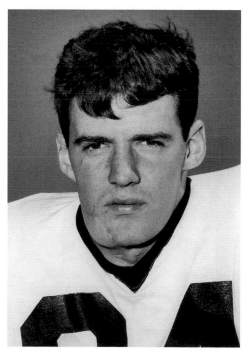

As a freshman at Virginia Tech, I had that determined look that I would give it my best each day.

My only pick-six: I "out-raced" Richmond quarterback Buster O'Brien to the end zone.

Cheryl and I on our big day—April 1, 1972—at First Baptist Church in Richmond.

Here I am with one of our defensive backs during my first full-time coaching job—at The Citadel. We didn't have the most talent, but we always coached tough, hard-nosed kids with great character.

Making sideline adjustments as the defensive coordinator under Mike Gottfried at Murray State in 1979. We had some good teams with the Division I-AA Racers.

Our family soon after Casey's birth in 1981. This was taken during my first season as head coach at Murray State—and plaid was in.

Ron Zook, my Murray State colleague, and I did a great job building this swing set—twice! Here we are celebrating getting it out of the garage.

My introductory press conference at Virginia Tech on December 23, 1986. I made some bold statements about playing for national championships, which raised a few eyebrows.

Looks like I'm not too enthused answering a question before our first bowl game—the 1993 Independence Bowl in Shreveport, Louisiana.

Celebrating our first bowl win—the 45–20 Independence Bowl victory over Indiana in 1993. It was only the second bowl win in Virginia Tech history.

My best buddy Shane has never been far from my side during my coaching career. He looks as pensive as I was before a big game at Murray State, and later, holding my headset cord at Virginia Tech.

Receiving the Bobby Dodd Coach of the Year Award at the end of the 1999 season.

the buses to go to the team hotel, I grabbed a seat in the second row. One of the seniors came on after me and the bus was full.

Coach Claiborne looked at me and said, "Frank, how about hopping up and standing over here by the window."

I thought to myself, *I don't know if this making the travel squad was such a good idea or not.*

It wasn't the first time I had been to New Orleans, because Tulane had recruited me. I think they recruited off these national lists without watching film and I had some very good passing stats in the state of Virginia. When I walked into their offices on my recruiting trip, the head coach, Tommy O'Boyle, looked at me and I could see in his eyes what he was thinking: *This guy is really short.* They put me up in a hotel and one of the players took me to Bourbon Street and I had a good time—but I never did see the campus.

We didn't score a point, losing 13–0 to Tulane in that 1966 opener; I didn't get on the field that day, either. Soon enough, I worked my way onto the field as the primary holder for extra points and field goals. Coach Claiborne wanted to practice a fake field goal before the Kentucky game, so he put Al Kincaid in for me as the holder. He would then take the snap and roll out and throw it. I think I mentioned something to him that Kentucky would know something was up if we substituted Al for me as the holder, but it didn't matter to him. Again I thought, *I guess they don't remember my 43 touchdown passes from high school.*

Al was a heady quarterback, very smart. But I still think I could throw it better than he did; I just never got the chance. We got to be good friends and I even took him home to Fancy Gap for a few weekends.

We played Vanderbilt in Richmond in the fifth game that season and they inserted me into the game in the first half. On the second play I was in there, I got an interception. I started from that point forward. The biggest game I remember that year was beating Florida

State at home 23–21 in a TV game. It was a big deal in those days if you played on TV, because there were only about two games televised each Saturday.

We won seven in a row that season to earn a trip to the Liberty Bowl to face Miami. That was another big deal for the school. Realize that back then there were just a handful of bowls, nine to be exact, and this was the second bowl game ever for Virginia Tech. The first was 20 seasons earlier in the 1947 Sun Bowl. You could almost say this was the first bowl for the school in the modern era. We lost it 14–7.

We opened my junior season at Tampa and I will never forget the night before the game. We stayed in a downtown hotel and I could hear all the traffic and the city noise outside my window. There were horns blowing and sirens sounding all night long. Because I grew up in the country, I guess I wasn't cut out for sleeping in a big city. I was sleep deprived, but we won the game the next day 13–3.

At the end of the fourth game of the season, we led Villanova 3–0 as they lined up to kick a field goal to tie the game. We blocked the kick and Frankie Loria picked it up and started running. I think the officials had blown the play dead for some reason, but an assistant coach came off of Villanova's bench and tackled Frankie. All of a sudden, both benches cleared and everybody was throwing punches. I started to jump right in the middle of this massive fight and my smartness suddenly took over—*Nah, I'll just stand right over here at a safe distance and watch this thing.*

Frankie, who was a year ahead of me, was one of my best friends on the team along with Ron Davidson and Lenny Luongo. Frankie was from Clarksburg, West Virginia, but the Mountaineers never offered him a scholarship. When we prepared to play them every season, we could tell he wanted to beat them pretty badly by the way he practiced that week. Everybody knew he wanted to win that game, so we took it upon ourselves to feel that way about West Virginia, too.

That's how much we loved Frankie. He was such a neat guy. He was very quiet, but he had a sneaky sense of humor and you couldn't help but love the guy. I think he was always two steps more mature than the rest of us. He married his high school sweetheart, Phyllis, while we were still in college.

Frankie was a great player, too. He was our free safety, while Ron and I were the corners. We played only three deep back then with the eight-man front. Unlike me, Frankie did have some good quickness and he could really hit people. Frankie could accelerate toward the ball better than anyone and when he hit someone, they stopped dead in their tracks. We played total zone in those days. I know I wasn't fast enough to play any man-to-man coverage and Frankie probably wasn't either.

We would do those rope drills and he would fall about four times, but as a free safety, his reaction was almost perfect. He was smart and had great instincts for the position. And when he hit those receivers, it was just like a karate chop—quick and powerful. He was a great punt returner, too, taking three punts back for touchdowns in 1966.

Frankie was Virginia Tech's first consensus All-American and became the first player in school history to be named an All-American two straight seasons.

We started the '67 season 7–0 before a pretty good Miami team came to town. The play I remember most that entire season involved me. We were tied 7–7 in the second half when Miami attempted a little curl route. As I came up to make the tackle, the receiver flipped the ball to a running back coming out of the backfield and they scored a touchdown on it. The ol' Hook and Ladder, as they call it, got me.

We then lost at Florida State 38–15 in a game where we couldn't cover their receiver Ron Sellers. He was the best player I ever saw in my three years playing college football. He was so tall and he could run like a deer. In three years against Florida State, I don't think we ever covered him. After that game, VMI, whom we had beaten 70–12 a year earlier, upset us 12–10 at Victory Stadium in Roanoke. We were transitioning at that time and our talent level was getting much better than VMI's, but we still lost to them somehow.

Three straight losses and no bowl: It was a disappointing way to end the season.

We opened my senior season, the first year without Frankie behind us at safety, against Bear Bryant's Alabama team at Legion Field in Birmingham. Alabama came into the season ranked No. 7 and we were big underdogs, but we should have won the game. We threw a couple of interceptions and lost 14–7 and I narrowly missed on a play that could have made a big difference. Their quarterback, Scott Hunter, threw a little outside route and I can see that football heading right to me to this day—I got a great break on the ball and I was ready to make the interception. I also was out far enough to the sideline that I knew I could have got it to the end zone once I caught it. But just before the ball reached me, our linebacker, Eddie Carter, tipped it and the ball went over my head right to the receiver I had cut in front of.

After we lost to Kansas State 34–19 on October 5, I had a blind date that night, of which I'll go into detail later. I wasn't much interested in getting serious with any girl, because one of the great things about my career at Virginia Tech was just hanging around all of my football buddies. We all lived over in Miles Hall and we just had a lot of fun together. Back then, Radford was an all-girls school and there weren't many females at Tech, so going over there was our best chance to find a date.

I would never want to admit this to my players, but I think the only time I ever missed curfew was when Al Kincaid and I were over there at Radford one night. That is when my roommate, Mike Widger, covered for me, telling the coaches at bed-check that I had gone to the bathroom.

Widger was a great linebacker, but he was always giving people grief about something or other. I was lying in my room one night at about two in the morning, sleeping, just minding my own business, when Jud Brownell, who'd thrown back a few that night, walked into our room. Mike got to messing with him about how little weight he could lift and how strong he was, or wasn't. So Jud walked over to our sink and said, "I'll show you how strong I am."

He lifted the sink right off of the wall and the pipes burst! Water started shooting out everywhere. It just kept pouring out and we didn't know how to stop it. Soon, the hallway was flooded and somebody got the bright idea to mix in a little laundry detergent. So here we were, at four in the morning, sliding up and down the hallway in this mix of water and soap suds. I think it flooded into the basement, but we somehow got it all cleaned up so we didn't get in any trouble.

All I wanted to do was get a good night's sleep and I ended up in the middle of that mess.

I was also a member of the Monogram Club and we used to have a picnic every spring. The guys would get a beer truck and back it up in a field somewhere and everybody would be having fun. When I became president of the club, I wanted to upscale this thing a little bit so I decided to find a park in Radford somewhere, instead of an empty field in the middle of nowhere. The picnic was a big hit with the guys and it became one of those all-night deals. Well, someone from the park called Coach Claiborne and told him his players were over there partying all night.

He called me into the office on Monday.

"Frank, were you responsible for that beer party the other night?" he asked.

"Well...I am president of the Monogram Club," I told him.

"I know that, but were you responsible for this beer party I heard about?" he asked again.

"Well...I am president of the Monogram Club," I said again, not tipping my hand one way or another.

"Listen, I had better not hear of anything like that again!" he told me.

"Yes sir," I muttered as I slowly walked out of his office.

Another time I had been out with my football buddies and had had a few and as I walked up the street at about seven o'clock the next morning, Coach Claiborne pulled his car up next to me.

"Frank, you're out early today…you wanna ride?" he asked.

"No, I am good Coach. I can walk."

"Come on! Get in the car!" he demanded.

I tried every excuse I could not to get into that car, but finally I had no choice.

So I got in the car, looking out the window and holding my breath the whole time. I didn't want him to see my eyes. I never wanted to disappoint him. Coach Claiborne was a guy who was everything I thought a coach should be back then. He was tough, demanding, and you always wanted his approval. For him to say, "Hey, you did a good job" meant the world to me.

I believed in him like you are supposed to believe in a coach. I feared him at times because he was so tough, but I think it was a good fear, if that makes any sense. As I got older I realized what a great coach he was. He could motivate us with the best of them.

That Monday after our loss to Kansas State, Coach Claiborne held one of those get-your-toughness-back practices. It was one of those practices where you really got after one another with constant tackling. I don't think the coaches even used whistles during that practice. The freshman quarterback was Don Strock and everybody tackled him. And by that, I mean *everybody*. We just wore him out that day. He would be down and you still had to participate in the tackle even as he was lying there under a big pile of players. Here was a guy who would set all the school passing records two years later, and we were just killing him. It's a good thing he never got injured from those get-tough practices.

The next week, we came back and beat Wake Forest 7–6, so it must have worked.

When we lost, Coach Claiborne always wanted to get our toughness back that following week.

The best moment of that season for me came against Richmond. Their quarterback, Buster O'Brien, who had transferred from Notre Dame, threw a pass out there in the flat and I intercepted it and headed to the end zone. I could see Buster had an angle on me to make the tackle, but I just slipped by him to score the touchdown, the only one of my career. Buster could really throw the football, but he was slow...even slower than I was.

You know how they say you should act like you've been there before? Well, I had never been there before, so I threw the ball up into the stands after I scored. There was no penalty for it back then, but they definitely would have flagged me for it today. Buster went on to become a state senator and now he's a prominent judge in Virginia Beach. Fortunately, they got a picture of me getting by Buster to score the touchdown, or not many people would believe it today.

We got back at VMI 55–6 at Victory Stadium to earn a bid to the Liberty Bowl again, this time to play Mississippi.

Still, I didn't enjoy it much, since I came down with the flu before we left and they put me in the infirmary for a week to recover. I got out on the day we traveled to Memphis, but I was still nowhere near 100 percent by the time we played the game on December 14. I remember we stayed at the Peabody Hotel downtown, where we watched the ducks come out of the elevator and parade around. That was something for all of us country boys to see.

We always ate steak for our pregame meal, but we were so fired up for that game that nobody ate their entire steak. I looked around at all the plates and saw that everyone had only eaten a few bites.

The game was played during the day, but it was so cold that it was the only time I can remember literally shaking on the field. It was 36 degrees when the game kicked off, but it seemed much colder to me, maybe because I was getting over the flu.

We ran a trick play on them and got up 17–0, but all that did was get Ole Miss upset. They had a quarterback you may have heard of, Archie Manning, and he brought them back, scoring 34 straight points to beat us. In that flurry of points I came up to make a tackle on one play…and I sometimes had a bad habit of ducking my head a little bit. Well that's what I did and after that I was seeing nothing but stars. I got knocked out of my final game. In today's world it would be called a concussion. In those days, they said I got my "bell rung" a little bit.

As I look back on it, and I compare our guys to today's athletes, few of us would be playing college football today. Today's players are so much bigger, faster, and more athletic. We played a lot of zone coverage then, which was good for me because I wasn't very fast. I always had a hard time keeping up with guys, but I like to think I had a good feel for the game and good football instincts. I was dependable and consistent. I know I didn't have great athletic ability.

TERRY STROCK, who played at Virginia Tech from 1957 to 1961 and coached the Hokies' secondary in 1968: *"I'd coached Frank when he was a senior and I remember he was a very hard-nosed, aggressive, tough player. He didn't have great speed, but he was very smart. He wasn't very talkative. He did more of his leading by example and by the way he played the game rather than any type of rah-rah talking. We had a great season with Frank Loria, who was an All-American that year, and Ron Davidson, who is in the Virginia Tech Hall of Fame."*

I think what I remember most about my career, in which I had nine interceptions, wasn't so much those wins and losses and the statistics, but all the great buddies I had like Frankie, Lenny, Ron, Al Kincaid, and Randy Treadwell. We had a good group of guys and we always got along pretty well. I became a pretty good student and got my degree in distributive education. That fear of farming and working in the fields paid dividends.

I didn't want the final moment of my football career to be getting knocked out in the Liberty Bowl. So when I heard that Roanoke was starting up a semi-pro team—I think I read about it in the newspaper—I mentioned something to Coach Claiborne about me possibly trying out. I always respected his opinion and wanted to see what he thought.

"Frank, if I were you, I would get on with my life's work," he told me.

That was Coach Claiborne—he could always cut to the chase without beating around the bush.

But he usually gave good advice, too. So I took it.

4

To Teach or To Coach?

CHERYL BEAMER: *"My daddy was a huge sports fan. He had two girls but no sons, so it was just natural that we would love sports and watch it with him. I was a cheerleader who paid attention to most all sports. We went to races together; I was a big Richmond Braves fan and a huge basketball fan—loved it more than football at the time. But my sister Sheila was dating a football player at Virginia Tech by the name of Waddey Harvey. I would come to Blacksburg and go to the games and sit with my mom and dad and sister. We would go out after the games and I would always be the third wheel, so I asked her, 'Next time I come over here, can you fix me up with somebody?' We literally went through the media guide and Waddy picked Frank out for me. They wanted somebody nice who wouldn't attack me and I knew right away he was the right type of guy. He did not have a line. He was as honest as the day is long and I could tell that from our first date."*

I mentioned having that blind date after that loss to Kansas State. Waddey Harvey had told me he had a nice girl he wanted me to go out with—Sheila Oakley's sister Cheryl. If I remember correctly, we just went over to a fraternity house that night and hung around my football buddies for a while. I could tell she liked sports, which was a big plus. We got along right away and she knew a little football, but I always told her it was a good thing we didn't meet earlier, because I was having fun hanging around all of my buddies.

Cheryl was down to earth and a very caring person. She was perfect for me in a lot of ways. We started dating regularly during the last half of my senior season.

Then I took a job after graduation, student-teaching at Newport News, Virginia. Cheryl was living in Richmond at the time and had attended North Carolina–Greensboro. One night, we were riding along in her car, which had a Carolina sticker on the rear bumper. Some guy started honking his horn, giving her the thumbs-up about that sticker.

I told her, "You need to get that Carolina bumper sticker off of your car right now."

"If that Carolina sticker comes off," she said, "then a Wake Forest sticker goes on."

We got to going back and forth about it and she finally said, "It's my car and I'll put whatever bumper sticker I want to on my bumper!"

I actually pulled the car over to the side of the road and ordered her out of the car, unless that sticker was removed.

She said, "You are not going to tell me what bumper sticker I can or can't put on my car! And it's my car! You get out!"

She had some spunk, but we laugh about that night now.

Cheryl knew I never got fired up about much. One of the few times she ever saw me mad was when we were dating and attended a Virginia Tech game the year after I graduated. We were sitting in the stands when a group of guys around us started in on Coach Claiborne. They continued on and on, calling him a "lousy coach" and saying he didn't know what the heck he was doing.

Finally, I had enough and snapped.

"Do you know the guy?" I asked, raising my voice. "Do you know what he's trying to accomplish on that particular play? You're just running your mouth, because you really don't know what you're talking about! Well, I do know the guy and I do know what he's trying to do. I played for him."

After that, they pretty much were silent. I guess part of me was standing up for Coach Claiborne and part of me just didn't like second-guessing from people who knew much less than the coach. I always respected Coach Claiborne and I would defend him to anyone.

At that point, I really wasn't sure what I wanted to do with my life. I had gotten my degree from Virginia Tech in distributive education. I added more math classes that following summer in 1969 so I could get certified teaching math. I liked math, I loved football, and I loved to teach.

I took Coach Claiborne's advice and had gotten on with my life's work, taking a job teaching math at Radford High. I was also working as an assistant football coach there under Harold Absher, making a total of $10,600 per year. I also started working on my master's degree at Radford College.

When Coach Absher decided to retire from coaching after the '69 season and go into the administration, I really thought I was up for the head-coaching job, but they hired Norm Lineburg instead. I was very disappointed at the time, but all these years later, Lineburg is a legend around these parts, and as I look back, he was exactly the right man for the job. I was too young and probably not ready for the job. (Under Coach Lineburg, Radford won the Class AA state championship in 1971.)

On November 14, 1970, I happened to be at Cheryl's house in Richmond, watching television, when the news came across the screen: the airplane carrying the Marshall football team had crashed while flying home after a loss at East Carolina. There were no survivors.

I instantly thought of Frankie Loria. He was only 23 years old and he was their defensive coordinator. It was a terrible time, one of the saddest days of my life. Frankie was just a wonderful guy and he had a heck of a career in front of him. To be the defensive coordinator at that age tells you something about his football mind. I always thought I had a gift for figuring things out on the football field, knowing what was coming next and all that, but I know for a fact that Frankie had it.

Ron Lindon and I went to his funeral in Clarksburg, West Virginia. Frankie's wife, Phyllis, was pregnant at the time and when the baby was born, she named him Frank Jr.

A few weeks later, Virginia Tech finished the season with a 5–6 record—Coach Claiborne's second straight losing season—and they let him go. That hurt me because I thought the world of the guy. He ended up taking a job as the defensive coordinator at Colorado for the 1971 season.

My buddy Wayland Overstreet, whom everyone calls "Street," and I shared a two-bedroom apartment back then and the monthly rent was $80 each. We lived in the bottom part of a duplex, most of which was underground. It had these cheap, cinder-block walls and when it rained, the water would seep through the blocks and flood our floors. We didn't have enough money to know the difference, but one morning, after it had rained hard the night before, I woke up and there was a huge puddle of water surrounding my bed. I heard a "ribbit… rabbit."

There was a frog hopping around my bedroom.

We called the owner and they sent someone over to inspect the damage. They saw all the water and told us they would make it up to us. We were thinking something along the lines of a free month's rent, but they handed us a case of beer instead.

I said, "Street, it's time to upgrade our housing situation."

Those were the good ol' days.

WAYLAND OVERSTREET: *"We had so much fun together. We would go to football games together, we played fast-pitch softball on the same team—Frank was a very good second baseman—played golf and went water-skiing up at the lake all the time. Frank drove an old green Mercury Comet back then and the vinyl top had come loose. We went to a Christmas party one night and when we came out after the party, it was snowing and blowing hard. I climbed into the passenger seat and fell asleep. Frank started to drive away, but the windshield wipers wouldn't work. So there he was, driving down the road with it snowing, his left arm out of the window manually moving the wiper blade so he could see, as the vinyl top flapped in the wind. He was absolutely the typical nice country boy with a big heart. We didn't have any money back then, but he would always try to do something to help others. We remained roommates until he and Cheryl got married and all these years later I consider him my best friend."*

Around Christmas that year, I planned to propose to Cheryl, so I bought a ring and hid it in my parents' house back in Fancy Gap. Cheryl took the bus from Richmond to meet me in Roanoke that Christmas Eve and we drove back to my parents' house. She was sitting in the living room. I told her, "I'll be back in a minute" as I got up to go get the ring.

Problem was, I forgot where I hid the darned thing. I talked to Mom and she didn't know where it was. I finally found it and I came back in and popped the question. She jokes now that my mom was peeking around the corner from the kitchen watching the whole thing, but if she did, I didn't notice her.

We were married April 1, 1972, at First Baptist Church on Monument Avenue in Richmond and I almost didn't make it there in time. I was riding with my Uncle Rufus and Aunt Charlotte and a couple of other people and nobody knew how to get to the church. I think we walked in with five minutes to spare, but I calmed down enough to get the job done.

My best man was Barnett and my groomsmen were Lenny Luongo, Ron Davidson, Waddy, and Dickie Longerbeam. Frankie Loria surely would have been standing there with us if not for the Marshall plane crash.

For a honeymoon, we drove up to Groundhog Mountain for a few nights.

After only one year as an assistant at Colorado, Coach Claiborne got another chance to become a head coach, getting the Maryland job. Before our wedding, I drove up to see him. He offered me a graduate assistant's position at a grand total of $150 per month, the standard pay then for a graduate assistant. I was thinking he surely would pay me more money, simply because I was one of his guys. I played for him. I was just sure he would increase the offer, as I explained how Cheryl and I were getting married, starting a new life, and probably needed more money to live on.

"That's great, Frank," he said. "I can give you $150 a month."

Good ol' Coach Claiborne—he didn't play favorites.

I enjoyed math but teaching five straight math classes each day was really not what I wanted to do for the rest of my life. First off, I thought football was something I knew a little bit about and I thought I would be good at coaching it. Most of all, it's what I really enjoyed doing. It seemed that coaching football would be the right route for my life.

I had no doubts when I took the job at Maryland that I was doing the right thing. As I think back on it, I probably wouldn't have made that move if I had become the head coach at Radford High, so not getting that job may have turned out to be a fortunate thing.

I was at the bottom of the coaching totem pole as a GA at Maryland. It was me, Ralph Friedgen, Charlie Rizzo, and two other guys. Bobby Ross coached the linebackers at the time. To tell you how low I was on the list: I didn't have my picture taken during the team photo session. Coach Claiborne wasn't going to let just anybody get in that team picture and I was very disappointed at being left out.

But I knew taking that job was still the exact right thing to do. In fact, I can even say that about all of my later moves: They were all exactly the right thing to do at the time. I imagine a lot of coaches cannot say they were so fortunate. Some of my moves, as well as others that I didn't get or didn't take, were by chance and just worked out that way.

I coached the freshmen that year and wanted to be more involved with the varsity, but I had to be happy doing what I was doing. And I was, despite my paltry salary.

BOBBY ROSS: *"I could tell right away that year that Frank was headed for big things in his career. He had great work habits, he was intensely competitive and he knew the game."*

Cheryl and I filled out a rental application for a one-bedroom apartment for $190 per month. That $150 per month salary of mine jumped out at the lady taking the application, because as soon as she read it, she looked over the top of her bifocals at me and said, "This isn't going to work."

I explained to her that my wife would be getting a job and we would be able to make the rent every month and she held steadfast, shaking her head.

"No, this isn't going to work," she told me.

We ran out and got Cheryl's parents out of the car to co-sign the application.

Fortunately, Cheryl got a job working as Russ Potts' secretary at the university (he later became a state senator).

Those were the days, I tell you. I remember being in the office one day with Coach Claiborne watching video of a high school player and the film was just awful. It was grainy and running sideways at times. I had just about stopped looking at it, because it was hurting my eyes. He said something like, "Boy, that number 12 really put a move on that guy. He looks good!"

I said, "How can you tell he put a good move on that guy—and how in the world can you see the number on the jersey?"

We opened the season with a 24–24 tie at North Carolina State and played North Carolina the next week in the home opener. One of the assistants told me to go up to the scoreboard on one end of the stadium and watch through a pair of binoculars to determine what front Carolina was using along the line of scrimmage. From the end zone, you could see it perfectly, so I was excited to be doing my part and relaying into a headset what their front was. I remember saying, "He's in a five, he's in a five," and an assistant coach would answer me, "Okay, Okay." I continued on like this for a few plays, but pretty soon, I wasn't hearing any response. Finally, I determined my headset and microphone did not work, so I put it down and watched the rest of the game.

I came home and told Cheryl, "I don't think I will be doing this for very long."

Randy White, who became a star defensive tackle for the Dallas Cowboys, and Tim Brant, who later became a top sports announcer, played on that Maryland team, which finished 5–5–1 that season.

Following that season, Bobby Ross got the head-coaching job at The Citadel and gave Ralph and me great news: he wanted us to join him as full-time assistants. I was thrilled to death, but Ralph started to ask him about benefits, insurance, and all of that. I gave him a look to say, "What are you, crazy? We got job offers here and you are asking about benefits?"

So that was it for being a GA; I was now the defensive backs coach at The Citadel. I realize some people go forever as a GA and our stint in College Park lasted only three months. We no longer had to get by on my $150 each month, either; I had a job as a full-time assistant that would be paying $11,000—about $400 more per year than I made teaching math.

Once we got to The Citadel, Ralph and I shared an office and got along great, and Cheryl and I liked Charleston, South Carolina, as soon as we saw it. It was a great city.

We had a nice stadium, but what I learned right away was there was one problem with that job: it was tough to recruit at a military school right after the Vietnam War. You could get tough, hard-nosed players who loved to be coached, but you couldn't get the real talented players that you needed to win consistently. They weren't always the biggest and they weren't always the fastest. But we really did have great kids at The Citadel. They were smart guys who would someday become doctors and lawyers.

I remember one game against VMI. Coach Ross was a graduate of VMI and he really wanted to win that game, but we couldn't stop them on the final drive and we lost the game. I just felt awful. We lived in an apartment on one end of campus and he lived in a house at the other end of campus. After the game that night, I thought, *Coach Ross must be feeling even worse than I do, so I will go over and see him.* It was one of the best things I ever did. I got there and discovered he needed someone to talk to and I needed to apologize for the way our defense played. At the end of the night, we both felt a lot better.

I almost left The Citadel at one point to return to Virginia Tech. Charlie Coffey became the head coach in 1971, replacing Coach Claiborne, and he gave me a call before the '73 season. Dan Henning was his offensive coordinator and Billy Clay had just taken over as defensive coordinator. I came up to visit and we talked about me becoming the secondary coach. Deep down, I really wanted to come back to Virginia Tech and coach at the major college level. But when I returned to Charleston, I called Coach Claiborne for his advice.

"Just be careful," he warned me. "Every move you make should depend on whether you can be successful, not how much more money you can make."

That was as good advice as I ever got, so I decided not to take the job. He knew that if you were on a staff that gets its pink slips, your career could suffer a setback that it may take a few years to overcome. From that point, I decided never to take a job unless I had a chance to be successful.

To show you how wise Coach Claiborne was: after that season (Virginia Tech finished 2–9), Charlie Coffey resigned. I was so glad I had stayed at The Citadel. Plus, Bobby Ross was a great coach to learn from. He was very precise in everything he did and how he coached the players. I had learned so much from Coach Claiborne, but I really needed to learn yet another way of doing things as well.

Following the 1976 season, Cheryl was pregnant with our first baby and Ralph's wife was about to give birth, too, so the four of us took the same Lamaze class. Those breathing techniques didn't help us too much and Ralph always joked that we needed some Styrofoam cups full of "coffee" to get us through them.

On March 31, 1977, we had a son.

Cheryl and I had narrowed our list of names down to Hunter, Christian, and Shane. She learned the meaning of the name Shane was "gift from God" and she also loved the Western starring Alan

Ladd, so that was the clincher. And Oakley was her maiden name. So that's how we came up with the name, Shane Oakley Beamer. After we named him, it dawned on us what his initials were, but I just said, "We're sticking with it, but he had better be a tough kid."

One night after the 5–6 season in 1977, our secretary was retiring so Ralph and I took her out for dinner and drinks to celebrate her retirement. The next morning, we get an urgent message that Coach Ross wanted to see us right away. We feared we were about to get fired for taking her out the night before. I walked in first to see Coach Ross as Ralph waited in the lobby. Both of us were nervous as heck.

Coach Ross' news was big all right: he was leaving to become the special teams coach of the Kansas City Chiefs.

At first, I was so relieved, hearing that we weren't in any trouble. Then it dawned on me—we may not have jobs since Coach Ross was leaving. I walked out of his office, rolled my eyes at Ralph as he was walking in to see Coach Ross. Then I started to worry about my future.

I interviewed for The Citadel's head-coaching job soon after that, but they hired Art Baker instead. The good news was that he kept us both on his staff. He moved Ralph from defense to offensive coordinator. Jimmye Laycock left for Memphis State, Charlie Rizzo went to Rice, and I was promoted to defensive coordinator.

Art wanted to keep our same eight-man-front defense, but he wanted the offense to practice against a five-man front in the spring. We practiced all spring with a guy over the center and then when we got to the fall, we went back to an even front, even though we hadn't practiced it much.

The result: we weren't worth a crap on defense.

That is when I formed another one of my philosophies: you cannot slow down your defense or change practices in the spring from what you plan to do during the season. You go full tilt and you practice exactly what you will use during the season. I have always liked to stunt and use full blitzing and everything in the spring. We just don't hit our quarterbacks, like most schools don't.

We were always kind of average at The Citadel. Just trying to get over .500 was a big issue. We finished 3–8 my first season there in 1973 and then went 4–7, 6–5, 6–5, 5–6, and 5–6. So that's average for you, but even though we weren't great on the field, those were fun years.

RALPH FRIEDGEN: *"Frank and I always had fun together. We shared an office, sat next to each other in staff meetings, played golf and tennis together. We would go out recruiting in the southern part of Georgia for three weeks every year. He would visit five schools each day and I would go visit five other schools and then we would go back to the hotel for dinner and a drink. Sometimes we had our own cars and sometimes we shared a car while recruiting. You get close with people when you are riding in a car with them all day. We would be riding along in the countryside, and knowing he was the son of a farmer, I would ask, 'Frank, what kind of cows are those over there?' He would answer with a straight face, 'Black and white cows.' You couldn't help but love the guy."*

In the spring of 1979, my coaching career changed with one phone call.

Ron Zook was a young secondary coach at Murray State under Mike Gottfried and he was about to be promoted to defensive coordinator. They hadn't been very good on defense the previous year and their coaches wanted to learn our eight-man-front defense. Ron had called me a few times during the season and I gave him some ideas. He asked if he could come down to Charleston when the season ended.

We spent three or four days together, and the night before he was to leave Charleston, he asked me, "Why don't you come back with me and take a look at Murray State?"

Heck, I had no clue where Murray State was. I knew it was a Division I-AA program, but that is about all I knew about it. But Ron kept on and on about it and finally I told him I would come just to shut up.

> **RON ZOOK,** the former head coach at Florida and Illinois: "*I remember Coach Gottfried was leaving town to watch a basketball tournament and he gave me this long list of things to do. One of them was 'Go to The Citadel and learn the eight-man front.' So I went down to Charleston and Frank and I really hit it off. When I came back, I told Coach Gottfried, 'We didn't just find our defense, we found our new defensive coordinator!' Coach Gottfried was skeptical, 'Hell, he won't come here,' he told me. But I worked and worked on him and got him to visit Murray. I consider Frank Beamer to be the biggest recruit of my career.*"

So I flew to Nashville and Ron picked me up at the airport and we drove to Murray, Kentucky, with me not knowing what to expect. I have to admit I was blown away by the place. They had a beautiful stadium. I saw their weight room and...wow! I saw their offices... wow! Their locker room...wow! Everything was modern and beautiful. I met with one of their vice presidents, Dr. Marshall Gordon, who oversaw football and he explained how they were emphasizing football to raise awareness of the entire university. Everything was just so positive toward football and the future of the program. By the time I left there to return to Charleston, there was no question in my mind that the right thing to do was to go to Murray State to become their defensive coordinator.

MIKE GOTTFRIED: *"I had heard Frank's name from Jerry Claiborne, who told me there's a guy down at The Citadel who knew the 'wide-tackle-six' defense that I wanted to install. So I sent Ron down there. I remember Ron telling me, 'I just found our defensive coordinator.' I told him, 'But I already hired you.' He responded, 'No, no…this guy is better. He would be better for us.' So Ron talked Frank into coming to Murray State for a visit. I had never met Frank Beamer and when I did I noticed that he was very quiet, but as I got to know him, I really liked him. He was a good guy, a good family man, and a good football coach. Soon, everybody at Murray State loved Frank. I always thought Ron giving up his promotion for somebody whom he thought was more qualified was the most selfless thing I had ever seen in all my years in the coaching business."*

Still, I wasn't totally certain and I felt I owed Art Baker a meeting before making the final decision. Ralph waited in the car for me, with our golf clubs in the trunk, as I went to see Coach Baker. We were headed to the course that day, no matter what I decided.

Ralph loves to tell the story that just as I walked out to the parking lot after talking to Art, I opened the car door and he asked, "Well?"

I simply said, "Go Racers!"

We laughed together and then went and played a round of golf, my last in Charleston for a long while. I thought about it later and Coach Baker was such an easygoing guy that nothing bothered him. I had gone in there with this big decision to make, probably thinking he would make a big fuss to keep me. Looking back on it, I don't think it was a big deal to him whether I stayed or did not stay.

Anytime I ever made a move, I always brought Cheryl with me to check out the place before I accepted the job. But when I left for Murray State for my visit, I wasn't serious enough about it to take her with me. It was the only job I ever accepted without her scouting the city and campus first. There is no easy way to get to Murray, Kentucky, so when we actually made the move, she had her doubts. We were driving along this two-lane road that leads there, winding around the hills of Kentucky.

Finally she looked at me and asked, "Frank, where in the world are we headed?"

I know she had her doubts about the place without seeing it, but I just continued to say, "It's going to be okay. It's a nice place. You are going to like it. It's going to be okay."

Fortunately, she did like it. Murray always reminded me so much of Blacksburg. There were so many good people there. It's in the southwest portion of the state, just like Blacksburg, and it has the same feel to it.

Mike was very good to work for and easy to be around. He handled the offense and I handled the defense and he let me coach. He was consistent. All the guys I'd worked for to that point were good to work for. Bobby Ross was even-keel, too. None of them flew off the handle or screamed and yelled for no reason. We tied our first game with me as defensive coordinator against Southeast Missouri and that was one of the teams we should always beat at Murray State. It was a road game at Cape Girardeau, Missouri, which is only about 60 miles from Murray. As we were riding back, I could tell that Mike was very down.

I continued telling him, "We are going to be okay. We are going to be okay. We'll get it squared away Monday in practice." I don't know if I believed it or if I was just trying to convince myself as much as I was trying to convince Mike.

Fortunately, I was right and we got much better. We were pretty good on defense that year. Bud Foster was a junior outside linebacker on that team and the guy always gave great effort. He ran sideline to sideline and never quit on a play. He didn't have great speed, but he was very solid and he knew the game as well as any player.

BUD FOSTER: *"Having Coach Beamer come to Murray was heaven-sent for me. Our previous defensive coordinator, John Sullivan, had played for Bear Bryant at Alabama and he was a bit old-school. Coach Beamer was a teacher and an educator and ahead of the game with what we were doing defensively. He knew the eight-man front and he was ahead of his time coaching our special teams, too. The other thing I noticed right away was that he always was the calmest when things weren't going well. He had perfect poise for a coach."*

I enjoyed two good seasons (9–2–1 and 9–2 records) working for Mike and I really liked him. He was a fun guy to be around—so entertaining when we had all of those long rides in the car. We would drive up to see his brother Joe coach basketball games at Southern Illinois. He would tell stories and have me laughing and I would think, *This guy would be perfect for TV someday, if he ever gets out of coaching.*

We had a good staff there, too. One of the funniest things I can remember in those two years was when Ron came over to the house to help me put together a swing set for Shane. We worked for hours inside the garage, following the directions and tightening every bolt. Finally, we had it ready. But by the time we had all of the attachments on it, Ron looked at me and asked, "How are we getting it out of here?"

We couldn't get it out of the garage! We had to take it apart, take it out in the yard and start over again. Ron will never forget that day. We had some fun times there. Another time, we had a big, strong, quick defensive tackle named Mike Watson. We didn't get many of those type of guys in Division I-AA, and for some reason, he wanted to quit the team. I knew he was just the type of player we needed to keep there, so as he tried to get to his car, I was playing safety—standing between him and his car.

"Mike, you need to think this thing over," I pleaded. "You don't want to quit. Please reconsider this thing. You're a good player and you have a good future, but only if you stay."

I lost that battle: Mike Watson got by me, got in his car, and we never saw him again.

In my second season at Murray, I interviewed with Kansas City Chiefs head coach Marv Levy for their special teams position. Coach Ross had arranged the interview for me, but they ended up hiring Don Lawrence, who used to be the Virginia head coach. It turned out to be another fortuitous turn in my career, because near the end of the season, Mike told me, "If we beat Western Kentucky, I may get offered the Cincinnati job."

Western Kentucky already was one of our rivals, so now there was even more riding on that ballgame. We were coming off two losses and it was one of those games where everything just bounced our way. We had that Racer mascot, which is a horse, running around the track every time we scored. After the game, the Western Kentucky coach, Jimmy Feix, said, "I thought they were going to kill the horse from exhaustion."

We won 49–0, and sure enough, Mike got the Cincinnati job.

I was happy for him, but a little excited for myself, too. I thought I just may have a shot at replacing Mike as head coach.

I knew I had one guy in my corner at the school when it came time to replacing Mike: Dr. Gordon, the school's vice president. He saw the big picture that if you are good at athletics, especially football, that could help put a school like Murray State on the map. I know Mike recommended me, too, which helped. And sure enough, I got the job.

I don't think they even interviewed anybody else.

And to think, two years earlier I wasn't even interested in coming to visit the place. But Ron talked me into it, fortunately, and now I was the head coach. That's how things have worked out for me. I looked back three years earlier and there was a week after Bobby left The Citadel when I didn't even know if I had a job. Then they gave the head-coaching job to Art Baker. I look back on it all these years later and wonder if I would have been able to win enough to keep that job if I had gotten it in the first place.

I was nine years into my coaching career, 34 years old, making $36,000 per year, and was now a head coach in college football. It was a great year for us, 1981, because Cheryl gave birth to our daughter on May 6. Now Cheryl already had named Shane, so I figured this time was my turn.

I always liked the name Susan because there was a Susan Beamer (no relation) in my elementary school and she was the sweetest, cutest little thing you can imagine. Cheryl liked the name Casey. I gave in at the last moment, so I was overruled in naming both of our kids.

There was never a question in my mind I was ready for the head-coaching job. I had worked under Jerry Claiborne, Bobby Ross, Art Baker, and Mike Gottfried, all of whom taught me things about the game and how to treat people. All of them believed in building good defenses with the eight-man front and they also believed the quickest way to win a game was with the help of sound special teams. They all varied a little bit on offense.

As soon as I got the job, I started to study offense a bit more, since I had played defense in college and coached defense throughout my career thus far. So I headed to William & Mary to visit with my friend Jimmye Laycock, who worked with us at The Citadel. He was named the head coach at William & Mary a year earlier and was having great success moving the ball up and down the field.

Ron left with Mike to become his defensive coordinator at Cincinnati. I retained Mike Dickens, who had played at Murray as a quarterback. I brought Ralph in as our offensive coordinator after he spent a year with Jimmye at William & Mary and we also hired Mike O'Cain as our quarterbacks coach. My other assistants were Keith Jones, Mike Clark, and Mike Mahoney (who later succeeded me as head coach).

As a head coach for the first time, I knew that I wanted my offense to be wide open. Coach Claiborne was a very good coach and he was my mentor, but he was a very conservative coach. He thought that when you threw it, three things could happen and two of those were bad. I was on the other end of that spectrum even then. That goes back to high school when we threw the football all over the lot in Coach Thompson's wide-open offense. That is what I said I always wanted to do when I became a head coach and this was my chance.

We started my head-coaching career with a 37–23 win over Southeast Missouri and won the first six games that season. I thought, *Man, this head-coaching thing is pretty easy.* The truth is, we finished 8–3 and had a pretty good team mainly because Coach Gottfried had built a good program and we had good players. All I had to do was not screw it up. I don't remember it being tremendously hard, I can tell you that.

That second year at Murray, I called the offensive plays after Ralph left to become the offensive coordinator at Maryland. I had trouble settling on a quarterback that season, and we lost five straight games and stumbled to a 4–7 record. I played one quarterback and then the other, and neither had the experience to lead us to a winning season, so a lot of it was my fault. I learned then that you had better pick one quarterback and go with him.

It wasn't a fun season. Morehead State upset us 13–10 in a road game and we faced a six-hour bus ride home. We stopped to get fried chicken but we had problems with the order. You can imagine what it's like getting enough chicken for more than 60 players and dozens of coaches and other team personnel. The restaurant didn't have our massive order ready in time, so as they prepared the chicken, we helped box it up for them.

All of our players got fed before I looked at the coaches and asked, "You guys hungry?"

"No, Coach," Bud Foster, then a graduate assistant coach, answered.

"Me neither. Let's get back on the bus and get home!" I said.

Those are just the type of things you did when coaching at smaller schools. You didn't have huge budgets paid for by bowl trips and television appearances. You didn't travel by airplane. You didn't stay at four-star hotels the night before games and the postgame meals were always on the run—fast-food chicken, burgers, or pizza.

I promoted Bud to coach our outside linebackers in 1983. I could tell he had what it took to become a very good coach some day. I knew one thing: if all of our players gave the effort Bud gave on the playing field, we would never lose a game.

We improved by three games to 7–4 that season, before the biggest win we had at Murray State came in the 1984 season opener. I had read in the newspaper that Louisville's coaches said they didn't cut-block much in preseason practice, so they wouldn't get anyone injured and they hadn't scrimmaged much, either, because they were opening the season against us.

We just cut-block them to death that day and their defensive linemen were falling like trees and we won 26–23. They finished 2–9 that year and their coach, Bob Weber, got fired after that season. They brought in Howard Schnellenberger the following year.

That taught me another lesson as a head coach: You had better practice full speed in camp no matter who you open up with each season. It's about getting your team prepared, not about who you play in the season opener.

Before one home game, a regional TV crew came into town to broadcast the game. We had a little reception the night before the game at a local country club. At the end of the night, one of those announcers came up to me and said, "I'm surprised you are here the night before a big game and I'm more surprised how relaxed and social you are."

I wanted to make sure they had a good time, because I thought they might return to televise more of our games.

It was at Murray State where I had my only real scare in an airplane. One time I was taking a flight from Paducah, Kentucky, to St. Louis in one of those 19-seaters. It was a morning flight and I was enjoying my coffee about 15 minutes after we'd taken off. All of a sudden, the plane turned about 50 degrees. My coffee ended up in the lap of the guy next to me. The pilot came on the intercom and mentioned something about getting into the wake of a big jet. That was about the only time I was ever really scared in an airplane.

I interviewed at a few places while I was head coach at Murray, because I thought I would have a hard time getting a head-coaching job at a Division I school coming straight from Murray. Not many guys had made that jump from Division I-AA at that point and I was convinced I had to take a step in between, somewhere. There just seemed to be a stigma about making that jump, even though Mike had just done it.

I had interviewed at James Madison, but didn't get the job. I wanted to interview at East Carolina and didn't get the chance. I wanted to interview at Ball State and I didn't get the chance. I never thought the administration at Murray State would have a problem with me putting out feelers. My philosophy was that having a guy working like heck while he is there, even if he is doing it to get another job to move up, is a good thing. He is trying his best to make your school a winner in order to reach a higher level.

It wasn't that I didn't love my time at Murray, because everyone there was so nice to us. We still have great friends who live there. But I always wanted to coach at a major college school.

One thing we really developed at Murray was a system that emphasized a way to win games with the help of our special teams. We blocked 34 kicks in those six seasons. I figured out that you could really gain an advantage on other teams, especially at that level, simply because they may not have emphasized their special teams or worked on it nearly as much as we did.

We had winning seasons in four of my first five seasons, but we started the 1986 season with a 2–3–1 record. We then ripped off a five-game winning streak to win the Ohio Valley Conference and make the Division I-AA playoffs by beating Austin Peay 24–14 in the final game.

We lost at Eastern Illinois 28–21 in the first round of the playoffs on November 29, 1986. It was a disappointing end to my sixth season as head coach, because we should have won the game and advanced to the next round. In those six years, my Murray teams had a 42–23–2 record.

I had no idea when I walked off the field that day in Charleston, Illinois, that it would be the last game I would ever coach at Murray State.

My life was about to change drastically.

5

Coming Home

Thomas Wolfe once wrote a book titled *You Can't Go Home Again*.

It became one of the classics of American literature and in it he wrote, "You can't go back home to your family, back home to your childhood...back home to a young man's dreams of glory and of fame...back home to places in the country, back home to the old forms and systems of things which once seemed everlasting but which are changing all the time—back home to the escapes of time and memory."

Well, Thomas Wolfe never coached football.

And he surely never played football at Virginia Tech, a place where I grew up watching the game with my Uncle Sharrell and my brother Barnett, where I became a captain of the team, where I met my wife and where I got my college degree.

No matter where my coaching career took me, Blacksburg would always be my home, as well as Fancy Gap and Hillsville, of course.

Virginia Tech had a pretty good season in 1986, winning nine games, losing one, and tying another to earn a trip to the Peach Bowl on New Year's Eve to play North Carolina State. It was Bill Dooley's ninth season at Tech, and I can't speak for him, but he would probably tell you it was one of his best teams.

He also was the athletic director. I don't know all the details, because I was about 530 miles away coaching in Murray, Kentucky, but apparently the school wanted Bill to drop his athletic director duties. There was an ongoing NCAA investigation into the football and basketball programs, which not everyone knew then, including me, and however it happened, it was clear by the end of the season that he wouldn't return as head coach for the following season.

Virginia Tech had hired Dutch Baughman as its new athletic director on December 12, 1986, and his first task was to hire a new football coach. Dutch called me that day, asking if I would be interested in interviewing for the job to replace Coach Dooley.

In my six years as head coach at Murray, as I said many times, I always felt I would have to take another head-coaching job at a lower-level Division I school and do well there before I would get a shot at a school like Virginia Tech, even if it was my alma mater.

On the other hand, there were issues at Virginia Tech. There was an NCAA investigation and I soon learned the school's administration also wanted to cut athletic expenses, increase academic standards, and play a tougher schedule. Now that's a formula that would make most football coaches cringe.

Dutch had narrowed his list for potential coaches to four or five people and arranged to meet me that week at the Opryland Hotel in Nashville for an interview. One of those four or five happened to be my good friend and mentor Bobby Ross, who had just resigned from Maryland because he felt the school had misled him on the future of the program.

I didn't know Dutch at all, but he was very low-key. He wore cowboy boots and had a Texas background. Right away when I listened to him in Nashville that day, I thought he was full of common sense and we just hit it off like two old friends. We met all afternoon that day, took a break, then came back and met for dinner. Then we met some more that night.

I went back to the hotel room very excited and told Cheryl, "I think he's going to offer me the job."

I figured one thing in my favor was that Dutch figured they probably didn't have to pay me as much as some other coaches would demand, since I was coaching at a Division I-AA school, and the fact that Virginia Tech was my alma mater. They probably knew I would have walked from Murray, Kentucky, to Blacksburg to get the job.

And they were right.

There were reports at the time that Coach Ross was the leading candidate, but Dutch gave me every indication he was focusing his search on me. Then Bobby called me one day.

"Frankie, I am thinking about taking this Virginia Tech job," he told me. "If I do, I need to know if you will join me as my assistant head coach."

Now I was really confused. I didn't know what to say, but I thought so much of Coach Ross, I said, "Sure, I would be honored to be on your staff there."

I called Dutch and told him what had just happened.

"Dutch, I don't know where to go here." I said. "The guy I think so much of wants to take this job. What's happening?"

He immediately told me, "No. No. You're the guy I want to come to campus and meet with the president."

Then I called Coach Ross back.

"They want me to come to campus to meet people, and if everything goes well, I think they will offer me the job," I told him.

"If that's the case, I don't want to stand in your way," he told me. "I need to get out of this thing. You are the right man for that job."

That's just the kind of guy Bobby was, and still is. He's a wonderful man and one of my closest friends in the business and I have always thought the world of him. He was so graceful to back out of it, but he would have been the popular choice as far as the fans and media go. And I know he would have done a good job.

It was the second time a guy had deferred a job to me that he could have had, the first being Ron Zook at Murray State.

BOBBY ROSS: "I had left Maryland and was looking for a job when I met with Dutch Baughman at a hotel in Richmond after I resigned. We talked about my situation and the Virginia Tech job and he also asked me about Frank, but I think he was baiting me. I figured he knew that I knew Frank well and wanted to see what I would say about him. I told him, 'You need to offer Frank Beamer this job.' And I think my wife told Dutch that same thing. He was one of my oldest and dearest friends and I was as happy for him when he got that job as I would have been for myself."

It all worked out for Bobby, too, because he got the Georgia Tech job almost right away. Then he won a national championship there in 1990.

I came to Blacksburg and met with Dutch again, as well as President William Lavery and Minnis Ridenour, a vice president who oversaw the athletic department. I had a good feeling about everything. They told me I just had to wait for the board of trustees' approval.

Dutch called me at the hotel and invited me to dinner at the Farmhouse Restaurant in Christiansburg. It was there he made it official: the board had approved my hiring and he offered me the job. It was December 22, 1986. We celebrated over dinner. The Farmhouse is still one of my favorite restaurants. To this day, we take our team to eat there the night before our home games, and also road games, before we bus to Roanoke and fly out.

My salary would be $86,000, which was pretty good money back then for a guy from Fancy Gap.

Not everyone was thrilled with me being named head coach at Virginia Tech. The next day, Bill Brill wrote a column in the *Roanoke Times* comparing hiring me to "waking up Christmas morning expecting a new bicycle and getting a sweater instead."

Cheryl was really mad about that column, but I shrugged my shoulders and told her, "Maybe he needed a sweater."

We had the introductory press conference that day, thanked several people, and introduced my family. I made a huge mistake: I introduced everybody but Cheryl. (Since then, I have always introduced her first to make up for that blunder).

I told the media, "This is a dream come true. We've got a winning tradition at Virginia Tech and we can build on that. I really think that someday we can play for national championships here."

I walked away from the podium and my brother Barnett approached me.

"Frank, what are you doing?" he asked. "These people would be happy winning six or seven games every year and going to a bowl every three years or so and you are mentioning playing for national championships? People may start thinking you're crazy for saying things like that."

I may have been crazy making those comments about playing for a national championship, but I believed it. We were an independent, but so were Florida State, Penn State, South Carolina, and Miami, and they all were not having much trouble winning 10 or 11 games each season. I knew we were a great academic school and Virginia had good high school football as a recruiting ground for us. I had confidence in my ability to turn the program into a team that could compete every season.

CHRIS KINZER, Virginia Tech kicker, 1985–88: *"I'll never forget sitting there in my dorm room in Blacksburg when Coach Beamer got the job. They were interviewing Beamer on TV and he said, 'I hope one day we can compete for and win a national championship.' I was sitting there thinking, 'This guy must be smoking marijuana or something.'"*

I knew there were doubters, but nothing could prevent the day I was hired at Virginia Tech from being one of the happiest days of my life. I just had no idea of the trials and tribulations ahead of me.

I remember Cheryl and I rushing to the Roanoke airport to catch our flight back to Nashville on Christmas Eve, because we wanted to be with the kids for Christmas. We barely made the flight—and it wouldn't be the last time I would scramble to catch a flight at the Roanoke airport.

We enjoyed Christmas with the kids before I returned the next week and started to work.

Of course, I didn't know about the behind-the-scenes storm brewing. I had no idea that we were about to be bit by some severe NCAA sanctions, either. In my first week, Dutch and I went to meet with several deans of the various colleges (or departments) for lunch. I went to get a salad and came back to the table, where many of them proceeded to tell me everything that was wrong with athletics at the school. They talked for some time and I never did get to eat my main course that day.

I just answered them this way: "Look, we're all at the same school and on the same team here. We will work with you to do things right. You have my word on that."

When I met with Dutch during our first interview, one of the things I told him when pitching myself was, "You are not going to find a guy who knows more about offense and defense and special teams than I do. I have coached them all."

When they asked me about my offensive philosophy, I said, "You have to be able to run the football, you have to be able to throw it, and then once you see what the defense is doing to defend both, you attack it in that regard."

I admit—and this goes back to my high school days—I loved having a team that could throw the ball around. At the same time, I am the first to admit there are games that call for toughness and you have to be able to run it. I never wanted to have a team that went out there and threw it all day long and I never wanted to coach a team that went out there and ran it all day long. Those one-dimensional teams don't win many national championships, at least not in the modern era.

Defensively, I wanted a team that could always get one more guy up front than the other team could block. I think you should build your defense with kids who can run fast and re-direct and play well fundamentally. You have be good gap-wise, have a fast defense, and have all 11 guys moving toward the football and get there in an angry mood—all the philosophies we had used at Murray State.

Therefore, it was just natural I would bring several of those assistants with me, such as Bud Foster, Steve Marshall, Keith Jones, Duke Strager and Larry Creekmore. They knew our system, they knew me, and they were good football coaches. We holed up in the old Red Lion hotel, where the Hilton Garden Inn sits today on the edge of campus, and got down to work. I remember all of us watched the Peach Bowl together that New Year's Eve as Virginia Tech beat N.C. State 25–24 on Chris Kinzer's 40-yard field goal on the final play.

It was Coach Dooley's last game and those players had rallied around him. I understood all of that. But now it was our team to coach.

I added Ron Zook—who was responsible for me getting the Murray State defensive coordinator job eight years earlier—as my defensive coordinator. Ron had been coaching the defensive backs at Tennessee for Johnny Majors. When I talked to people once I got to Blacksburg, I asked about Coach Dooley's staff members and the name that kept coming up was Billy Hite.

Everybody loved Billy, and I heard he was a very good recruiter, so he was the only coach I retained from the previous staff.

Before we ever coached a game in 1987, however, I got hit right between the eyes with shocking news. Dutch called me into his office one day and announced, "I'm sorry Frank and I hate to do this, but they didn't tell me the whole story when they hired me. I am planning to resign."

I was stunned.

Apparently, as I said, the football program and the basketball program were being investigated by the NCAA. The football program had over-signed the number of scholarships it was allowed, and very few people even knew about the basketball trouble. Dutch said he didn't know anything about it when he was hired. On top of that, they wanted the athletic budget balanced and the academic requirements for recruits were being increased.

Then I made a mistake of my own before we played our season opener against Clemson.

Two days before the game, I had the coaches stay in the office until 2:00 AM because I wanted to change some things on defense. I had a defensive staff which had worked their butts off getting ready for the season and here I was making changes at the last minute. It was exactly the wrong thing to do. I learned from this mistake later. Ron Zook knew the defense I wanted from us being at Murray State together, but I messed it up trying to change things at the last minute.

And no matter how much football you know or how well-prepared you are, it's impossible to win without enough able bodies.

We went into that first game without four starters because of injuries. Six more players were ruled ineligible for academic issues, so it's no wonder we lost 22–10. We did get one loud cheer that day. Coach Dooley had a conservative offense, sort of a "high-diddle-diddle, we're coming up the middle," as Billy Hite called it. Almost immediately, we threw a deep pass, which fell incomplete but the fans cheered it anyway.

We then lost to Virginia 14–13 and Syracuse 35–21. We were 0–3, and every day I would wake up and wonder who we would lose to injury or academic problems.

We beat Navy 31–11 on October 3 at Lane Stadium for my first win at Virginia Tech, before losing to South Carolina and East Carolina. I remember in the Friday walk-through at South Carolina, we had these old, gray warm-up suits with the numbers marked out and the new ones marked in. Here came South Carolina with these silky, black warm-ups. I looked out there and saw Sterling Sharpe running around in those and I told our equipment man, Lester Karlin, who has been with the program since 1978, "Lester, next week we are going to have us some good-looking, silky warm-ups like South Carolina."

South Carolina beat us pretty good, 40–10, and after the game, Ron and I had a disagreement about how to run the defense. I said something he didn't agree with. Then he blew up at me and asked something like, "Then why did you hire me as your defensive coordinator?"

We smoothed it over, but I probably was getting too involved in everything. I can see now that I tried to do too much during that first season. I tried to be everywhere at once, coaching all three phases of the game. I would be in a staff meeting trying to make a decision and I would have to take a call or leave for an appearance, normal things a head coach has to do, and the staff would be left hanging.

We were 1–5 and headed to play Tulane in New Orleans. We played a sloppy first half and I had held my emotions in check through the first half of the season. As I walked into the locker room at half-time, one of my assistants, Tommy Groom, told me, "Coach, you've got to get in there and go off on them."

I thought about it a moment and figured, *Maybe this is what they need.*

So I spent the halftime ranting and raving and screaming and yelling at my players. I think I even kicked a chair. It must have really fired them up because Tulane, which was coached by Mack Brown, returned the second-half kickoff for a touchdown and went on to beat us 57–38. I figured out then that halftime speeches weren't going to get it done that season.

I also knew that blowing up at them just wasn't me. I have done it a few times over the years, but it usually was reserved for an off-the-field incident. I would rather be calm at halftime even when things are going wrong, just to keep a level head and try to think our way out of the mess. After that game, I always felt that halftime was a good time for making adjustments, not for losing my temper.

Shane was just 10 years old that season and he always asked me to be on the sidelines with the team. I let him come down there and when things weren't going well, certain words were used on the sidelines that wouldn't be accepted in Sunday school. Shane came home one night and started to tell Cheryl about what went on down there and what was being said during moments of frustration.

I pulled him aside and said, "Listen, son, you can't be telling Mom everything. What happens on the sideline stays on the sideline, you got it?"

He agreed and stayed mum after that point.

Virginia Tech's longtime trainer in those days was a guy by the name of Eddie Ferrell, who came to Virginia Tech in 1971. Now

Eddie was a great guy, but he had one of those senses of humor that if you didn't know him, you may have wanted to punch him out sometimes. Eddie would walk into our Sunday meetings and update us on who was injured, how severe it was and his chances for practicing and all those things.

At one of our home losses that season I noticed a helicopter hovering behind the stadium. When Eddie stuck his head in the door that Sunday morning, I asked him, "What happened over there yesterday?"

"Y'all finally got a first down," Eddie said straight-faced, "and someone was so excited that they fell right off the back of the stadium!"

With that, he walked away without even smiling or laughing. If it were anybody else, I would have wanted to take a poke at him, but Eddie could get away with it. Everybody on the staff just loved the guy. Both of his sons, William and Daniel, became part of the program later. William played for us and Daniel became a graduate assistant coach. Sadly, Eddie died the week before our 1998 season began. Today, there is an annual sports-medicine clinic and a scholarship named in his honor.

Someone did fall off the back of the stadium that day, but fortunately, the person survived the fall.

Eddie cracked us up often in those days when we needed a laugh most.

And we needed it often during that first season.

Dutch had resigned, I'd stepped on some of my assistants' toes, and we had started the season with only one win. But it was about to get worse—much worse.

On October 26, the NCAA hit the school with severe sanctions, limiting the scholarships we could offer to 15 for each of our next two recruiting classes. The NCAA allowed 30 per class at the time, so that meant we would lose 30 total scholarships over a two-year period. People can talk about not having your games on TV or not going to a bowl as tough penalties, but those don't hurt nearly as much as scholarship reductions. A bowl ban may be one year, but having scholarships pulled hurts a program three, four, or even five years down the road.

Those were some harsh penalties as far as a football coach is concerned. I know some people at Virginia Tech told me they believed the NCAA made the penalties more severe because of what had happened two years earlier.

The NCAA had announced that Bruce Smith, who was an All-American at the time, would be ineligible for the 1984 Independence Bowl, but Bruce got a lawyer to fight it. The case went back and forth in the courts and was at a standstill when the bowl was played, so Bruce was allowed to play in the game. They believed that didn't sit too well with the NCAA and if they ever got the chance, they would make the school pay for it. Therefore, the NCAA got its chance two years later, and subsequently hit Virginia Tech hard with those sanctions. At least that was the theory.

Whether that was true or not, it was definitely a real mess. At the same time, I knew it was a troubling situation, but I always felt like I could solve it. Maybe I might have been a little naïve back then, but I still believed we had a bright future once we got through it all.

That is why I made all those statements about playing for a national championship in the first place when I was hired. I knew Virginia Tech was a great academic school. Virginia was a great state for high school football. What would keep us from winning a national title? I had just wanted to send everyone a message that I believed in Virginia Tech and that's why I said what I said. I was confident in my ability to turn things around. I had coached on both sides of the ball and special teams were important to me. I knew I could recruit. I felt this was the perfect place to win and win big.

But maybe I didn't know what I didn't know.

Anyway, the administration was more than fair to me because of the NCAA probation. They added a year to my contract for every year we were on probation. And I think that also is one of the reasons they were very patient with me as the years went on and we were trying to turn the corner.

We lost three straight games on the road after the probation was announced—at Kentucky, at West Virginia, and at Miami—but weren't blown out of any of them. We were competitive for three quarters in most of our games, just not deep enough or talented enough to win them in the fourth quarter. After 10 games, we had a 1–9 record.

We won our last game of the season, beating Cincinnati 21–20, when the Bearcats failed to convert a two-point conversion in the final minutes. It was freezing cold and the students were away on Thanksgiving break—there were only 10,000 or so fans at Lane Stadium.

I told the media, "When we get this program back to where it should be, the people I am going to appreciate are the 10,000 fans out there today."

The thing that was unique about the situation was the fact that when you get hired somewhere, normally you replace a coach who was fired or resigned because the football team was not successful. Instead, we had replaced a group of coaches who had just won 10 games, including a bowl game. By comparison, that made that first season even worse. It was an eight-game swing in the wrong direction.

After that final game, Ron Zook left us to join Ohio State's staff. He was from Ohio and I kind of knew he always wanted to coach there. We parted on good terms, even though we had gotten into a few arguments earlier in the season. I still think highly of him and will always be appreciative of him for what he did helping me get the Murray State job.

All in all, it was a miserable first season. But the one thing I have always said is, "Even if I knew about the NCAA sanctions and the penalties that were coming, I still would have taken the job."

But now we would be trying to bounce back from a 2–9 season with two years of NCAA probation ahead of us and without the guy who hired me there to support me as we tried to turn things around.

Maybe Thomas Wolfe was right after all....

Nah.

5

Turning It Around

I knew the name, but didn't really know much about Dave. When he got the job and started to work following our first season, I trusted him right away. I never doubted anything he told me. I knew the university brought him in to clean things up and make sure there would never be another NCAA scandal. He had been around a bit and had coached football, so I think that helped me tremendously.

Four years later, that fact would be crucial to my future at Virginia Tech.

When he was first hired, Dave was quoted as saying, "I want to make sure what we tell recruits and student-athletes is within the rules. I don't expect a coach to learn the entire NCAA rulebook, but I do expect them to know certain areas. My job is to help them not cross the line on the rules. The university has said, 'We're embarrassed. We want to do things the right way.'"

I know one thing: they never had to worry about Frank Beamer breaking the rules. I would rather lose by 50 points and play by the rules than win if I had to cheat.

We weren't losing by 50, but we were still losing football games in 1988. We improved by only one game to 3–8, mainly because we were playing young kids and our overall numbers were down because of the scholarship reductions. We signed only 14 kids in that recruiting class. We also played a brutal schedule that season, losing to West Virginia, which played for the national championship; Florida State, which finished 11–1 and beat Auburn in the Sugar Bowl; and Clemson and Syracuse, which each won 10 games.

During our first five years, I think we faced 29 bowl-bound teams and 18 Top-20 opponents. Eight of our first 27 games were against top-10 teams, so the administration had accomplished one of their goals: upgrading the schedule.

We were beaten 35–13 at Southern Miss by a quarterback you've heard of: Brett Favre. Southern Miss also won nine games that year. We lost by two points to South Carolina, which ended up winning eight games. Our schedule was like murderer's row that season.

We made progress in our third year, beating Akron, Temple, West Virginia, Tulane, Vanderbilt, and N.C. State.

Before the West Virginia game, Shane had stumbled upon their student newspaper, which referred to Virginia Tech as "a second-class program." As a coach, you use anything you can to motivate your team, especially when you are a big underdog, and this newspaper story was perfect. I held up that newspaper the night before the game and told our players, "This article here says Virginia Tech is 'second-class.' I am from Hillsville and we didn't have much growing up, but nobody ever called us 'second-class.'"

That second-class thing really got them riled up enough to play well. West Virginia was ranked ninth in the country at the time, coming off that national championship loss to Notre Dame in the previous Fiesta Bowl. They still had Major Harris at quarterback and were 16-point favorites over us.

But our defense was lights-out that day, and Mickey Thomas kicked four field goals, as we surprised the Mountaineers 12–10. It had to be the highlight of my first three seasons.

Mike Gentry, our strength and conditioning coach—one of the best in the country—told me later that was when he knew the players had accepted me as their coach. They weren't thinking of the days when Bill Dooley was here and they weren't feeling sorry for themselves after two straight losing seasons.

That Monday, my high school coach, Tommy Thompson, walked into my office carrying a plaque that included the date of the game and the score. He had it engraved and presented it to me. It was great to see him again.

Later that week, he had a heart attack and died. I will never forget how his coaching helped me get to where I was. It was a terrible week, because on that Wednesday, Cheryl's father also died.

Three days later, Florida State handed us a 41–7 loss at Lane Stadium—the Seminoles were loaded that year.

Next up was East Carolina, which always seemed to give us trouble, especially at their place.

We were fighting them tooth and nail in the second half when I suddenly felt severe tightness in my chest. I called the team doctor over and told him, "Something's not right. I have some tightness in my chest and think I need to get checked out after the game."

We lost the game 14–10, we flew home and he arranged for me to get tested that Sunday. Then the doctors sent me to Roanoke Memorial Hospital for more tests. They told me I had severe blockage and needed an angioplasty. The doctors inserted a tiny balloon into the artery and inflated it until the blockage was cleared. A reporter had asked me if football-related stress caused the problem and I cracked, "No, stress is lying on the operating table and realizing three of the four doctors are West Virginia graduates."

That was a good one on the banquet circuit. I never had a heart attack, but the doctor, Robert Rude, told me I probably would have if that blockage hadn't been caught in time. I had started smoking a little bit in college and then continued on through the years. From that day, October 21, 1989, I never smoked a cigarette again (although I will have a cigar once in a while on the golf course).

SHANE BEAMER: "I was holding his headset cord on the sidelines at the time and I could tell something was wrong with him. It was a wakeup call for him to take better care of himself. He was smoking then and he didn't want me or my sister to know about it, so he would hide a pack of cigarettes under his car seat. I would sneak out to the garage in the middle of the night and take them out of his car and throw them away."

Billy Hite took over for me as head coach as we beat Tulane in the eighth game of the season. I returned and we beat Vanderbilt to improve our record to 5–3–1 before losing 32–15 at Virginia, our third consecutive loss to our rival since I got the job. In the final seconds of that game, one of our defensive linemen, Jimmy Whitten, was getting into it with a Virginia offensive lineman. After the final play of the game, I ran out there to grab him and prevent a fight. Jimmy reared back to hit the guy and his elbow hit me in the mouth and knocked out my right front tooth.

I fell down like I had lost a heavyweight fight. While I was down there, I thought I might as well try to find my tooth. Above me was mass chaos as players were pushing and shoving each other and their students had run onto the field to celebrate. (Today, I have a nice solid bridge where that tooth was.) We just got our butts kicked, people are swarming all around me, and I'm on my hands and knees looking for my tooth.

First it was my heart, then it was my tooth—all in about a two-week span. Cheryl told me later that when she saw me fall to the ground after catching that elbow, she thought I may have been dying of a heart attack.

It took a 25–23 win over N.C. State in the season finale to give us a 6–4–1 record, our first winning season.

Through those first few years, the program was evolving and we made several changes as we went. For example, the upperclassmen always had a tradition of shaving the head of all the incoming freshmen during training camp. It was done long before I ever came back to coach and it had continued during our first couple of seasons.

Jim Pyne was a highly recruited center we had just signed when he walked into my office one day just as the 1990 camp started. He was clearly upset. He had thinning hair to begin with and he told me that when his head was shaved once in prep school, it didn't grow back as well as he would have liked.

"If they shave my head," Jim told me, "I may not stay around here."

That is when I put a stop to the head-shaving tradition.

Good thing he stayed, too, because Jim became an All-American for us.

Quarterback Maurice DeShazo was part of that class, too, along with receiver Antonio Freeman, cornerback Tyronne Drakeford, and linebacker Ken Brown.

I could tell we were on the fringe of becoming a pretty good team that season, because we won six games and yet three of our losses were by seven points or less. We could have beaten Florida State on the road when the Seminoles were ranked No. 2. We lost 6–3 at Georgia Tech to my old buddy Bobby Ross' team, which ended up sharing the national title with Colorado that season.

The loss that really hurt came at Temple, 31–28, at the old Veterans Stadium. I just hated playing in that place. The artificial turf had seams everywhere because the Phillies played there. It was like playing on bad carpet that was laid on top of cement. And it was always 90 percent empty. They would have about 200 fans in the stands and then we would have some fans, but you could hear the conversations in the crowd. I would rather play in a packed stadium with everybody against us than to play there.

We played with absolutely no intensity that day and I could tell we were not ready to play from the first play of the game. We had guys dropping with injuries on that old nasty turf as the game wore on. I think by the fourth quarter we were missing quarterback Will Furrer, safety Damien Russell, Pyne, tailback Vaughn Hebron, and a few others. It's always terrible to lose, and you always hate losing guys to injury—but when you do both in one day, it's the worst possible scenario.

The next week, we came home to face Favre and Southern Miss again. They had beaten us soundly two years earlier when he was a sophomore. When he was a junior, they had shocked Florida State to open the season and now he was a senior and no longer a secret. Will Furrer had a great game for us and we had a 20–16 lead in the final minutes. We faced a third-and-short and Southern Miss was out of timeouts. We discussed what play to run on the sideline and Will headed back to the huddle.

Then I called him back to the sideline.

"Now Will, remember, if we get this first down, the game is over," I told him.

He looked at me and sort of rolled his eyes.

"No shit, Coach," he said and ran back to the huddle.

I guess I had stated the obvious.

But that was Will. He never minced his words.

We got the first down, ran out the clock and after beating N.C. State a week later, we were 5–5 with a home game against Virginia, which had beaten us three straight times since I had returned to Blacksburg. They entered the game ranked No. 17. We wore all-maroon uniforms for the first time and I don't know where they got the idea, but the kids painted their shoes black for the game. That night was electric at Lane Stadium and everything worked for us as we won 38–13.

More than two weeks after our first win over Virginia had given us our second straight winning season, Big East commissioner Mike Tranghese announced that the conference would be adding football, with Temple, Boston College, Rutgers, and West Virginia joining Pittsburgh and Syracuse. The big additions as far as I was concerned, were Miami—and us.

Tranghese invited us to join the Big East on December 13. (Our acceptance didn't become official until February 5, 1991.)

I wanted to celebrate, just knowing this was the piece of the puzzle that Virginia Tech had lacked all those years. Having a conference affiliation, especially with a powerhouse program like Miami joining, too, would now give us a recruiting advantage we never had as an independent. The potential of the program had suddenly increased dramatically in one day.

That week, Chet Gladchuk, who had just been hired as the Boston College athletic director, called me. He wanted to talk with me about becoming their next football coach. They had just fired Jack Bicknell, so Cheryl and I flew to Boston. Chet talked to me about the numbers of a six-year contract, starting at $160,000 per year. I was making $103,000 at Virginia Tech, but he never really came out and said, "I am offering you the job."

It was just sort of a given that it was mine if I wanted it.

But one of the first things we noticed there was the housing situation. They told us, "Now the head coach can afford to live here near campus, but the assistants will be living about 45 minutes away in a suburb."

In other words, none of the assistants could afford housing near campus and would have to drive an hour or more to work every day. Right away, I knew that was not the perfect situation. The city of Boston was not me. And it wasn't Cheryl, either. We couldn't leave Blacksburg for the big city like Boston. It surely wasn't the people— Cheryl and I both liked all the people we met at Boston College.

We flew back to Blacksburg and Virginia Tech immediately offered me a raise, but I turned it down. I didn't want it to appear as if I talked to Boston College just to force them to give me a raise. I called Chet back and said thanks, but no thanks.

Then the news broke in the *Roanoke Times* that Boston College had offered me the job, but Chet was quoted as saying, "We never offered him the job."

Anyway, he ended up making a great hire in Tom Coughlin.

Following our 5–6 record during the 1991 season, I felt I had to make a few changes. I let go two assistants who had been with us for the first five seasons—Duke Strager and Larry Creekmore. It was a tough thing for me to do because they were good, loyal coaches. I hired Terry Strock, a Virginia Tech graduate who coached me in college, to coach our defensive ends.

One of our graduate assistants at the time, Todd Grantham, who played offensive line here from 1985 to 1988, had what it took to become a great coach. All he needed was experience, so I decided I was going to give him some. I hired him to coach the defensive tackles.

I knew we had to make improvement in 1992 or we all may be looking for jobs in a year.

Little did I know I was about to begin the most trying, most frustrating year of my coaching career.

We beat James Madison and Temple, surrounding a terrible 30–27 loss at East Carolina—I was now 2–4 against the Pirates. The truth is, we should have won all three of those games for a 3–0 start.

We then lost to West Virginia 16–7 at home. We traveled to Louisville and played well, taking a 17–6 lead early in the fourth quarter. But they scored two late touchdowns to beat us 21–17. It had to be about the toughest loss I'd ever experienced to that point in my career. We were 2–3 and a team in turmoil. Two players had gotten into a heated argument in the locker room after the game while I was talking with the media.

The night of the game, the telephone rang at the house—we always had a listed number back then—and Casey, who was only 11 years old, picked up the phone. Some guy just went off on her, telling her what a lousy coach I was and calling me names. She listened and listened and listened before he hung up.

She walked into the living room with tears running down her face.

Cheryl asked, "What's wrong, honey?"

"Somebody wanted to talk to Daddy," she said. "He said he was a terrible coach and he should be fired."

"Why didn't you just hang up, honey?" Cheryl asked her.

"Because that would have been rude," she answered.

When I arrived home that night, Cheryl greeted me at the door and told me the entire story. I sat Casey down and said, "Look, honey, sometimes in life's work, we're up here." I held my hand at eye level, "and sometimes we're down here." Then I lowered it to my waist. "And right now we're down here. But Daddy's a good football coach and we're going to be up here one day."

We made sure our phone number was unlisted from that point on.

N.C. State scored on the final play of the game to tie us 13–13 in the next game, before Miami, then 6–0, came to Blacksburg. It was the first-ever trip to Lane Stadium for a No. 1-ranked team. We fell behind 37–3 and eventually lost 43–23. The next game was the real heartbreaker. We jumped up on Rutgers 28–7 before they fought back to cut our lead to 49–37 with about seven minutes left in the game.

They scored again to make it 49–44 and forced us to punt. They took possession at their 22-yard line with only 1:32 remaining. We just needed one stop to win the game. We gave up a few short completions before they completed a Hail Mary to our 15-yard line. They spiked the ball to stop the clock with only five seconds remaining. On the final play, they connected on a pass to the corner of the end zone to beat us by one point.

It was about as miserable as I ever felt after losing a football game. We were 2–5–1 and had blown another game we never should have lost.

We rolled up 558 yards and 49 points and forced five Rutgers turnovers and came away with a loss. We followed that up with a

28–9 loss at Syracuse and two more heartbreakers at home—13–12 to Southern Miss and 41–38 to Virginia.

By the end of the season, of our eight losses, we had led in six of those games at some point in the fourth quarter. That had to be some kind of record. We just couldn't finish. We also had committed 88 penalties for 755 yards, a big chunk of yardage for 11 games, which led us to show videos of our penalties in front of the entire team on Mondays. Many of those penalties came at the worst possible times. It became a great teaching tool as we singled out the offender in front of his teammates. I found that peer pressure helped eliminate mental mistakes.

We were a soft team, too, and I knew we needed to become tougher, more hard-nosed, starting with the off-season program.

It was one of those seasons when we really felt the scholarship reductions, too. I always said back in 1987 that they would hit us three, four, and five years down the road and they were hitting us hard in 1992.

Fortunately, I had an athletic director who knew all of that. I was not making excuses; those were just the facts.

Dave Braine has told the story often, but it is one of the best stories of my career and one of the most important of my life.

Dave had always attended church every Sunday. But during the early part of the season, some man would approach him every Sunday, tap him on the shoulder and ask, "When are you going to get rid of Beamer?" Each and every Sunday this went on.

So Dave tired of that guy's question and he stopped going to church. Instead, he started to come into the office with us on Sunday mornings. He would arrive with a bag of donuts, watch film with us, and sit in on our staff meetings. Then he'd come to my office and ask me questions about every decision I made and why I made it. Some head coaches may not have liked that, but I never took any offense to it at all.

And I never once asked him, "Am I safe here?"

That is not the way I thought. I wanted to know: what can we do to get better? That was my entire thought process. I always felt like Dave was in my corner, and as it turned out, I was right.

It probably was a good thing for me that he sat in on all of our meetings, because he saw we were doing a good job and he stood up for me at the end of the season. He also had a very good football background.

DAVE BRAINE: "During that 1992 season, I knew it was a tell-tale year for Frank. We would either extend his contract or start over with a new coach. That was before cell phones and the Internet, and letter after letter about firing Frank Beamer flooded my office. After I got tired of seeing that guy in church, joining Frank and his staff on Sunday mornings was the best move I ever made. I would listen to Frank critique the coaches, the offense, the defense, and the kicking game. I would sit in his office and ask him questions and he always had a great answer for every question. Never one time did he get upset with me or resent me being there. I thought to myself, 'Hey, this guy is a good coach and we have to keep him.' Sometimes, he didn't always hire the best people and that's the easiest way to fail, if a coach doesn't surround himself with good people in every area. But there was no question he was the right man for that job. At the end of the season, the president, Dr. [James] McComas, called me in. He always called me 'Mister AD.' He asked, 'So Mister AD, do we need to change our football coach?' I answered, 'No sir, we just need to give him the money to get some good assistant coaches around him.'"

We had a Monday morning meeting in Dave's office after our final game and his exact words to me were, "I don't think you can survive this unless you make some [staff] changes. There needs to be change for change sake."

The bottom line: I still had a job.

At the time, I probably never realized how serious the situation was as far as my status was concerned. My thing was just keeping my head down and working hard every day to get this program to where it needed to be. There were obstacles, and I was tackling the obstacles. When you hear the words "two, eight, and one," you think, *Ouch, that's a bad team.* But it was a deceiving 2–8–1. We were so close to winning many of those games and we were a lot better than what you would think a 2–8–1 football team would look like.

At least that's what I told our administration.

Fortunately, they believed it as much as I did.

All these years later, this turned out to be the turning point in my career. Three men—Dr. McComas; vice president Minnis Ridenour, who oversaw the athletic department; and especially Dave—stood behind me when I needed their support most. It took a lot of guts on their part to do that, because there were people out there who wanted me fired. I'm sure of that. It comes with the territory when you're 2–8–1.

I also think a big part of their decision was coming from the fact that those sanctions from probation hit us hard and they knew it wasn't our doing. They were more patient than maybe they would have been if there never had been NCAA probation.

Now came the hard part and the part of the job that every coach hates. I knew Dave was right and I had to let some people go. Sometimes, you just have to do it for the betterment of the program. I let go of tight ends coach Tommy Groom, who had played at Tech from 1964 to 1966; I also let go of defensive coordinator Mike

Clark and secondary coach Keith Jones. Offensive coordinator Steve Marshall left to coach at Tennessee. It's just business and I think they knew that. It would not be the last time I would make changes to my staff, but it was still tough to do.

Any time you blow six fourth-quarter leads, I guess that becomes the obvious thing that needs fixing.

A few weeks after the season, I hired Syracuse secondary coach Phil Elmassian, whom everyone would call "Elmo," to run our defense. Elmo was familiar with the 4-3-4 defense, somewhat of an advanced version of the wide-tackle-six defense that I wanted to run. It was an attacking-style of defense in which we label an outside linebacker "whip" and strong safety "rover"—two positions which can drop into pass coverage.

I hired Rod Sharpless from Cornell to coach the defensive line and J.B. Grimes from Arkansas to coach the offensive line. I also promoted a bright young graduate assistant, Bryan Stinespring, to coach the tight ends. We moved Terry Strock from coaching defensive ends to the wide receivers and promoted Rickey Bustle from quarterbacks coach to offensive coordinator.

Another change I made in 1993: I revamped my role in preparation for Saturday. During the week, I had been with the offense, defense, and special teams. I thought to myself, *Look, I hired good people and they know what I want to do in our system, so just let them make these decisions without me involved and do their jobs.*

And that's the way I've done it ever since.

That allowed me to come in on Sunday mornings and spend most of my day working on special teams. It freed up my assistants to do what they had to do without my interference. Our special teams got better, too, so I really think that was a large reason we turned things around that season.

There's no question about it: winning is much more fun than losing. When you are winning, everybody is in a better mood. Food tastes better. People smile more. Life is good. We had been through enough losing through those first six seasons, so now it was time to enjoy the winning.

We started something called "Friday Night Video" and it was sometimes the highlight of each week. I got this idea from Bobby Ross, who used it with the San Diego Chargers. Every Friday night, we would show the team a video of great plays our players had made from the previous week. We always put great blocks on the video, because a block is an unselfish play that benefits the team even though the player—usually an offensive lineman—doesn't get as much publicity. As it evolved, we added some funny clips to get the guys laughing. I would be in the front of the room, narrating the action, sort of like a movie director previewing my film.

Over the years, we've had some real funny stuff on there. One of the things about having 18- to 23-year-old players is that many of them are not experienced fliers. We had two kids—Gennaro DiNapoli and Billy Conaty—who just hated to fly. We were flying into Washington, D.C., right over the Potomac River to play Temple one Friday and Gennaro started screaming. It just happened to be the spot where an Air Florida flight had crashed years earlier. Well, the guys were filming Gennaro as he screamed and that somehow got on Friday Night Video the next week.

We stopped doing the video in 2007 because the guys had turned it into one-upmanship of who could bust whom the most. It became too loud and too disruptive for a Friday night, a time when I want the kids somewhat quiet and focused on what they have to do the next day.

When we started practices for the '93 season, I could tell right away that Elmo was the perfect hire. He had a different personality and was very fiery—just what we needed at that time.

I really believed we had laid a good foundation for the program in those first six years, but it hadn't translated to wins. My record was 24–40–2 at Virginia Tech. But now we had some new assistants, we probably cracked down on our players a bit tighter when it came to discipline, and it carried over to the field, where we committed fewer penalties. We also installed a period during practice when the first-teamers would go against the first-teamers, which made all of our starters better.

I could tell that we had a different type of team after we accumulated a school-record 675 yards (which is still the school record) and 63 points in a win at Pittsburgh for a 2–0 start. We then scored 55 points on Maryland, 55 on Temple, 49 on Rutgers—again, but we won this time—and 45 on Syracuse.

By season's end, Dwayne Thomas had rushed for 1,130 yards and 11 touchdowns; Maurice DeShazo had passed for 22 touchdowns and had only seven interceptions in 230 attempts. We'd cut down on penalties and our special teams play had been very good. We blocked four punts and two field goals and scored five non-offensive touchdowns.

Our only losses were to Miami, which was ranked No. 3 at the time; West Virginia, by one point on a missed field goal at the end of the game; and to Boston College 48–34. That really was the only bad game we played all year. We just couldn't stop them that day. That would be the same Boston College team, coached by Tom Coughlin, which would upset No. 1 Notre Dame in South Bend at the end of the season.

After the win over the Orangemen at Lane Stadium, players dumped Gatorade on me—my first Gatorade bath ever—and we rushed into the locker room to celebrate. We were 7–3 and it was about to get much better.

Dave had been working behind the scenes with the Independence Bowl chairman, Mike McCarthy, during the latter part of the season, crossing his fingers with each win. Virginia Tech's previous trip to the Independence Bowl, and the entire issue about Bruce Smith's eligibility, had left a bad taste in their mouth and Dave had to overcome that. But he was pretty sure he had worked out a deal for us to receive a bid to the game, as long as we beat Syracuse.

As we celebrated in the locker room, sure enough, Mike McCarthy invited us to play in their game on New Year's Eve. Now I am telling you, we would celebrate Sugar Bowl and Orange Bowl invitations in years to come, but nothing matched that day.

It was our first bowl berth and it felt just like we had won the Super Bowl.

Those were the days when they extended bowl bids before the regular season was finished. We still had one regular-season game to play, at Virginia, meaning the Independence Bowl people were taking a risk on us because we could have arrived in Shreveport with four losses. Fortunately, we hung on to win that one, 20–17, for my first win in Charlottesville. It was just the type of close game that we would have lost a season earlier.

The Independence Bowl trip couldn't have gone better. The people there were so gracious to us. Virginia Tech fans, hungry for their first bowl trip in seven years, flocked to Shreveport. We had to guarantee the bowl we would sell 8,000 tickets; we sold 12,000. Even Virginia Governor George Allen, who was a UVA graduate, made the trip to support us.

With less than a minute remaining in the first half, we had a 14–13 lead over Indiana. The Hoosiers had the ball, trying to get into field-goal position, when DeWayne Knight busted through the line clean and forced the quarterback to fumble. The ball got kicked backward and bounced up perfectly into the hands of Lawrence Lewis, who ran it back for a touchdown.

We kicked off and Indiana moved into field-goal range in the final seconds. They hit a short pass and the Indiana receiver ran out of bounds, and I thought the clock had run out, but the official signaled for one second to be put back on the clock. I went after him, arguing up a blue streak, yelling and screaming.

"The clock should be at zero!" I screamed. "The time ran out!"

I used some other choice words, but I didn't win the argument, and just as Indiana lined up to kick a 51-yard field goal on the final play of the half, I continued to yell about it. I was ranting and raving as the Indiana kicker approached the ball. Defensive tackle Jeff Holland just got a hand on it, deflecting it before it fell perfectly into Antonio Banks' lap. He caught it cleanly and ran 80 yards for a touchdown. Just like that, we scored two touchdowns without our offense stepping on the field, turning our one-point lead into a 15-point lead at the half.

As I ran to the locker room after that blocked field goal, ecstatic with a 28–13 lead, I smiled at the referee.

"Great call, Ref," I told him. "You got it right."

We won the game by a score of 45–20 for our first bowl win. We would go on to win bigger games and bigger bowls and have better records, but looking back, nothing was as sweet as that 9–3 season in 1993.

We followed that historic season—I call it historic now because it began our streak of winning seasons and bowl games—with an 8–3 record, losing only at Syracuse, at No. 1 Miami, and to Virginia in our final game. It was good enough to get us to the Gator Bowl, which had been moved to Gainesville because the Jacksonville stadium was being renovated for the NFL's Jaguars. We faced Tennessee, which had a freshman quarterback named Peyton Manning.

Just like his old man Archie did to us in my final game as a player at Virginia Tech in the Liberty Bowl some 26 years earlier, Peyton picked us apart. He passed for 189 yards on 12-of-19 passes to beat us 45–23, so I like to think that we gave Peyton his confidence to go on and have a great career.

We lost the game, but the Gator Bowl's payout of $1.5 million was the biggest Virginia Tech had ever received and we needed it to pay for better facilities to compete on a national level. Proof of it was losing Elmo to Washington's staff after the Gator Bowl.

"I want to compete for a national championship," he told me then.

Phil was right in his feelings back then. We had put together two good seasons, but we still didn't have the type of facilities other top football programs had at the time.

We took one major step toward achieving those goals in 1995.

To begin that season, we lost 20–14 to Boston College and 16–0 to Cincinnati in a muddy mess at Lane Stadium. We committed five turnovers that day and Cincinnati turned three of them into points. After the game, one of our seniors, Jim Baron, stood up and yelled, "WE WILL NOT LOSE ANOTHER [EXPLETIVE] GAME THIS SEASON!"

We were 0–2 and, after 9–3 and 8–4 seasons, the critics were expecting us to take a big step backward. I could just sense it. That next Friday, the day before Miami came to Lane Stadium, the *Collegiate Times* ran a headline: "Lost! Lost! Lost! Hokie Football Team. Last seen playing in the first half against Rutgers in November of 1994. Big reward if found."

I have to admit it was clever.

We found inspiration that night during Friday Night Video, and we upset Miami 13–7 the next day. Looking back, that one game may have been the turning point in the program. It was the beginning of a nine-game winning streak which earned our first major bowl bid—against Texas in the Sugar Bowl.

That was the first season of our famed Lunch Pail, which co-defensive coordinator Rod Sharpless' mother-in-law had found at a garage sale somewhere in New Jersey. John Ballein, our director of football operations, had painted our VT logo on it and the defense brought it to every practice and game. It symbolized a working man's approach to the game, sort of "bring your lunch today, because we're going to work."

Our special teams made huge plays in the Sugar Bowl. Bryan Still returned a punt 60 yards for a touchdown to get us out of a 10–0 hole and Jim Baron returned a fumble 20 yards for another touchdown. We scored 28 straight points to win 28–10.

Jim's proclamation was correct—we hadn't lost another game that season.

But we did lose Coach Sharpless, who took the defensive coordinator's job at Rutgers. I removed the "co-" off Bud Foster's job title. He didn't share the duties with anyone from that point on. He has been our only defensive coordinator since.

Beating Texas in a bowl like the Sugar Bowl was a big deal for us and our "firsts" were starting to accumulate. We had played and won our first bowl game two years earlier; now we put together our first 10-win season and won in our first major bowl.

I was happy my parents got to go to New Orleans to see the game, because 11 days later, on January 10, 1996, my father, Raymond H. Beamer, died.

We followed that season with another first—our first 10-win regular season—in 1996.

We had beaten Miami 21–7 for the second consecutive year, we had beaten Boston College 45–7, and West Virginia 31–14, before ending the season with a 26–9 win over Virginia at Lane Stadium. Our only loss came 52–21 to Syracuse in the Carrier Dome, which was rocking loud that day.

Those 10 wins earned Virginia Tech's first-ever Orange Bowl bid, and it happened to coincide with the game's move from the old Orange Bowl stadium to the new Joe Robbie Stadium farther north. Our opponent that night on New Year's Eve, Nebraska, was coming off back-to-back national titles in 1994 and '95. I always had great respect for Tom Osborne and the way he coached his teams. They were a hard-nosed, tough group that pounded people and tried to wear them down by the fourth quarter. And that's exactly what they did. We had taken a 7–0 lead at the end of the first quarter and they scored 41 of the next 55 points. The final score was 41–21. Nebraska just happened to win another national title the following year, giving Coach Osborne three titles in four seasons before he retired. But let me tell you, his team that didn't win it during those four years was pretty good, too.

That was Jim Druckenmiller's final game for us. Jim was a big, strong, tough guy for a quarterback. You don't have many quarterbacks who are your strongest players, but he was. He was one of strength coach Mike Gentry's favorite workers.

Jim had a particularly good senior year, completing 57 percent of his passes—his touchdown-to-interception ratio was 17 to five. I'll never forget Jim's first career start a few years earlier. It was a night game at Boston College, televised on ESPN. Jim had lost his voice during the week and he couldn't call the signals. We didn't know what to do and offensive coordinator Rickey Bustle was in a tizzy. We couldn't figure out if it was nerves or something physical. We worked out a system where the center would call the signals and Jim would slap him for the snap. Nowadays, that's common with some teams in college football and even in the NFL, especially for teams on the road.

Anyway, Jim's voice came back just in time, even though we lost the game.

The Orange Bowl was also the final game for Cornell Brown, our first consensus All-American. I will always be grateful to Cornell for signing with us after that disastrous 1992 season when he could have gone anywhere to play college football.

We now had put together two consecutive 10-win seasons and had played in the Sugar and Orange Bowls.

Just as I had described my visions of the program to Cornell when I recruited him, we had turned the corner.

Virginia Tech was now a winning program and there was no turning back.

7

A Special Player, a Special Season

JIM CAVANAUGH, former Virginia Tech assistant coach: "*I was coaching at North Carolina in 1994 and went to recruit a defensive end at the old Ferguson High School [which closed in 1996] in Newport News. I remember it was on a Friday morning. The head coach there, Tommy Reamon, gave me five tapes to watch and I went into an office and turned on the tapes. On two of them, this left-handed kid came in the game in the second half and just was slinging the ball around the field. Tommy walked in and said, "Well Cav, what do you think?" I told him, "I don't think the defensive end is quite good enough, but who the hell is this left-handed quarterback?" Tommy said, "That's my guy—and he's only a freshman." I stayed for their game that night and this freshman left-handed quarterback started and ran around and nobody could catch him. That was the first time I saw Michael Vick. From that night on, I kept his name to myself and the other North Carolina coaches. Then Ferguson closed its doors and he and Tommy ended up at Warwick High School. I didn't tell other college coaches about him, not wanting the secret to get out to other coaches at other schools. Then Coach Beamer hired me and I came to Virginia Tech two years later.*"

It was February of 1996 when Cav mentioned something about this left-handed quarterback nobody could tackle.

In 1996 and '97, everybody in Virginia knew about Ronald Curry. Heck, everybody in the country knew about him. He was a *Parade* All-America quarterback from Hampton, Virginia, and every college coach in the country wanted him. I watched plenty of tape on him and I always thought I could spot a good player from just a few plays. I didn't need to watch the whole tape or the whole game to tell if someone was special. I would call a great player a "four-play guy" when I spoke with our coaches, meaning I had to watch only four plays to decide if I wanted him.

Well, when I watched tape of this left-handed kid from Newport News, I told one of our coaches, "Turn it off. He's a *three*-play guy." I needed only three plays to tell that Michael Vick was the most different player I had ever seen. How quickly he got rid of the ball was amazing. How much zip he put on the ball for his size was amazing. How he ran around and the speed and quickness he had…it was even more amazing. He would run around and nobody would be able to tackle him.

I watched Michael's tape with Warwick coach Tommy Reamon the first time and I told him right away, "Tommy, *this* is the guy I want."

I wasn't sure what type of shot we would have had with Ronald Curry anyway, but the decision was easy for me. I said right there and then, "This guy will be a better quarterback than Ronald Curry."

Now don't get me wrong, I am not saying Ronald Curry was not a great player by any means. Curry got all the publicity because he played on the better team and they always beat Michael's Warwick team. Curry was the all-district quarterback; Michael was voted all-district as a utility player.

As the recruiting process progressed, it became apparent that not only would they not go to the same school, but they would not even visit the same schools.

Tommy had one rule: if you recruit Michael, you can't recruit Curry, too. That was no problem for us. We didn't want to recruit both. Michael had visited East Carolina and Syracuse, where Donovan McNabb hosted him. They became big buddies and that became our biggest fear: Donovan would talk him into signing with the Orangemen.

I remember meeting Michael for the first time near the gymnasium of his high school, and he had a big ol' smile on his face and he was very polite. The guy just lit up the room with his smile. That night we went to visit him and he lived at this modest apartment with a yellow school bus outside. Michael's mother, a lovely lady named Brenda Boddie, drove the school bus for a living. We walked in and right away I could tell what effect she had on Michael.

She was a sweet, caring lady and I could tell she had reared him well. He worshipped her and obeyed her and he was very polite and attentive as we talked. We never had any dealings with his father or knew if he was in Michael's life. When I left there that day, I was more convinced than ever that we wanted him. Not only could he play, but he had character.

Cav thought if we didn't get Michael, East Carolina would. Steve Logan was running a wide-open offense down at East Carolina and Michael had some friends on their team. But I worried more about Syracuse because of McNabb.

And I really think Tommy had a lot to do with Michael's final decision. Cav's relationship with Tommy also was big for us. He trusted our staff and I think he knew that Virginia Tech would be good for Michael.

I really believe those are the main reasons we signed Michael Vick on February 4, 1998.

Grant Noel, another quarterback in that class, had committed to us already and I think Syracuse tried to use that against us. But

Michael told the media, "I don't care if Virginia Tech signs 10 quarterbacks, I *will* be the starting quarterback."

That is, after his redshirt season. We had to stick to our promise to Tommy, who didn't want Michael on the national stage until he was good and ready.

Well, from the first time I saw Michael run the scout team that next fall, I knew he was good and ready right then and there. We had a great defense that year and nobody could tackle him in practice. Heck, nobody could *touch* him, but we gave our word to Tommy and we weren't going back on it.

Michael's story was a perfect lesson in not recruiting according to those ratings or recruiting services. Nobody who did those ratings back then had ever seen him play, because if they had, he would have been a *six*-star guy, if there was such a thing. I think we timed him at 4.33 in the 40, which is unheard of for a quarterback, and he had a vertical jump of over 40 inches. The guy was a freak athletically.

We started the 1998 season 4–0 but by the time we prepared to play at Boston College, our senior quarterback, Al Clark, had a twisted ankle and then our second quarterback, Dave Meyer, also got hurt. In our Monday meeting before the Boston College game, I said something like, "You know…Michael Vick really gives us the best chance to win this game."

"Remember our promise to Tommy," Cav reminded me.

He was right: our word was more important than winning a game.

MICHAEL VICK: *"That was the right thing to do. I didn't want to play early. I needed the time to figure out what I had to accomplish academically. So I was fine with it."*

We brought Nicky Sorenson, our safety who played quarterback in high school, over to offense that week. Here we were at Boston College on national TV on a Thursday night and I think we committed about six turnovers.

I stood there on the sideline, frustrated. I looked next to me at Michael standing right there. I knew if we put him in the game, he would pull us out of this mess, but we had to keep our word about redshirting him. You can't imagine how tough that is, to have a weapon like Michael standing there watching, and to not stick him in the game.

Fortunately, it was like a miracle when we blocked two kicks and had a goal-line stand and somehow won 17–0.

We were 5–0 and a 29-point favorite the next week at home, but lost to Temple 28–24. It was an excruciating loss because we had dropped the winning touchdown pass in the end zone in the final minutes. We then beat UAB and West Virginia to climb to 7–1 before Donovan McNabb threw a touchdown pass on the final play as Syracuse beat us 28–26. That was one of the most heartbreaking defeats in all of my years at Virginia Tech. In the final game, we lost to Virginia 36–32 on one of the final plays, before we beat Alabama pretty good, 38–7, in the Music City Bowl to finish 9–3.

We not only lost three games but those three were devastating, rip-your-heart-out losses—and all of them may have been avoidable if we had decided to play Michael Vick that season.

The next season, Al Clark had graduated and we entered the spring with Dave Meyer listed first on the depth chart and Michael second. On the 10th practice of camp, Michael was elevated to the top of the depth chart. It was April 5, 1999.

As we started the season, when I gave my talk to the team I mentioned something like, "Let's not worry about our opponents this year…who we should beat, who could beat us, etc. Let's just win Game No. 1 and then win Game No. 2 and so on."

We even placed a sign on the fence of our practice field that read: "Prepare to Win No. 1." John Ballein would climb up a ladder to update the sign each week by replacing the number. We started the season ranked 11th in the country and I really felt we had the makings of a top-10 team.

But I'd never seen Michael Vick in a real game against live competition. Nobody had, at least not on the college level.

If I had, I would have ranked us much higher.

I knew Michael would be a great quarterback, but I honestly didn't know he would have the effect on the team that he had. His first four completions in the season opener against James Madison went for 110 yards and he rushed for three touchdowns. We won easily 47–0. It was the game of the "Flip," as it became known around Blacksburg. Michael scrambled out of the pocket to the right, made two or three guys miss, got hit, flipped head-over-heels and landed on his feet in the end zone. You can find that play on YouTube today.

I just smiled and shook my head, until I realized he was hurt. When he landed, his ankles buckled, but fortunately his injury wasn't too serious.

That spectacular play was just a sign of things to come.

We let Michael recover from his leg injury the next week and beat Alabama-Birmingham 31–10 with Meyer at quarterback. Dave was a steady guy who wouldn't make many mistakes. He completed 12-of-21 that day for 144 yards.

Michael struggled in his comeback game, throwing three interceptions against Clemson, but Corey Moore, our senior defensive end, was unstoppable. He had two sacks, three tackles for loss, forced a fumble that he recovered and returned for a touchdown, and we won 31–11 at Lane Stadium.

Our fourth game, we traveled to Charlottesville to face Virginia, who was 3–1, coming off a huge win at BYU and ranked 24th. They had beaten us two straight years and the pressure was on us to prevent another loss to our biggest rival. This is the game in which Michael and André Davis really began to find a rhythm. Michael hit him in stride for a 60-yard touchdown to give us the lead and we never looked back. It was 31–7 after three quarters and neither team scored in the fourth.

We pounded Rutgers 58–20 to get to 5–0 and jump to No. 4 in the polls. Our next game, at home against Syracuse, was homecoming. It also would be televised nationally and ESPN's *College GameDay* was in town. Syracuse had a 5–1 record, was ranked 16th and had broken our hearts on the final play a year earlier in the Carrier Dome.

It was much easier than expected, as we cruised to a 62–0 win.

The margin of victory even made some history. It was the largest shutout margin of defeat for a ranked team since the Associated Press poll began in 1936. It was also probably the game in which the rest of the nation began to notice Virginia Tech.

Michael did his thing in every game, just as he had for the scout team the year before, running around and throwing darts as we rolled to a 6–0 record.

We had a week off, but jumped a spot from No. 4 to No. 3, because undefeated Nebraska was shocked at home by Texas and my buddy Mack Brown, who was in his second season coaching the Longhorns.

After Nebraska's loss, only Florida State, which was ranked No. 1 from the beginning of the season, and Penn State were ranked above us. I told our players not to worry about the polls and the future. I told them, "Just remember our sign—prepare to win No. 7."

That would be Pittsburgh. We didn't play our best game of the season by any means. Pittsburgh quarterback David Priestley passed for 407 yards, but we won 30–17 and that was the name of the game—just keep winning. Our secondary wasn't at full speed that day at Pittsburgh, either, since cornerback Anthony Midget had a groin pull and Ike Charlton got poked in the eye.

I think we all knew the game at West Virginia, the eighth game of the season, would be pivotal for us. We headed to Morgantown where I just knew we would be in for a battle from the time our bus rolled into the stadium. There were students mooning us and Mountaineer fans throwing things at the bus.

When we arrived in the locker room, somebody announced that Penn State had just lost to Minnesota 24–23.

We had the game under control, leading 19–7 when Shyrone Stith, who hardly ever fumbled, fumbled at about our 30-yard line. That was so unlike him. Then they threw a little hitch route and Nicky Sorenson came up and missed the tackle and they scored. They kicked off and we fumbled the kickoff. Then they scored again and all of a sudden, we were trailing 20–19 with only 1:11 remaining.

After the kickoff, we started deep in a hole at our own 15.

I told Michael, "We need to get to their 35 to give Shayne Graham a chance" to win the game with a field goal.

The rest is Virginia Tech history, I guess. Michael completed a pass for 14 yards to Terrell Parham and then a pass of seven yards to André Davis to get us out of the hole. But only 36 seconds remained and we didn't have any timeouts.

The next play is what made Michael Vick so special, so *different*, as I like to say.

He dropped back and got flushed out of the pocket and he rolled to his right. He was right in front of me near the sideline, and I think the defender really thought he was going to run out of bounds. At that moment, Michael hit another gear. He was already running fast, but he ran even *faster*. He ran right by that guy down the field, jumping out of bounds at West Virginia's 36-yard line. Looking back all these years later, this one play may have been the biggest of my coaching career, and I am convinced no other player but Michael Vick could have made it.

He then completed a nine-yard pass to their 27 before spiking the ball with only five seconds remaining.

With his legs and his arm, he had gotten us eight yards closer than what I told him we needed.

I always thought Shayne was one of the most dependable kickers I ever coached and he proved it—drilling the 44-yarder right down the middle on the final play. As I walked over to shake Don Nehlen's hand—he was one of my best friends in the coaching business—I knew then we were on to something special that season and it was largely because of Michael Vick.

We left Morgantown 8–0 and assured of a No. 2 ranking when the polls were released that Monday.

The West Virginia game was one of those thrillers which almost every national championship team experiences. If you look back over the history of our game, almost every champion won at least one game that could have gone either way. If the ball bounces the wrong way, they lose it. If it bounces the right way, they win it. And that was just the type of game we had with the Mountaineers.

Six years earlier, we faced a final-play field goal on that same field, and it drifted wide of the uprights, resulting in a 14–13 loss. Those two outcomes show how narrow the margin of winning and losing can be in the game of football.

I knew each win meant the next game would be even bigger. There would be more attention nationally and perhaps more pressure. Now that we were ranked No. 2, I just told our players something I had told them often: "When things seem big, think small." By that, I meant focus on the little things, like finishing off a block or looking the ball into your hands. That is the best way to take care of the big picture.

The next week, we fell behind Miami, who was ranked 19th at the time, 10–0 in the first quarter. But we ripped off 43 consecutive points to end the game. It was our fifth consecutive win over the Hurricanes. Michael took care of any worries I had the next week about us taking Temple lightly. He had touchdown runs of 53 and 75 yards and we won easily 62–7.

All that was left between us and an 11–0 record, as well as a Sugar Bowl appearance for the national championship, was an 8–2 Boston College team—at Lane Stadium.

I think we saved one of our best games for last. Michael hooked up with André Davis twice on long passes—69 and 59 yards for touchdowns—in the second quarter. We rolled up a season-high 555 yards and Michael was at his best, accounting for 366 of those. We sacked Boston College's quarterback six times.

When the clock ticked down to zero, Shayne Graham and Jimmy Kibble came up from behind me and each grabbed one of my legs. Suddenly I was on their shoulders getting carried to midfield. I could see our fans storming the north end zone to tear down the goal posts. Then they moved to the south end.

They had set up a platform with a microphone so I could say a few words to the crowd. I didn't have much time to put together a speech, but I said something like, "How about these players out here?" and the crowd roared.

Then the question popped out: "How many of y'all am I going to see in New Orleans?"

The crowd roared again.

It was a great feeling, knowing that you were 11–0 and had no game to prepare for the next week. Our work was done and we had at least five weeks to prepare for our next battle.

That next Thursday, the cover of *Sports Illustrated* was everywhere. André Davis was pictured carrying the football high and tight and headed toward the end zone. The headline read: "THEY BELONG! Why Virginia Tech Deserves A Shot at the National Title."

I didn't think there was any question about it since we were one of only two teams who were undefeated, along with No. 1 Florida State.

But it wasn't official until eight days later when the final BCS standings were announced: we were No. 2 and headed to New Orleans to play the Seminoles for the national championship. As it turned out, Nebraska was only 1.3 points behind us at No. 3, even though the Cornhuskers had lost that game to Texas.

Thirty-five years after my first somewhat-forgettable recruiting trip to Tulane, when the head coach took one disapproving look at this undersized quarterback from Hillsville, Virginia, I was headed back to New Orleans.

This time, I was taking an 11–0 football team with me.

8

One Night in New Orleans

Remember what I said when I was introduced as Virginia Tech's new football coach on December 23, 1986?

"I really think that someday we can play for national championships here."

Many people laughed at that, including some of the coaches and players on that 1987 team, which finished 2–9. Even my brother Barnett questioned me. What was this guy saying? I admit there were a few moments during those first six seasons I wondered why I said it myself, especially during that 2–8–1 season in 1992.

We had a 24–40–2 record in those first six seasons and the possibility of Virginia Tech playing for national championships probably seemed like a mirage to most people. But I never thought that way. I just knew if we could weather the storm and keep plowing ahead, all the reasons I originally felt that way would prove to be true.

Thirteen years after that first press conference, almost to the day, that statement became a reality.

As the No. 2 team in the country, we were headed to New Orleans to play No. 1 Florida State for the national championship on January 4, 2000.

I guess it proves if you do things right, if you work hard and if you keep your head down and plow through it, no set of problems is insurmountable.

We were an 11–0 team for the first time in Virginia Tech history and now we just had to get by one more hurdle—the talent-laden Seminoles—to hold that crystal football as national champions.

This Florida State team wasn't much different than any from the recent past—the Seminoles were talented, deep, explosive, and very fast. They had scored at least 30 points in all but one game and had scored 40 or more seven times that season. They started the season ranked No. 1 and stayed there after four months.

We'd played Florida State four times since I returned to Virginia Tech and lost all four—by scores of 41–14 in 1988, 41–7 in '89, 39–28 in '90, and 33–20 in '91 in a so-called neutral site game in Orlando.

In that first game, our first-ever trip to Tallahassee, I thought we would have an incident before the game ever started.

Every college football fan has seen that pretty horse they have with their Chief Osceola mascot riding atop holding his flaming spear. Well, one of our linebackers, Don Stokes, was a pretty emotional guy who could get fired up. He came into the locker room after warm-ups and started swearing up a storm and punching the lockers. He said he was going to tackle that horse before the game and he was using words that were meant only for the locker room. I watched him rant and rave for a while and he wouldn't stop.

I got to worrying that he actually might go try and tackle that huge horse before the game. Can you imagine the scene that would have been? I walked over to Billy Hite and asked, "Billy, you want to take care of Don for me?"

"What exactly do you want me to do?" Billy asked.

I really just wanted him to calm him down, but Don never did approach that horse. He probably saw how big it was up close and thought better of it.

That one ended in a 27-point loss to a Florida State team that would finish 11–1 and ranked No. 3 in the country.

The next year, in 1989, they were one of the best teams in the country again and clobbered us again, 41–7, at Lane Stadium. Their quarterback, Peter Tom Willis, had one of the best days a quarterback ever had against us, passing for 338 yards and three touchdowns.

The one time we had a chance to beat them came in Tallahassee the following season when they were ranked No. 2 in late September.

We jumped up 21–3 and had quieted their crowd. They fought back with three touchdowns, but we still were clinging to a 28–25 lead late in the game and we had just stopped one of their drives with an interception by Roger Garland.

Then their All-American cornerback, Terrell Buckley, picked off Will Furrer and returned it 53 yards for a score to put them ahead 32–28 with less than four minutes remaining. Suddenly, we put together a pretty good drive and I thought we would punch it in and pull off a big upset.

We had a third down at their 33 and handed off to Vaughn Hebron. He was fighting for the first down, and just as he turned to get that extra yard, their linebacker, Kirk Carruthers, knocked the ball loose. The ball bounced into the arms of one of their defensive backs who ran 77 yards for the clinching touchdown.

Just like that, two turnovers turned our three-point lead into an 11-point loss. If we'd held on, it would have been the biggest win of my career to that point. Our offense gained 418 yards that night and really only stopped ourselves with turnovers.

After the game, I was drained and disappointed from coming so close to beating the No. 2 team in the country. When I met Bobby Bowden at midfield, he asked in his Southern drawl, "Frank, wasn't that just the *best* game?"

The *best* game?

For whom?

I really didn't know how to take that. I didn't know Bobby that well to know if he was joking, rubbing it in, or just stating a fact. But it certainly wasn't the best game to me, because we had lost it. I would rather win a boring game any day than lose an exciting one. After getting to know Bobby later, I think that was just him.

In 1991, our athletic director, Dave Braine, sold one of our October home games against Florida State to the city of Orlando for $800,000. I didn't want to do it, but that was a pretty good paycheck in those days for one football game. Dave told me it would be a neutral site and I asked whether Florida State would have their horse at the game. I just didn't want that horse running around at one of our "home games."

"No, no," he told me. "This game will be completely neutral."

Florida State was 5–0 and ranked No. 1. We were 2–4.

I walked out of the dressing room and I looked up there to see their fans had filled the stadium. I looked over to the field and there was that gigantic horse with the Seminole on top of it with his flaming spear lit. Their fans were going crazy, doing that tomahawk chop thing. Our little gobbler stood next to that huge horse, bobbing his head up and down.

I thought, *Yeah, this is a real neutral field!*

I think that was the only game in which I actually rooted against our offense—for one play anyway. Florida State had a great defense and they were very hard to score on, but I had noticed something in their field-goal rush team which left them open for a fake. We got down there and had a third-and-short at their 10-yard line and I actually whispered to myself, "Please don't get this first down."

I wanted to run that fake field goal so badly and it was the only time I ever pulled against my own team. We came up just short and ran the fake: Scott Freund, our holder, took the snap in field-goal formation and ran off tackle and got the first down. We scored a few plays later, but we lost the game 33–20.

That wasn't the last time we ever sold a home game to another city, but it just seemed to me that giving our players a chance to win the game trumped any amount of money the athletic department could take in. I think Dave realized it afterward, too.

Anyway, being 0–4 against Florida State and Bobby Bowden wouldn't normally allow a coach to be confident going into the biggest game of his career. And Florida State had a run going of 13 consecutive seasons with top-five teams in the final polls. The Seminoles also had a pretty good bowl record going—they were 12–2–1 in their last 15 bowl games under Bowden.

But this time I was confident. I thought we could win. But I also figured, just like in the 1991 game in Orlando, we would have to take some chances to win.

Everyone knew we had Michael Vick, who was spectacular that season. But we also had a group of seniors who gave us great leadership and experience. I didn't think any stage—even the Sugar Bowl at the Superdome for the national championship—was too big for them.

Kicker Shayne Graham had won the West Virginia game on the final play. Corey Moore and John Engelberger were the two best defensive ends in the country. Defensive tackle Nathaniel Williams had overcome so much to reach his senior season. He had battled alcoholism at a young age and whipped it and become a different guy, doing everything we asked of him and more. I was so proud of him. Linebacker Michael Hawkes was the glue of that team. He was a great leader who led by his actions, working hard every day. My son Shane was a senior, too, as were punter Jimmy Kibble, linebacker Jamel Smith, defensive tackle Carl Bradley, cornerback Anthony Midget, defensive end Chris Cyrus, and offensive linemen Tim Schnecker and

Keith Short. It was one of those years when we had great leadership and almost perfect chemistry.

As we started our preparations in Blacksburg, I told the team to lay low: make no comments to inflame Florida State's passion or get them mad at us. Be respectful, I told them. Act like the underdog. I knew Florida State had been there before and might take us lightly. If they did, we had them right where we wanted them.

That is, until I opened the newspaper one morning and read where Corey had boasted, "We are going to beat their ass."

Now Corey was a great, great player. He was the Big East Defensive Player of the Year that season. But still, I didn't want him or anyone popping off before the game.

I called Corey in and asked, "What were you thinking?"

"I was trying to take the pressure off of our quarterback," he told me.

"You let me worry about the quarterback," I said. "You just worry about yourself."

Well, I worried that would motivate Florida State.

Corey took some heat for that, and he also had an episode with a camera being too close to practice that week at Tulane. But I wish the critics could have seen him when our seniors visited a children's hospital early in the week in New Orleans. Seeing those children made our players appreciate the blessings they had in life. Corey spent about 20 minutes coloring a coloring book for a sick little girl who was about six. He brought a smile to her face.

Those are the parts of bowl trips fans don't get to see and it's another reason I have always been behind the bowl system. Players get to do things they don't normally get to do during the course of a long, grinding season.

We gave our players great lectures about not getting into trouble in New Orleans. The chief of the New Orleans Police Department met our team as he does before every Sugar Bowl. He told our kids not to stray more than two blocks off of Bourbon Street and to respect the drinking age. Make sure if you're talking to a girl, it's really a girl, he warned them. That got a big laugh from everyone. We had maybe only 10 players who went to New Orleans as freshmen in '95 when we beat Texas, so it was a new experience for almost everyone.

Before that game four seasons earlier, I'd sent home center Keith Short, who was a freshman, because he had broken a team rule. This time around, now a more mature senior, Keith stood up and warned his teammates about making curfew and not getting into trouble.

When we send someone home in those cases, we don't give them first-class airfare—we send them by Greyhound.

"How long was that bus ride?" I asked him in front of the team.

"Twenty-six hours," Keith answered.

That was enough to get their attention.

This time, I didn't think anyone would get into trouble because no player wanted to miss the game. On New Year's Eve, Corey stood up at the end of practice and said, "We've had our fun down here but this is game week now. I had better not see anybody out tonight. If anybody has a problem with that, stand up and tell me now."

Nobody stood up. That illustrated what a leader he was.

In our final preparations, I thought going in that we were good enough to beat them in the kicking game, on offense, and on defense. Our deal that night would be to bring pressure on defense and match up with them one-on-one on the outside, win the kicking game, and don't turn the ball over. And take a chance or two if the opportunity presented itself. That was the formula to beat Florida State and win the national championship.

In the past, Florida State usually beat us because they were so much more talented, plain and simple. And they never let up. In the 1988 game when we were down in Tallahassee, they were pouring it on in the fourth quarter—they ran a reverse and were throwing deep balls with a big lead when Billy Hite yelled sarcastically across the field, "Run it up! Run it up!"

I always respected Bobby Bowden, but I must say he never let up once he had a big lead.

People have asked me about my philosophy toward that issue over the years. First of all, I always want my kids to play hard, no matter how much time is on the clock. But I just think that after we have enough points we should run the ball for the most part, and maybe mix in a pass or two, but I do want to get the game over and not embarrass the other team.

The guy across the field is trying to get his program right and he's got a family, too. I have never been interested in running anybody out of the business or making a guy's job worse or embarrassing anybody. Now some people may question, when does a team have enough points? We've all seen comebacks by teams which are 21 points, or more, down.

Let me say, I like having to make that decision. If I was getting hammered, I took the approach that it was my job to get my team better so it didn't happen again. I never really held any grudges about it when it happened to me. It was my job to right my ship.

I certainly didn't think that would be an issue as we prepared to play Florida State this time. I thought we matched up well.

Our defense entered the game ranked No. 3 in the country in both total defense and rushing defense. On average, we had allowed just 247.3 total yards and 75.9 rushing yards per game. Having Corey and John Engleberger—who had seven sacks, six other tackles for loss, and 16 quarterback hurries that season—as bookends on the line of scrimmage was invaluable. Some scouts even projected Engelberger as the first of our players to come off the board in the draft that next April.

Those two defensive ends were very instrumental in helping our program jump to the next level that year.

In the Superdome locker room before kickoff, I noticed some of our players were upset that some of the Florida State players had mouthed off to them and ran through our stretching line during pre-game warm-ups. It was as if they were trying to intimidate our players.

I thought I would use it.

"That's a team that doesn't respect you," I told them.

After we took the opening kickoff, we committed a false start on the first play and then Shyrone Stith lost yardage on the first official play—not a great start by any means. Then Michael scrambled 25 yards for a first down. We moved inside their 10, but I didn't want to settle for three points and I decided to go for it on fourth down.

As I made the call, passing up the sure three points, Bryan Stinespring asked over the headset, "You sure you want to do this?"

I was. I just thought coming into the game that we needed to take some chances when the timing was right, but Michael fumbled into the end zone on the fourth-down play and Florida State recovered.

Chris Weinke, who would win the Heisman Trophy the following season, hit their fast receiver Peter Warrick on a 64-yard touchdown pass as we fell behind 7–0.

Then we did something we rarely did—we failed to protect the punter. We were punting out of our own end zone and one of their interior guys kind of grabbed one of our inside blockers. That allowed Tommy Polley to come through clean to block the punt. They recovered it at the six-yard-line on the bounce and trotted into the end zone for a 14–0 lead.

Michael hit André Davis for 49 yards for our first score before another special teams breakdown in the second quarter led to them building a 28–7 lead. We were backed up deep when Jimmy Kibble hit a low punt. Warrick caught it in stride and never slowed down.

Our punt coverage people got out of their assigned lanes and a guy like Warrick just needed a crack and that was what we gave him. Fifty-nine yards later he was in the end zone and we were in a three-touchdown hole.

Michael ran three yards for a touchdown to get us to within 28–14 at the half. I told our players, "We've got them right where we want them."

I always have to be positive at halftime, even if we are getting whipped 35–0. Since that previous time in the same stadium during my first season, when it didn't work against Tulane, I hadn't ranted and raved much at halftime. I didn't want our players to get down on themselves. I wanted them to think positive, knowing they could fight back and win this game. Of course, I would have rather been ahead 28–14, but I came out of the locker room pretty optimistic. We scored last in the half to give us some momentum and we hadn't played very well at all and we still trailed by only two touchdowns.

And we had Michael Vick on our team. We just had to stop giving them big plays and not make any more mistakes in the kicking game.

Our defense did its job on the first two series of the second half before Michael got us moving. We got inside their 10, but couldn't get any movement in the running game and had to settle for Shayne's 23-yard field goal to cut it to 28–17. The defense stopped them again and we got a great punt return 45 yards to Florida State's 36-yard line. Two players later, André Kendrick busted off a run of 29 yards for a touchdown to make it a one-score game.

It was 28–23 and I decided to go for two to make it a field-goal difference, but we didn't convert.

The defense did it again on the next series as one of our seniors, Anthony Midget, intercepted Weinke. Michael then did what he did best, ripping off two runs that got us to their 7-yard line. We went to Kendrick again and he scored to give us the lead. Again, we had to go for two since the margin was one point. Most fans don't realize this, but coaches carry a little chart that details when to go for two and when to kick the PAT. It's simple math, really (remember, I taught math). If you trail by five points late in the game, you go for two to cut the lead to a field goal. If you lead by one point, a two-point lead is not a big help, so you go for two to make it a field-goal lead. But we didn't hit on a pass play again.

Still, with 2:13 remaining in the third quarter, we had a 29–28 lead and were just 17 minutes away from Virginia Tech's first national championship.

We just had to finish the game.

We then committed a personal foul that helped them on their next possession, which led to Weinke passing to Ron Dugans for 14 yards for a touchdown. He then passed to Warrick for a two-point conversion that put us behind 36–29. Michael ran to the left on our next possession and had some running room, but he fumbled. Our defense stopped them inside our 10, and they settled for a field goal to make it 39–29.

I could feel the momentum getting away from us and I wanted to get it back.

On our next possession, we got a couple first downs and crossed midfield. We faced a third-and-8 when Michael lost a couple yards. I knew it was a little too far to go for an ideal fake punt to work, but I felt like our fake was good enough to make it. Jimmy took off running and picked up seven yards, but came up short of the first down. The way the game was going, I just believed that we needed to do something, being down 10 points and running out of possessions.

As I look on this game all these years later, I think we may have been good enough to beat them by playing by the book and not taking those chances. But we'll never know.

After that, Weinke threw deep to Warrick, who bobbled the pass before catching it for a 43-yard touchdown that put the game away.

On our next series, their defense knew we had to throw and Michael got sacked a few times. We moved to their 2-yard line on our final drive, but couldn't get it in and it ended 46–29.

Frustrating. Disappointing. Surprising.

It was all of the above. I hated to lose any game, but I especially hated to lose this one.

Warrick just killed us, turning his six catches into 163 yards. He took a punt return back for a touchdown and caught the long touchdown that clinched the game. We got beat in the kicking game. Florida State rushed for only 30 yards that night, on 23 attempts, and if you had told me that I would have been sure we would have won the game.

Despite the loss, Michael gave a great effort in the biggest game of his freshman season. He passed for 225 yards and ran for 97 more and you could tell that Florida State respected him after the game. Many of their players hugged him and complimented him in the press.

"Michael Vick already has my vote for next year's Heisman," Florida State safety Sean Key told the media. "Who out there is better than him? Who out there is even close?"

Bobby Bowden said this: "There ain't a darn thing you can do about this guy. You put four or five guys on him and he runs 50 yards.... Boy, is he something! Better than I thought. I knew he was good. I didn't know he was this darn good."

Many fans and media who had not followed us probably had not seen Michael play until that night, but they got a glimpse of what we had seen the entire season. Michael was special and now he was no longer a secret.

The locker room after a loss always is a tough place to be. It's quiet, unless a swear word or two is thrown around in frustration, and people are generally in a bad mood.

This one was worse than most.

We knew this team and these seniors would never be together again. And we knew we had our shot, our chance to win a national championship, and didn't take advantage of it—and that's what probably hurt the most. It seemed everybody was crying that night. The governor of Virginia, Jim Gilmore, waited to greet me outside the locker room as we honored our seniors, something we always do following our final game. Then, just as we broke down our final team meeting, I headed to the coaches' area to gather myself before meeting with the media.

John Ballein walked up and told me, "The president's on the phone."

At first, I thought he meant the Virginia Tech president, but I knew Paul Torgersen was at the game. I learned later that one of our student trainers, Dana Bottiglieri, had taken the call earlier and John had mentioned that the president would have to wait a moment because "Coach was honoring our seniors."

That's how much our seniors meant to me.

I headed to the training room and picked up the phone. President Clinton was on the other end.

"I really enjoyed the heart your football team showed. This wasn't the first time I've seen you play this year. I really enjoy your style," he told me.

I thanked him and said something like I appreciated his call, but I really don't remember exactly what I said. The disappointment of losing the game trumped any possible thrill of talking to the president, but it was nice of him to call the losing coach. I know my mom and dad would have been thrilled I was taking a call from President Clinton, because they were big Democrats.

That loss ended an amazing ride for us on a sour note. Getting there for the first time was big, but losing hurt more as the years went by. After the game, I thought we would be back again very soon—and again and again. Now I realize it was a unique opportunity and those don't come along very often. I still think we would have been good enough to win if we had played them over again. We just had to eliminate the mistakes we normally didn't make during the course of the season.

I know one thing: I never watched the tape of that game. Not once. It still hurts and it would hurt to watch all of those big plays gone wrong on tape. Maybe one of these days when I retire and the pain of it doesn't hurt so much, I will watch it.

Then again, maybe I never will.

9

Two Years and Out

I could tell you that the task of getting over that loss to Florida State had been accomplished by the time August camp started to begin the 2000 season, but the memory and pain of losing it never really goes away completely.

The pain eased a little, mainly because we had another season to prepare for, but it will never go away completely. National championship opportunities don't come along every day like the mail man.

We had lost all of those seniors, such as Corey Moore and John Engelberger, which is probably why we opened the season ranked only No. 10 in the country. I know I thought we would be a better team than that.

The good news was that we had Michael Vick back for his sophomore season. He had redshirted two years earlier, so we anticipated three more seasons of Michael dazzling us and frustrating opponents with his feet and his arm. And I naturally figured we would make several more national championship game appearances.

The next step was to win the darn thing.

The bad news: we weren't going to sneak up on anybody anymore and no opponents would overlook us.

One thing hadn't changed: Opposing coaches gushed about Michael. After our season opener, a 52–23 win over Akron, Zips

Coach Lee Owens said, "If Michael Vick is not the greatest football player on the planet, then I don't know who is."

I agreed.

Michael was spectacular against Akron, scoring on touchdown runs of 16 and 63 yards in the first quarter. He then threw two touchdown passes before we pulled him from the game. There was no sense risking an injury when we had a big lead. Our defense was young and it showed, allowing Akron 410 yards.

We beat East Carolina 45–28 and Rutgers 49–0 before Michael rushed for 210 yards in our 48–34 win at Boston College. In that game, there was one play when the offensive coaches had called a pass play. He dropped back from our 18-yard line, about three defensive guys had Michael dead to rights and were about to make the sack. Michael moved to his left, making them all miss, then he took off running, swerving near our bench to juke three more guys. He took off down the sideline, cut back to the middle of the field, and made about another guy miss at their 10-yard line. By the time he glided into the end zone, I think the entire Boston College defense had their chances to tackle him.

I just turned calmly to Billy Hite, our running backs coach, smiled and said, "Nice call."

That's how it went with Michael. He could make plays that made you shake your head. He could make plays no other player could make. I imagined defensive coordinators who faced us really shook their heads at times.

Michael and our top receiver, André Davis, both sustained ankle injuries in the 37–34 win over Pittsburgh, which gave us an 8–0 start. Here we were, about to travel to Miami with a shot of playing for a second consecutive national title, but with two of our top players not at full strength—and one of them was Michael Vick.

Some media billed it as the biggest game in Big East history because it was the only time two Big East teams ranked in the top five
had met on the field. But we knew we would be nowhere near full
strength.

As our bus pulled into the Orange Bowl that day, fans were shooting us the bird and screaming at us. Casey was only nine years old and
sitting next to me on the bus. I leaned over to her and said, "Casey, I
don't think those people like you very much."

The Orange Bowl was one of those places, like West Virginia,
where I always knew we were nowhere near the friendly confines of
Lane Stadium. A year later, Rick Neuheisel, then the Washington
head coach, called me. His team was headed to the Orange Bowl to
play the Hurricanes.

"What's the atmosphere like in the Orange Bowl?" Rick asked me.
"What should we be prepared for?"

I told him, "Just protect yourself. The thing you really have to
worry about is the bus ride into the stadium. They will be throwing
stuff, flipping you off, and cussing you."

Miami, undefeated and ranked No. 1, defeated Rick's team 65–7.
He called me back after the game. "I wish one of those bottles they
were throwing at us would have hit me in the head and knocked me
out *before* the game," he told me. "What a nightmare!"

I had to laugh at that one.

I felt the same way after our game against Miami that day. We
started Dave Meyer at quarterback, but fell behind 14–0 at the end
of the first quarter. That's when I asked Michael if he could go. He
wanted to try it, but he just wasn't himself out there. The ankle obviously limited his mobility. He played 19 plays in the second quarter and had only 14 total yards, before we pulled him from the game
at halftime. By the end of the third quarter, we trailed 28–0. We lost
41–21, ending our 19-game regular-season winning streak. I still

believe we would have won had Michael been at full strength and André played.

Both of them also missed the game at Central Florida the following week, so we just stuck to the ground, rushing for 313 yards. We threw only eight passes (completing two) and still won 44–21.

Michael returned as we beat Virginia 42–21 to finish 10–1. He immediately said publicly after the game that he would come back for his junior year. Since he had redshirted and had been out of high school three years, he was eligible for the NFL draft following his sophomore season, but we never even considered that he might leave at that point.

We went about our business at the TPC Sawgrass in Jacksonville preparing to face Clemson in the Gator Bowl when some media guys started asking me about Michael leaving for the NFL.

I asked John Ballein, "Have you talked to Michael? People are asking me about him coming out. He already said he was coming back. What's going on?"

We were getting ready to go to the dog track that night and we called him in for a talk.

"Yeah, I am kind of thinking about it now," he told us.

I said, "Look, that's fine, but let's do some research when we get home and see what the NFL guys say and go from there. Don't make any rash decisions right now."

As the media picked up on the story, it grew bigger and bigger by the day.

We beat Clemson 41–20 as Michael passed for 205 yards and Lee Suggs scored three touchdowns on New Year's Day. After the game, our radio analyst Mike Burnop, who was a great tight end at Virginia Tech, asked Michael on the air about his plans for the following season.

Michael Vick was a one-of-a-kind quarterback.
His release was as quick as his feet.

Standing behind President Bill Clinton in
the Rose Garden in 2000. I was invited
to the White House to join a select group
as the president made remarks on the
Conservation and Reinvestment Act.

That's a look of pride in having my number
retired September 12, 2002, during a
home game.

My postgame speeches usually are not very long—win or lose. This one is from the 2002 season.

Celebrating with Vinny Fuller after he scored on a blocked field goal return in our 19–13 win over West Virginia in 2004.

Celebrating with Victor "Macho" Harris. We had a common bond in recovering from severe burns.

I'm not sure if I like the play being called.

We walked to midfield to greet East Carolina before the 2007 season-opener, our first game since the April 16 shootings. We won the game 17–7, but the most important thing of the day was bringing the Virginia Tech community together again.

On September 3, 2007, two days after we beat East Carolina to open the season, we placed the game ball at the memorial for the 32 victims of the April 16 shooting. From left, Carlton Weatherford, me, Eddie Royal, Xavier Adibi, and D.J. Parker. It was the most emotional game ever at Lane Stadium.

The game ball: September 3, 2007.

A day hardly goes by when I don't think of April 16, 2007. My daily walk around campus usually takes me by the memorial at the head of the Drillfield.

Here I am giving instructions to our special teams.

Those Gatorade baths are colder than they appear on TV. Here I am receiving one after our Orange Bowl win over Cincinnati on January 1, 2009.

Waving to Hokie fans after our 2009 Orange Bowl win over Cincinnati.

Leading the Hokies from the locker room to Lane Stadium before a game. Of all the walks I take each week, this is my favorite.

Michael's answer: "There's a good chance you're going to see me around here next year, but I've got a lot of thinking to do. It's going to be a tough decision. Me being 20 years old and having the chance to be a millionaire sounds almost too good to be true. No matter how it turns out, I am going to be the one who's going to have to deal with everything."

Burnop then asked him about the possibility of us making another run at the national title, if he returned for his junior season.

"Hopefully, if I stay, we can make that run," he said. "I hope I can be a part of it."

We left Jacksonville and I still thought Michael would be coming back.

When we arrived home, I immediately called an old friend, Bill Polian, then general manager of the Indianapolis Colts, who knew the NFL as well as anybody. This was before the league installed the current system where underclassmen can submit paperwork to receive feedback about their draft status. We had to conduct our own research on Michael's behalf.

Michael had finished third for the Heisman Trophy as a freshman behind Wisconsin's Ron Dayne and Georgia Tech's Joe Hamilton. His numbers were down in 2000, largely because of his injury, when he finished sixth in the voting. I thought he could win it the following year and that was one of the reasons I wanted him to stay. You don't get many opportunities to become an All-American or win the Heisman Trophy.

He had accounted for 4,276 total yards and 36 touchdowns in only two seasons, but I wasn't thinking about the past. I knew we could beat anyone on the schedule the next two seasons, if only we could convince him to stay. But at this point, I would have taken one more season of having Michael on our team.

I made my pitch to him and we got Bill on the phone with him. He advised him to come back.

I added, "Michael, if you would be the first pick of the draft, then I agree—there is no reason not to go."

But deep down, I never thought he would be the No. 1 pick of the entire draft. I didn't know if the NFL was ready for a quarterback like Michael, because he was such a great runner as well as a great passer. Remember, there weren't quarterbacks back then in the NFL running the read option and all that like they do today. Coaches wanted quarterbacks to stay in the pocket and deliver the ball on time.

We met with Michael and his mother down at Johnny Lawson's business in Newport News to lend our support when Michael announced his decision to the media: he declared early for the NFL draft. I didn't think it was a great decision, but as it turned out that next April, he became the No. 1 pick by the Atlanta Falcons, who traded up to take him, so I had been wrong.

I was happy for him, especially since he signed the largest rookie contract in NFL history—a six-year contract for $62 million.

He was gone, but he sure made an impact in only two seasons on the field. It is safe to say that Michael Vick changed everything for Virginia Tech. Our school admissions, largely because of our national championship appearance against Florida State as well, tripled because of the exposure Michael gave us.

We suddenly had a following that expanded way beyond Blacksburg and even beyond Virginia.

It was much easier to get into kids' homes to recruit after that. Kevin Jones was the perfect example. He came here because of Michael Vick. From that 1999 season on, I could walk into about any high school and say the words "Virginia Tech" and some kid would say, "Oh yeah, that's Michael Vick's school."

Along with Cornell Brown, Michael was obviously the most important recruit we ever signed. He changed the whole culture here. He made Virginia Tech a name brand. He made Virginia Tech *cool*.

The best thing is that anyone here who knew Michael liked him. A lot of great players, you just don't want to be around them for very long because they are full of themselves and they act special. But you wanted to be around Michael. He was very genuine, very real, and he was a good person while he was here.

I know Michael left here in good academic standing, but he never got his degree. It has always been something I wished he would finish.

Everyone knows Michael's life hasn't gone smoothly since he left Virginia Tech, but we never in our wildest dreams imagined he was into anything like dog-fighting. It absolutely shocked everybody on my staff. He never got into trouble here. He went to class. He obeyed our rules and his teammates loved him. In fact, he was as well-liked as any player who ever came through here. He never played the superstar role or acted bigger than anybody else.

We never had reason to suspect anything like that. We never heard a word about dog-fighting, and really, we had no clue.

I did say to him, "Be careful who you hang out with. Don't let your old friends take advantage of you and get you into trouble. You have a lot more to lose than they do."

He would tell me, "Coach, I'm not turning my back on those friends I've known my whole life."

Deep down, I really admired his loyalty, but that conversation and his response became very relevant later when the dog-fighting thing was brought to light.

The thing is, Michael had a dog when he was here and he loved that dog. He absolutely loved it. He had it with him all the time and he would bring it around the football facility.

When I started to read the stories about his involvement and about all of the gory details, I had a hard time digesting it all. I am a dog-lover myself. One of the saddest days of my life was when our dog Jock died. Cheryl will tell you I cried like a baby that day.

We all know dog-fighting was one thing, but the way they killed the dogs was another. That was by far the worst part of it all. When I read about the details of the cruelty, I just thought, *Whoa, Mike....*

The whole thing was tough on me and on anybody who was close to Michael. I also hurt for his mother.

The one thing we weren't going to do—and I told my staff this— we weren't going to turn our back on him. I knew he was a good person with a good heart. Even though millions of people across the country saw Michael as a bad person because of this, I never did. I knew everyone had an opinion on this and I understood it. But good people do terrible things, sometimes because they don't know any better.

Earlier, Michael had donated $100,000 to our program and we had named a portion of our football facility "Michael Vick Hall." When his crimes became public, we were under great pressure to take his name off that wall. I think his high school removed his name and trophies from their trophy cases.

I stood up then and said, "We don't turn our back on one of our own. We will stick by him."

Michael Vick Hall remains here today.

I could never justify what he did, which was definitely wrong. It was definitely cruel to animals. There was no arguing that point, and I would never argue it, either. But I told him, "Your story will be a great one someday. You are a guy who once had nothing. You then had it all, lost most of it, and you will come back stronger and change your way of doing things. You have a chance to impact a lot of people after this. You can tell young people about making good decisions and they will listen to you."

I have used his story many times in the talks I give to younger kids. If they have made mistakes, they can always turn something bad into something good if they work at it.

When he was in Leavenworth Federal Prison, we stayed in touch with him. John Ballein would write him notes and Michael always wrote back, asking about the coaches and the team. This is what he wrote in one of his final letters from prison in December 2008, shortly before his release:

> …Be sure to tell Coach Beamer and Tyrod [Taylor] they did a fabulous job going down the stretch. My time has come for my exit from prison and my entrance back into society. I look forward to getting my second chance at life, to be with my family and to play football again. Thanks for all of the encouraging letters and please remind everyone of my appreciation. I will see you soon and will call you as soon as I am home. Tell everyone I said hi.
>
> A Hokie For Life!
> Thanks for everything!
> Michael.

I knew he could prove himself all over again if somebody in the NFL would give him a chance after prison. Ironically, it was Philadelphia quarterback Donovan McNabb who really helped him when he was getting back into the league, and then it was the Eagles who ended up signing Michael. Not all starting quarterbacks would have gone along with that situation, but those two had a bond all those years from the time Michael had visited Syracuse.

The best that I can tell, Michael is doing just what I thought he would do: making the most of his second chance. On March 4, 2011, I received the Joe Paterno Award from the Maxwell Football Club in Atlantic City. That night, Michael received the Bert Bell NFL Player of the Year Award.

It was a great moment for both of us.

"It's a huge deal for me," Michael told the assembled media. "I knew at some point I would have to step up to the plate, accept responsibility, and do things the right way."

"I am real proud of him," I told the media that night. "He made some bad decisions, but I always knew he was a good person with a good heart. I think he's well on his way toward helping a lot of young people and I know that's what he wants to do."

I really believe Michael learned his lesson and will continue to do good things for the rest of his life. I am happy to see that he also is getting his due for turning his life around.

When cyclist Lance Armstrong publicly admitted to doping, USA Today ran a cover story on January 18, 2013, about famous athletes, scandal, and atonement. One paragraph read: "Michael Vick, once in prison and in disgrace for his role in dog-fighting, has worked with the Humane Society of the United States to combat cruelty to animals and has spoken at inner-city schools to tell students of his mistakes. His rehabilitation has been commended by many, including the president."

That is exactly the kind of redemption I pictured for Michael. He's impacted people in a positive way with his actions. He is coming back stronger than ever. I will always hold him in a very high regard, not because of his on-field achievements but because of how he's battled back from this terrible adversity and turned his life around.

Michael's departure from Virginia Tech, however, didn't mean it was the last time I would visit the Vick household in Newport News.

10

My Loyalty Is Tested

Our win over Clemson in the Gator Bowl put the finishing touches on back-to-back 11–1 seasons. Dating back to our win over Alabama in the 1998 Music City Bowl, we had won 23 of our previous 25 games. Since the end of the 1994 season, we had a 58–14 record and had played for a national championship. The program was on a roll.

It was the type of success I had envisioned when I took the job.

But I learned there is one derivative of a program's success: your name is mentioned as a candidate for other coaching jobs.

I already told you about the flirtation with Boston College back in 1990 and how and why I turned down that offer. Now other people were calling me.

When we were staying in New Orleans for the Sugar Bowl following the '99 season, Green Bay Packers general manager Ron Wolf called me to set up a meeting for the following January. I agreed to meet him in Roanoke, where he had booked a room. The Packers were in the process of firing Ray Rhodes and were looking for a coach. The name "Green Bay Packers" just grabbed my attention, as it would most any coach, because I immediately thought of their tradition and Vince Lombardi.

We sat down in his hotel room that day and visited for a while, just talking football. I think he was just feeling me out and it was a very preliminary meeting. I was flattered by the interest, but I really didn't think pro football was for me. The money would have been great, but there are so many other things you have to deal with in the NFL. Bobby Ross always told me the worst thing about pro football was that the head coach was not in control of the personnel. Our talks never got serious—from either side.

A year later, following the 2000 season, when we were in Jacksonville for the Gator Bowl, Alabama athletic director Mal Moore called. They had just fired Mike DuBose. I wasn't much interested in that job, either, because I worried I could never do better as a coach than what the Bear had done. Any coach there would always be compared to the Bear. (Of course, as we know now, they are mentioning Nick Saban's three national championships more often than anything the Bear did years ago. It is amazing what Nick has done there.)

Another time, Vince Dooley, then the athletic director at Georgia, made overtures to me during the annual College Football Hall of Fame banquet in New York, but the talks didn't amount to anything.

Only once did I ever come close to leaving Blacksburg.

In November of 2000, we had just lost that heartbreaking game at Miami 41–21, largely because we didn't have Michael Vick and André Davis, both hobbled with ankle injuries. We bounced back to beat Central Florida in Orlando and returned home with a 9–1 re-cord and a week off to prepare for the regular-season finale at home against Virginia.

North Carolina athletic director Dick Baddour called me, wanting to talk about the Tar Heels job. He was about to fire Carl Torbush. We talked a while and I was very intrigued with what he had to say and with the prospect of taking the Tar Heels job.

Cheryl and I wanted to get away to our house at Lake Oconee, Georgia, and Dick told us to meet him in Charlotte. We talked through a third person in Charlotte, and Cheryl and I drove to the lake house to think about our future, knowing we had an off week ahead of us. I took a few days, I talked to him again, I talked to Cheryl, and on Saturday, November 18, I told Baddour I would accept the job.

It would be one of the biggest mistakes of my life.

I didn't tell a soul other than Cheryl and my trusted assistant, John Ballein.

We prepared well and beat Virginia 42–21 the next Saturday to finish 10–1. Cheryl and I then flew to Chapel Hill on Sunday morning, November 26, to work out the details. I had totally convinced myself it was a great opportunity. In fact, I knew it was. I also knew we could win big at North Carolina. They had great facilities and support from the administration.

Once we arrived that Sunday, we toured the Dean Dome and all the football facilities and met everybody in the administration. They took me to meet the president and offered me a glass of hot cider, somewhat as a toast to the future.

I never signed a contract and they wanted me to stay that Sunday night and have the introductory press conference on Monday morning.

"No, we have to get back to Blacksburg tonight," I told them.

I know they were thinking if we got on that airplane to come home, I would change my mind.

And that's exactly what I did.

That Sunday night at my house, I got to thinking about everything. North Carolina had great facilities and great potential to win football championships to go with the many they already had in basketball. I knew we could win there. Some football coaches may have been scared off by what great basketball North Carolina always had, but I always thought that would be a plus. I never worried about basketball. What was most important to my decision-making process was the fact that those football facilities were built on somebody else's blood and sweat. They weren't built from my work.

What we had at Virginia Tech at that time, on the other hand, and what we have built for the future, were built largely because of the success we had since 1993.

Another thing was that our daughter, Casey, was in school at Virginia Tech at the time. How would she feel if we up and left for North Carolina while she was a student here? And how would she be treated if I left to take another job?

But most of all, I realized how much I loved Virginia Tech. I loved the people at Virginia Tech and the relationships we had developed over the years. I loved the town of Blacksburg. I knew that was—and always would be—my home. I realized there was no other place I would rather be.

I didn't sleep at all that night, weighing both sides of the decision.

"Whatever you decide, we will do," Cheryl told me. "You always make pretty good decisions."

I woke up Monday morning, or basically got out of bed since there is no waking up when you don't sleep, and I thought to myself, *This is my alma mater. This is where I want to be. And this is where we will be as long as I am coaching.*

I headed to the office, where everybody waited on my decision. When I walked up to the football facility, I noticed a few people carrying signs, such as "Don't Go Frank" and "Honk If You Want Frank to Stay." It felt good to be wanted.

By now, I had alerted my staff about what was happening. I think my assistants expected me to take the job even though they didn't know how far the discussions had gone. It wasn't very long after I arrived at the office when Dick Baddour called me. I didn't take the call, because I was a flat-out mess, a real basket case. I went upstairs to Jim Weaver's office and met with him, along with the school president, Dr. Charles Steger, and Minnis Ridenour.

As we talked, it became clear that if I stayed, they would offer what I wanted all along—for my assistants to be taken care of with more money and better contracts. I received a raise, too, but my staff being taken care of was my main concern. I thought they had been vastly underpaid and that was the one issue that led me to listen when people called asking me to interview for other jobs.

I came back downstairs to my office and I called Cheryl at home.

"I can't leave honey," I told her. "We're staying."

I called all of my staff into a meeting.

"We're staying," I told them. "I just feel like I want to stay and get it done here—not somewhere else."

At this point, Michael Vick hadn't decided whether he would return for his junior season.

"Whether Michael does or doesn't come back, it doesn't matter." I added, "I just can't leave."

I immediately felt support from all of them. One by one, they told me they would have supported me no matter what my decision was. That meant a lot to me.

Then came the hard part: I had to tell North Carolina.

I called Dick and I started my explanation, "Listen, this is nothing to do with you. It's me. I just can't leave here. I love this place and it's my alma mater. I want to tell you that you did everything right. It was perfect, but I just can't do it."

There was silence on the other end. I could tell he was upset and I understood why he would be, but he didn't say too much. He never yelled at me or anything like that. It was very cordial. He was a professional and I appreciate that to this day. Dick ended up hiring John Bunting and I think he has forgiven me over time, but it took a while. He was very cordial to me in recent years during the ACC meetings before he retired.

After the entire thing was over, I was relieved. I knew I made the right decision and I had no regrets. Not only did I not have regrets over the years, but every year that passes reinforces my belief that I made the right decision.

As a competitor, I may wonder "what if?" as far as how many games we would have won and all that. But then again, I would have wondered about the past 12 or 13 years here at Virginia Tech if I had gone to North Carolina. I also know that I just can't live my life with "what ifs" in my mind. Nobody should.

The fact is, we were in the process of building something at Virginia Tech that was very special to me and I wouldn't have been able to say that had I gone to North Carolina.

Of course, the one regret I do have is that I went back on my word. My word has always been solid my entire life and this was the one time I broke it. But I broke it for a good reason, probably the best reason: loyalty.

That is a word I mention to my coaches when we meet to begin every season in August. Be loyal to each other. Be loyal to yourself and be loyal to your school. My loyalty to Virginia Tech, and everything it stands for, won out in the end. Virginia Tech stuck with me after that 2–8–1 season and I never forget that. And I never will.

Following the 2012 season, I wanted to interview a great young assistant coach who happened to be working for his alma mater. He agreed to fly to Blacksburg and we sent the school's airplane to pick him up. As the plane sat on the runway, motor running, preparing to fly back here, he wouldn't get on it.

He called and I picked up the phone.

"Coach, I just can't do it," he told me. "Although I appreciate the opportunity and I want to thank you for it, I went to school here and I love the people here. I just can't leave."

"If anybody understands that, I do," I told him. "No hard feelings."

How could I ever be mad at him? I knew exactly what he was going through.

The North Carolina thing concluded any talk I would ever have with any general manager, athletic director, or president at any other institution. This has been my home since I arrived here as an unsure freshman quarterback in the summer of 1965, and it will remain my home until the day they put me in the ground.

I have come to determine the best things in life are sometimes right under your nose. There are no better people anywhere. And there is no better place to live than Blacksburg, Virginia.

This is my final word on the subject: I will remain a Hokie 'til the day I die.

And I can guarantee you that my word is solid on that.

11

The Quarterback Closest to Michael Vick

"Coach Beamer, I have the next Michael Vick for you."

Since Michael Vick left for the NFL following the 2000 season, I don't know how many times I have heard high school coaches tell me that. I've probably heard it dozens of times over the years. They didn't have the next Michael Vick, of course, because there wasn't one. People with Michael's speed, arm strength, and quick release don't grow on trees.

I never saw another Michael Vick. The only guy I ever saw who was close was his little brother, Marcus.

Marcus had a lively arm. He was competitive and he could run. Now he wasn't as fast as Michael—who was?—and his release wasn't quite as quick, but there was no question in my mind that Marcus could become a great college quarterback some day.

He just needed some college-level experience, as do all quarterbacks coming out of high school.

The big difference was that when I made a return trip to the Vick household to recruit Marcus, things had changed somewhat. This wasn't a modest apartment complex with twin beds and a yellow bus outside anymore. Michael's family lived in a very nice house in a very nice neighborhood. There were big-screen TVs and king-sized beds.

All of a sudden, due to Michael and his NFL income, the family had a fantastic life and Marcus was enjoying every bit of it. The desire to make their lives better was part of Michael's makeup when he was young. But as I would learn, I am not sure if the drive to succeed was there for Marcus.

I know that when we recruited Marcus, he hinted he wanted a bigger city in which to play college football. I am not sure how much he loved Blacksburg, because of its smaller size. All the things we love about Blacksburg weren't the things he was looking for. He wanted to be his own guy, maybe not follow in Michael's footsteps. And he wanted to have a bigger social stage to experience when he was off the field. He considered Tennessee, Miami, and N.C. State, but in the end, he signed with us.

There was another thing that I learned pretty quickly once he arrived on campus: unlike Michael, Marcus just didn't seem to care if he disappointed me.

If Michael did something wrong—and he rarely did—he was hurting inside because he hated to disappoint people. He hated to disappoint me and our staff. It really bothered him. But I don't think it ever bothered Marcus when he disappointed us.

Sadly, that would be often over the next four years.

Just like with Michael, we redshirted Marcus (for the 2002 season). Bryan Randall was our quarterback and we felt pretty set with him, although Marcus had passed for five touchdowns in our spring scrimmage. All the offensive coaches believed he was about to become a very good quarterback. All he needed was experience.

Bryan passed for 2,134 yards and 12 touchdowns as we finished 10–4.

The following season, Marcus and Bryan were sharing time on the field. We got to alternating them, and sometimes it got messy. We were also playing Marcus at receiver when Bryan was at quarterback, but I knew we had to make a decision and stick with one guy at quarterback. I decided to go with Marcus near the end of the season.

We had beaten Temple 24–23 in overtime to give us an 8–2 record when I called Marcus in for a talk.

"I want to name you the starter for the rest of the season," I told him.

"No, no," he said. "I'm comfortable right where I am."

That took me back. In my mind, he was more talented than Bryan and he was the one who I wanted to get on the field at quarterback. He may not have been a better quarterback than Bryan, but I was looking down the road to what he would become with experience: one of the top dual-threat quarterbacks in the country. As I thought about it later, Bryan brought all the things to the table that I want in a quarterback—dependability, leadership, and the intangibles. If we only could have blended all the ingredients from Marcus and Bryan together, we would have had a Heisman Trophy winner.

We finished 8–4 in the regular season, but got beat by Cal 52–49 in the Insight Bowl in Tempe, Arizona, in a game in which Marcus caught a touchdown pass.

DeAngelo Hall had returned a punt to tie the game 49–49 with just over three minutes left, but our kicker kicked the ball out of bounds on the ensuing kickoff. And Cal had a guy you may have heard of at quarterback—Aaron Rodgers. He took them right down the field to set them up for the game-winning field goal on the final play.

Rodgers passed for 394 yards that night and probably was more impressive to me than all those other great quarterbacks we'd faced, or would face in the future: the Mannings, Favre, McNabb, Chris Weinke, Jason Campbell, Matthew Stafford, or Andrew Luck.

All those guys went on to have NFL careers, but Rodgers was something that night. Every time the ball came out of there, it went to the right receiver.

That 2003 team was one of the most talented teams we ever had. We had two first-round picks that year (DeAngelo Hall and Kevin Jones) but we had no chemistry. We had some selfish guys and we had too many off-the-field things happen that year, too. And that is one of the reasons we lost our final three games to finish 8–5.

Following the season, Marcus got into some trouble involving under-age girls at his apartment. Another time he was found with marijuana in his car, so we suspended him for the 2004 season. People often asked me if I ever talked to Marcus or tried to reach him. Let me tell you, he knew the way to my office.

We called him in quite a bit. I would talk and talk and talk about doing the right things, about avoiding trouble, and being accountable for his actions. He would listen and always respond, "Yes, Coach… yes, Coach."

One of my assistants joked that his "Yes, Coach" answers really meant "Screw you, Coach."

That next season, our chemistry changed completely. It's really odd when the chemistry on a team changes that much from one season to the next, but everybody got along real well and we won the ACC championship. We beat Miami 16–10 in the final game for our 10th win and we went to the Sugar Bowl to play Auburn. Our team had less talent than the year before, but much better chemistry, and a lot of the credit goes to Bryan. He'd completed 170-of-306 passes for 2,264 yards and 21 touchdowns and had cut his interceptions down to nine. Bryan finished his career with 6,508 passing yards, now second on Virginia Tech's all-time list behind Tyrod Taylor, who would come along three years later. Bryan's 48 career touchdown passes are still a school record. He also is second on the list in total offense with 8,034 yards.

I learned something right there, or actually reinforced what I already knew: when the leader of the team is also the best player, you've got something special. And good chemistry trumps good talent every time.

By the time Marcus returned for the 2005 season, we had demoted him to third on the depth chart, but he was so talented that it was just a matter of time before he won the job with Bryan now gone. He had a great season, passing for 2,393 yards and 17 touchdowns and rushing for almost 400 more as we finished 11–2.

But there were many bumps in the road for Marcus that season.

The first came in the 34–17 win at West Virginia, when he flipped off the Mountaineer fans and the TV cameras caught it with a close-up view.

We didn't find out what Marcus had done until we returned home after the game. When somebody asked me about it, I once joked, "Have you ever been to West Virginia's stadium?"

That bus ride in and out of there is as daring as it gets in college football. Opposing team's buses pull in there along the fraternity houses and trailers and everybody is drinking. One time we won a game there and as we pulled out on the bus, I could hear our players saying, "I think they're going to do it" and "Yeah, they're getting close."

I wondered what the heck they were talking about and I looked out the window just in time to see several guys dropping their pants to moon us. Our players erupted into applause.

I may have made a joke about the middle finger, but I knew that Marcus' actions were not the type I wanted representing our program. I don't want our players engaging with the other team's fans and I don't want any of them flipping off anyone.

I didn't condone Marcus' actions and never will, no matter how hostile the environment. I asked him about it later and he said, "But coach, they were calling me names."

"But Marcus, you *can't* do that."

How Marcus played was never the issue. I can't think of a time where I thought after a game, *Well, Marcus really stunk today.* His issues were always his actions off the field—and one time on the field.

We started that season 8–0 before losing 27–7 to No. 5 Miami. We beat Virginia and North Carolina to finish 10–1 and win the ACC's Coastal Division. We played a 7–4 Florida State team in the ACC Championship Game in Jacksonville. We committed 17 penalties for 143 yards in that game, one of the worst displays of discipline ever, and lost 27–22. Marcus committed one of the 15-yard unsportsmanlike conduct penalties.

It wasn't the normal Florida State team we were used to seeing. The Seminoles were very beatable. They had lost five games coming into the game and we had the better team, but they played better that night than they had all season—and we self-destructed.

Instead of a BCS Bowl, we headed back to Jacksonville the following month for the Gator Bowl.

In that first half against Louisville, Marcus stomped on the leg of one of their defensive ends, Elvis Dumervil. Although the officials never saw it, once again the TV cameras caught it clearly.

At halftime, quarterbacks coach Kevin Rogers asked, "Should we play him in the second half?" and I didn't know what he was talking about. I didn't see it and didn't know about it until I overheard some of the coaches talking about it at halftime.

I asked Marcus about it after the game.

"Coach, he was twisting my ankle," Marcus told me. "I just retaliated."

"But Marcus, you *can't* do that."

It seemed to be a common refrain for me while talking to Marcus Vick.

After the game, when I realized completely what had happened and then saw the replay—I wasn't so sure Marcus' explanation held up—I grabbed him and we headed to the Louisville locker room to apologize. Marcus apologized to the other kid and he accepted it gracefully. We also asked the Louisville sports information director if their coach, Bobby Petrino, could come out of the locker room for a minute so we could apologize to him, too.

A minute later, the director appeared and told us, "Coach Petrino doesn't want to see you. He said there's nothing he needs to discuss."

Later, I heard about a nasty remark Petrino had uttered after we shook hands at midfield following the game. I must have turned away and didn't catch it at the time, but my buddy Greg Roberts, a local television sports anchor, told me he called me a two-word insult that began with the letters "M" and "F." And they didn't stand for "most friendly."

I planned to suspend Marcus for our first game for next season. I met with Dr. Steger and it was decided that it should be a three-game suspension. Together, we also determined that if there was one more transgression of any kind, he would be kicked off the team.

I flew to Newport News to break the news to Marcus and Brenda that he was facing a three-game suspension to begin the 2006 season. By the time I landed, another storm was brewing with Marcus. Apparently he had loaned his car to his girlfriend earlier and she had received a ticket for driving without insurance. She never paid the ticket. So a court date was set in his name, and Marcus, not knowing about the ticket, never showed.

When Jim Weaver learned of this, he said it constituted another strike against Marcus and according to the policy that was now in place, he had to be dismissed from the program. He called Dr. Steger and informed him. Then he told John to call me when my plane landed and give me the news: I had to tell Marcus he was being dismissed from the program.

I met Brenda and Marcus and the first thing I said was, "Marcus, I am sorry but we've got to let you go."

It was one of the toughest things I ever had to do. I saw the look on Brenda's face and I knew she was heartbroken. I think my news shocked them both. I know I had tears in my eyes. Still, I think she understood our position. It wasn't like she said, "How could you do this to my son?" or anything like that. There was no great emotion from Marcus, but I do think he was disappointed.

And that was that.

We would have loved to have him back for his senior season. Sean Glennon took over at quarterback in 2006 and we finished 10–3, after losing to Georgia in the Chick-fil-A Bowl.

To this day, I have a very good relationship with Michael Vick and his mother. She called the office just the other day to say hello and to tell us she was thinking about us. She is a wonderful woman. And Michael has turned his life around after the dog-fighting thing, just like I knew he would.

But Marcus?

I think he only cared once he crossed the white lines and stepped onto the field. I don't think I ever reached him. I can honestly say this: I never reached him to the point where he got the most out of his athletic ability or as a student. He had the ability to be in the NFL for many years. Now I worry about his future.

I know he never got his degree and never reached the heights he should have reached on the football field.

And that truly saddens me.

12

Winning off the Field

My 100th win at Virginia Tech came in the opening game of my 15th season—a 52–10 blowout of Connecticut at Lane Stadium. We entered the season ranked No. 9; Michael Vick now played for the Atlanta Falcons, and Grant Noel had replaced him at quarterback.

Grant was almost perfect that day, completing 16-of-20 passes for 267 yards and three touchdowns in his debut, but I wasn't much in a mood to celebrate a win or any milestones after the game, because Lee Suggs had suffered torn knee ligaments during the game.

The next week, the defense pitched a shutout as we beat Western Michigan 31–0. We had an off weekend coming up, so I wasn't rushing to the office early that Tuesday morning since our next game, at Rutgers, was 11 days away.

Cheryl had NBC's *Today Show* on television while I was getting ready for work. I overheard Katie Couric and Matt Lauer mention something had happened at the World Trade Center in lower Manhattan.

It was September 11, 2001.

I quickly drove to the office and turned on the TV. All of us in the football offices had trouble focusing on work that day as we sat there stunned, watching the devastation. It showed me how vicious the people who hate us can be and also how well-organized they were. It was a horrible day.

The next few weeks we could see people in this country pulling together. Many people stood up and said that they wouldn't live in fear. Similar feelings would come back to us at Virginia Tech less than six years later.

Every college and pro football game was canceled that next weekend and we were very anxious to get back on the field the next week. By resuming our games, it was almost as if we told the terrorists, "This is how we do it in the United States—and you are not going to dictate how we live our lives over here."

I liked that message.

I think football, and all sports for that matter, was a unifying force for us at the time. In the big scope of things I knew it wasn't important whether we went out and beat Rutgers, but it was very important that Virginia Tech and Rutgers University were playing a football game in the state of New Jersey in the United States of America.

During that next week, John Ballein suggested one of our players should carry the American flag out of the tunnel before the game. I loved the idea. Then we had to decide which player would receive that honor. There was no better choice to carry the U.S. flag than Brian Welch. Brian was a great kid whose father Kenneth Welch was a marine who died in the U.S. Embassy bombing in Beirut in 1984, when Brian was only six years old.

Our team plane flew into Newark on Friday, September 21, and we could see the ruins from the World Trade Center still smoldering—10 days after the attack. It was an unbelievable sight. There was a stunned silence on that airplane. I looked around and noticed coaches and players looking out of those small windows in saddened disbelief.

Brian carried the flag the next day as we entered Rutgers Stadium and on the second play of the game, who intercepted a pass and ran it back to Rutgers' 1-yard line? That's right, Brian Welch. We won the game 50–0 and awarded Brian a game ball.

When the media asked Brian about it after the game, he placed carrying the flag way above his interception.

"It was amazing," he said. "That meant so much to me. Football will come and go, but that will stay with me always."

That tells you a little bit about his character.

When I met with the media following the game, I said, "I think we were like most Americans—we had an empty place in our stomach and a hurt in our heart. But once the game started, I thought our guys did their best to play football at full speed."

The next week, we decided to have a second player carry the state flag of Virginia, and before long, it seemed like every team in the country carried flags onto the field before the start of a football game. I do think we were the first to do it, and we've been doing it ever since that day. During the 2007 season, we added a third flag—the Hokie Spirit Flag.

What September 11 helped us realize is that Brian was right: football will always come and go, but there are much bigger things in life, things you can learn or experience that will stay with you forever. It spurred an era of renewed patriotism, but it also got everyone thinking in larger terms.

As coaches and administrators at Virginia Tech, I think we have always tried to take that approach with our players.

We want to help our players become better people, not just better football players. We want them to see the big picture in life and teach them how to be successful off the field. I like to think we have a lot to offer a prospect, things way beyond learning how to execute a perfect form tackle or seal block.

We know we cannot recruit players or continue our success without great facilities to offer them. And by that I mean nice offices for the coaches, meeting rooms for the players, nice practice fields, a big and modern weight room, and a luxurious locker room. And of course, a beautiful stadium that is modernized and full of loyal fans on Saturday afternoons.

I take great pride in comparing what Virginia Tech had in 1987 to what we have today.

We built something here. We built something substantial that future Hokies will enjoy and benefit from long after I am gone.

I am really proud of what my alma mater has become. We have great people working here and we have great fans. All in all, I can honestly say we have a great program and I think Virginia Tech is thought of in a much different light than it was 20 years ago.

The one thing I have tried to develop here is a family atmosphere built on long-lasting relationships. I want a staff that cares about each other, and that includes support personnel and secretaries. That was part of my thinking when we abolished hazing after Jim Pyne, then a freshman, came to me with his concerns in 1990.

I have made some adjustments in the details of running a program and developing a team over the years, usually with our players' best interests in mind.

For example, in preseason camp, I have eliminated two-a-day practices, which once were the norm for every program during the month of August. The NCAA has a "20-hour" rule anyway, which prevents any student-athlete from participating in his or her sport for more than 20 hours per week, and that includes the time the game is played.

That never really affected us much, because we always did things to fall under the 20-hour limit anyway. I never believed in getting carried away with three-hour practices and hours and hours of meetings. The reality of it is that the kids are here to get an education first, and football comes second. Our coaches have families, too.

In recent years, we practice in camp only during the afternoon. I think we can always learn the most by going back over the film and seeing what was good and what was bad and correcting those mistakes. In the old days, we would practice in the morning, look at the video, install what was needed for the next practice, and then go at it again in the afternoon. It seemed like we were always in a rush.

With that schedule, we discovered that the kids' legs were gone. We wanted them to go full-tilt in practice and they couldn't. So we changed, alternating with two practices one day, one practice the next and so on. Then that wasn't making sense to me after a while, either, so we just reduced to one practice per day.

I tell the kids, "We will practice only once each day, so make it a good one. Be completely ready, physically and emotionally."

This way, our kids have more time to recover from each practice.

Discipline—on the field and off—has always been a key element between winning and losing football games.

The one thing I hate to see is guys making it all about them and not about the team. I tell our guys up front that I am behind any rule that prevents them from taunting our opponent. I hate to see them do something that even *seems* like taunting. I think the game ought to be played this way: players line up and play as hard as they can between the whistles; knock the other guy down legally, and then help him up if he's right in front of you. Then get ready to do it again.

All of that side stuff with players pointing and talking to each other, I don't think that's a good part of the game.

That doesn't mean we have been immune to selfish penalties, either. We've had a few personal fouls cost us dearly. Marcus' transgressions at the Gator Bowl were embarrassing to us, even though the officials never noticed it. One of our defensive ends, Cols Colas, shoved Miami's quarterback after a third-down play, giving them a first down in a crucial part of a game in 2001. Miami was ranked No.

1 at the time and they ended up winning the game 26–24. (Ironically, Cols later became Miami's strength and conditioning coach.)

The next year, we were leading Pittsburgh 21–7 and had forced them to punt after a third-down incompletion, but Ronyell Whitaker hit a receiver late near our bench. Pittsburgh was given an automatic first down, scored a play or two later and went on to beat us 28–21.

I am not picking on these guys by any means, but showing that no matter how much we preach about not being selfish and not committing selfish penalties, it still happens. If it is a late hit or a personal foul, it is a selfish play in my book. And the good thing is that's exactly how it comes across to the kids, too. They know when a teammate is being selfish.

We hand out fines, such as $100, for these types of penalties. Now before you get the idea we pay our players, the money comes from their stipend when we get to a bowl game at the end of the season.

We show all of our penalties during our weekly film sessions on Mondays with the team, something we started in 1993 and which really helped cut down on our penalties. I tell the kids if it's a bad call. I tell them if it's a good call. If they were holding a guy, I tell them they must not be as athletic as the other guy, since they had to hold to do the job.

We also issue fines for wearing the wrong shoes, or having one sleeve too long. I am a big believer in having every player dress the same and act the same. We travel in our warm-suits and if they wear a hat, it must be a Virginia Tech hat and it cannot be worn backward.

About our kids being interviewed on TV, I tell them, "You never know who's watching. You have 15 seconds to impress people who are seeing you on TV."

When I see a kid on TV with his hat on backward, I wonder what message he is trying to convey. What image is he representing? Is it about his team and program, or is it all about himself?

We go over all these rules in the preseason.

We have established a team-educate program by hosting guest speakers during camp. These people either are experts or have first-hand experience on issues which our players may encounter, such as drugs, sexual assault, gambling, agents, underage drinking, and steroid use.

Recently, we hosted Ray Jones, whose wife, Jill, and oldest son, Nicholas, were killed by a drunk driver. She was a professor at Liberty University. The one thing that really struck me about his speech to our team is when he said, "The truth of the matter is, you always know the right thing to do. The hard part is *doing* it."

RAY JONES: *"It's obvious, but I still love that quote. It's originally by General Norman Schwarzkopf. After giving the Virginia Tech team the general's quote, it was pretty easy for me to tell them that everyone would agree that drinking and driving is not the right thing to do. And I didn't want to be hypocritical and tell them not to drink, because I like a cold beer with my pizza and I like a glass of wine with my pasta. But, I told them that if they were going to make the choice to drink, then they can make the next choice to choose not to drive. That's simply the right thing to do."*

I am telling you, there weren't many dry eyes when Ray was done speaking to our players. I know I had tears in my eyes. And the most important thing is that I believe he had an impact. We haven't had a player with a DUI since he told the team his story, knock on wood.

We should educate our players on what is right and what is wrong with every topic that they may face. They should know it. Then they are responsible for knowing the difference and doing what is right. If they do not do the right thing, they will be punished.

And I will say this, too: It all goes back to recruiting. If we recruit the right kind of kids, we won't have as many issues. If there were issues with the player in high school, there likely will be issues with him in college. It doesn't change. At least that's my experience.

I have noticed over the years that when our best players were our best kids off the field, then the kids who were on the fence between right and wrong would usually follow that lead and go the right way. Bryan Randall, Tyrod Taylor, Logan Thomas, Cody Grimm, Danny Coale, and John Graves—and I could name dozens more—have been some of our best players and our best people.

When we have that combination, we usually have a team with few off-the-field issues. We usually have a team with good chemistry, which normally translates to winning.

At the beginning of each season, I tell the players during a meeting on the field, "It's *your* team, not mine. You seniors will be seniors only once. You had better think about what you want from your team. What do you want this team to be?"

I don't have any of those "senior councils" which report to me or anything similar. My approach to the players is, "You know the rules. You know what is right. So do the right thing."

The fact is, as Ray Jones told them, most everyone knows what is right, but the hard part in life is doing what is right.

During our final team meeting after spring practice, which is the final meeting before the kids leave for the summer, I give the "that guy" speech. I always tell them that they will read in the newspaper or hear in the media about a well-known athlete who has screwed up in one way or another. I tell them, "There will be at least one per week." And most of the time, this guy has done something that will affect his life forever.

I always finish my talk with this line: "Don't be 'that guy.'"

After I gave my talk in the spring of 2012, we monitored the sports pages and there was a mention of a famous athlete in some sort of trouble on six of the first seven days.

I know as a head coach, there's nothing worse than getting the news that one of our players is in the news for all of the wrong reasons. It just tears at me and causes me sleepless nights, probably as much as any losses.

We've had a few fights between our players and other students or townspeople. On the final day of summer camp before the 1996 season, I had just lectured our players about staying out of trouble—and that night there was a fight over at the Squires Student Center between a few students and a few of our players. There had been a big party and when it ended, two guys got to mouthing off to our players. Cornell Brown pushed a guy and they arrested five or six guys. He happened to be one of them. He missed the East Carolina game that season because of it.

When I found out about it, I really laid into them.

CORNELL BROWN: *"We were just finishing practice when I noticed the campus police car pull up to the edge of the stadium. We were gathered around Coach Beamer as he began his post-practice speech. 'Now you guys have really worked hard and you are on the path to great things...,' he started. I saw John Ballein talking to the cop as Coach Beamer talked to us. Then John walked up, 'Coach, you got a minute?' They talked for a minute. Coach Beamer turned around and his face was beet-red. His whole demeanor just changed instantly. 'Are you shittin' me?' he screamed. 'We go out on the last night of camp and half the team gets in a fight?!' He then went down to the end zone and said,*

'Whoever was involved in this fight get down here with me!' But nobody went—nobody owned up to it. He exploded again, 'Next time you want to fight somebody, you invite them down to the sheep field and fight them there!' I had never seen him so mad. And I don't think I've ever seen him as mad since."

When it comes to fighting, I tell our players, "You gotta walk away! That guy wants to fight you, but he doesn't have nearly as much to lose as you do. And secondly, what are you going to do after you whip his ass? What are you going to do now? Do you feel better about yourself?"

I just think unless they are insulting your mother or your girl-friend, it takes more of a man to walk away from a fight than to respond to one.

Of course, I remember when I got into one as a junior in high school. This kid in school would always purposely bump into me and I never knew why. It would be in the hallway or after school. It happened all the time. Finally, we agreed to meet outside, and just as he walked up, I decided I was going to get the first lick in. I let him have it and I don't remember ever seeing him again, but he would probably beat me up if we met today.

Off-the-field problems became a big issue during that entire '96 season. There just seemed to be something every week. How we continued winning through it all, I will never know. We went to play Nebraska in the Orange Bowl and a headline in the *Miami Herald* that week read: "Virginia Tech 21, Nebraska 18—*Arrests*." I don't know if that number was accurate, and I can't speak for Nebraska, but it probably was very close on our side of the scoreboard.

Then we had a player test positive for pot during the trip, so we sent him home. I was embarrassed. We didn't have bad kids; they were just doing dumb things.

Following the season, the university initiated the Comprehensive Action Plan, which put in a place a defining punishment for off-the-field infractions for the entire athletic department. It was a much better way of doing things. This way, a tennis player and a football player would be punished the same if they committed the same infraction. Most importantly, it took the coach out of the decision-making process. I was all for that. I don't want to make those decisions.

Previously, the athletic director and I would talk about each kid and what he had done on a case-by-case basis. Then we would agree on the punishment.

This new system took it out of my hands.

Under this plan, if a player is charged with a felony, he is off the team. Then various misdemeanors bring various punishments.

Marijuana seems to be the drug of choice these days; it's all around us. It's easy for kids to get, because it's cheap and they grow it in Virginia.

The good thing is, we are aware of it and we are very pro-active in education and testing for it.

I tell our kids: "We are going to test you and you will get caught, so if you need an excuse when you are at a party and everybody else is doing it, you just say, 'I can't do that because I might get tested tomorrow.'"

Our athletic department has a uniform policy for each positive test. After the first positive test, they receive counseling. With the second offense, they miss three games. With the third, they miss a certain percentage of their season. On the fourth, they are dismissed.

Fortunately, I don't think we've ever had anyone have more than two positive tests.

MIKE GOFORTH, Virginia Tech's associate athletic director for sports medicine: *"One of my jobs is drug-testing our players. When one of them fails, even just once, it breaks Coach Beamer's heart. Once we were having a rash of shin splints and very tired legs on the team by the end of each week. He arranged for a softer practice field and all of a sudden, our shin splints went away. He wanted a cold tub installed, so they would feel refreshed by Friday and Saturday. All this shows that he cares for their health and well-being—not just to win games, but so they are healthy people. I have friends in my position at many programs across the country who tell me some coaches may push them to get a player onto the field before he has fully recovered from an injury. Coach Beamer would never do that. The player's health comes before winning a game with him. What drives me to do my job every day is the fear of disappointing him, because I respect and admire that man so much."*

When it comes to our kids and injuries, I have three expectations from our training staff: First, I want to know the details of the injury and I want the player to know the facts of the injury as well; second, I want a plan for the rehabilitation; and third, I want the plan communicated to the parents so they are aware of their son's situation.

We have a great training staff here and our players would tell you that, too. One time, our quarterback, Al Clark, had sprained his ankle during a game at Miami. Mike Goforth had spatted (that's taping over the outside of the shoe) both of his shoes. We have a Nike contract and those executives out in Oregon never like it when you cover that famous logo.

I asked Mike, "Why did you spat both of Al's shoes if he had one sprained ankle?"

"Coach, I didn't want Miami to know which ankle was hurting him," he told me.

Made sense to me.

As far as alcohol goes, if they are old enough to drink legally, we just tell our kids to be responsible. We check curfew at 11:00 PM on Thursdays, and on Fridays of game week we're checked into a hotel. Obviously, they are not drinking those nights and we don't want any of our players drinking during the season. It can affect their weight, overall health, and their performance.

When it comes to agents, I warn them: "The only way that agent is going to make money is if he gets you to come out early. He may not be telling you accurate information, because he wants you to come out early, no matter where you might be taken in the draft. Now if he is doing something illegal [according to NCAA rules] to sign you, how can you trust that guy after you sign with him?"

We haven't had many guys come out early when they shouldn't have because of an agent's advice. Shyrone Stith is about the only one I can think of. He should have stayed for his senior year, but he listened to an agent. (Stith was selected in the seventh round by Jacksonville in the 2000 NFL draft and played three seasons with the Jaguars and Colts.)

We have noticed that these agents have runners who work for them. They hang out in the social areas or the bars where players may be known to visit. We are fortunate to claim that we have never had a kid lose eligibility because he signed with an agent early. I think that is because we've always made it a big issue and educated our kids about it.

Now that the NFL slots its salaries according to when the player was taken in the draft, the agent can only do so much good anyway. I sometimes think kids just like the sound of, "Let me talk to my agent."

This all goes back to education, which again, is something I think we emphasize as well as anybody.

Most importantly, I would tell anybody that we are legit in our academics.

Our approach has also helped us with the school's admissions department when we are recruiting a borderline student. Over the course of time, I think we have proven ourselves. When our admissions people hear us say, "Now this kid is borderline, but we will work with him and give him extra attention," we have credibility with them.

We have done it in the past many times and been successful.

I have told our coaches: "If a prospect is borderline, then he needs to be a great player. Otherwise, why would we take him and take the risk?"

Not all borderline students remain borderline after they get here and adapt to college. All some of them need is a little structure, motivation, and guidance. I think of kids like Waverly Jackson, who was from a small school in southeast Virginia. He had a learning disability, but we had a tutor named Derita Ratcliffe who took an interest in him and he worked his butt off. He never missed a class, always sat in the front row, and got his degree. He now coaches high school football in Virginia. Cordarrow Thompson was another. He was a great kid, a lovable kid. And Wayne Ward was another.

None of those kids would have gotten into college without football, but all they needed was a chance. We gave them that chance and now they have a college education and are living productive lives. That's the biggest thing about this job to me: How did we affect people's lives?

Wins and all of that are nice, but seeing a guy like Waverly come through here and accomplish what he did makes it all worthwhile.

If you walked into our main meeting room right now, you would see a big board with all of our players' names. Next to the names would be the color green, yellow, or red. Green means they are taking care of their business academically, yellow means they need to improve, and red—which is where all freshmen start—means they need to work and improve. We check such things as class attendance, test schedules, and tutoring schedules.

As a staff, we meet every Thursday to discuss each of our players and what is happening with them academically over the course of the past week. What's different—good or bad? If it's good, we tell them, "Way to go, Joe! You got a 90 on that math test." If it's bad, we say, "Joe, you missed a tutoring appointment and that's not going to happen again."

This way, we have no surprises. We know who is doing well and who needs help. We stop bad habits before they begin and before they become a serious issue. I like to think that approach tells the player that we care about him. We care deeply whether that player gets a degree by the time he leaves here.

On Friday nights, our players eat according to GPAs. The kids who already have graduated eat first and they are followed by the highest GPAs to the lowest.

Which brings me to the end result: graduation rates.

The NCAA uses a percentage system called "Graduation Success Rates." The Graduation Success Rate is the percentage of athletes who graduated within six years after starting college, not counting transfers. Our GSR has been between 70 and 80 percent each year since 2006. In recent years, we have been at 79 percent, while the NCAA average is somewhere between 60 and 65 percent.

Of course, I would love to have a GSR of 100 percent every year, but even the Vanderbilts, Northwesterns, and Dukes do not achieve that. There are too many obstacles which get in the way for some kids. Sometimes, players are on course to graduate but playing in the NFL, and the big money that comes with that, gets in the way. Then they never return to finish their degree.

In the old days, even the guys lucky enough to make an NFL roster didn't make the type of money that made their lives comfortable enough not to get a degree. Times have changed and players are receiving multi-million-dollar contracts with huge signing bonuses.

I know one thing: we still push them to come back and finish their degree, no matter how big their bank accounts are.

To show how old-school—or out of touch, some critics would say—I am, I don't tweet or text, so I have to rely on other people close to me to understand and monitor this Twitter thing. I tell our players, "Be responsible. Know what you are putting out there. Don't hurt yourself, your team, your teammates, or your coaches."

We had two guys recently who were tweeting back and forth and John would call them out during our meetings. He will stand up there and say, "Now so-and-so tweeted this and it was plain stupid. It looked ridiculous. Don't do it again!"

With all the potential problems that could put a student-athlete's name in the newspaper for the wrong reasons, it is important to note that the majority of our players give back to our community. It just doesn't gain the public's attention the way that an arrest does. But they don't do it for publicity.

John came to me with an idea in 2008 and I loved it instantly. As I already told you, my mom, Herma, was a fifth-grade teacher and reading was one of her passions. I met this attorney in Richmond, Frank Cowan, who suggested to me, "You know, there are a lot of children in Richmond who need the ability to read and need access to books. You could start a program and honor your mom's teaching legacy by naming it after her."

So we started a program, and called it "Herma's Readers," in honor of my mother.

Our goals are to reach kindergartners through third-graders, providing books and the opportunity to learn to read. With that ability, kids also learn to write better. With texting these days, there are so many abbreviations and kids are not learning proper English, so I think this program is more important than ever. Research has shown that students who are actively reading by the third grade are more apt to succeed in life.

I enjoy going out to schools and reading to these kids and we've had several of our players do it as well.

To raise money to buy books, we purchase our own game-worn helmets and then auction them off. We used that money to purchase books for schools throughout the state of Virginia. At last count, by the summer of 2013, we had purchased more than 53,000 books for Virginia's elementary schools.

I know Mom would be proud and happy about it. We are affecting these kids in a positive way, getting them started in the right direction. That would bring a smile to her face. Her whole life was about education and teaching kids. It's exactly the right thing to do to honor her memory. I know she'd be honored to have her name attached to this program.

My door is always open when a player needs to see me and that is about the only thing that would ever stop one of our staff meetings. It's important for our players to know that. If you walked down our hallways any day, you would see players in our assistant coaches' offices. I tell our coaches I like it that way, because these kids have to feel that they can come around anytime to talk to us. It doesn't have to be just about football, either. If we have an open door and we talk—and especially listen—to these kids, I think we will develop the kind of relationship we need to be successful as a team and they will be successful as people after football.

We must treat our players right every day and a large part of that is educating them. In the end, kids have to know we really do care about them. And we do. They need to know that there is a respect and a genuine caring for them as people first, athletes second. We ask them to work hard and to sacrifice. Football is not easy. We ask them to give the best that they have every day, and I don't think we can receive it unless they know we are doing the exact same thing on the other end.

And as coaches and administrators, that is what we try to do every day.

13

Darkest Day in Virginia Tech History

SHANE BEAMER: "I was coaching at South Carolina and was on the golf course at a booster outing on that Monday morning. When we made the turn after nine holes, somebody mentioned there had been a shooting at Virginia Tech. When I finished the round and walked into the pro shop, everybody was gathered around the TV. I turned on my cell phone and had a million messages. We all love this community, but it hit Dad very hard. He loves Virginia Tech so much and it shook him to the core. There are two things he still doesn't talk about much—the Marshall airplane crash in which he lost his good friend Frankie Loria and what happened on April 16, 2007."

We were busy planning a practice—our 12th practice of the spring—on the morning of April 16, 2007. It was a cold and snowy Monday and we had been discussing how terrible the weather was and how it would affect practice later that day.

John Ballein had just gotten back from his daily run when he told me that he saw an ambulance pulling into West Ambler Johnston Hall, just about a hundred yards from our football offices. He'd walked down to the office of our equipment manager, Lester Karlin, who had access to a police radio since he was a member of the Blacksburg Volunteer Rescue Squad.

"Lester, what's the ambulance for?" John asked.

At first he mentioned he heard someone had "a cardiac arrest" problem.

John came back to the football office, and Lester called a few minutes later.

"There's been a shooting," he said.

I was writing on the grease board, preparing for our morning staff meeting, when John walked in. He had heard it may have been a "boyfriend-girlfriend" incident, but at this point, nobody knew anything for sure. He said there was a shooter on the loose and somebody from the administration had called to tell us to secure the building and to lock our office doors.

All of our players live in Cochran Hall, which is close to West Ambler Johnston, so we were obviously concerned.

A short time later, John walked in again.

"We're not having practice today," he announced.

I asked, "Why? What's going on?"

He looked at me with a blank stare and said, "More people have been shot."

We turned on the television to CNN and we heard the voice of one of our kickers, Matt Waldron, giving an interview. He had called into the network and was describing the scene.

By 12:20 PM, we knew more than just two people had been killed. The media was now reporting there were 20 shooting victims in Norris Hall.

I could not comprehend that number. Twenty.

I told every assistant coach to call each of his position players and John called our academic advisers to check our players' class schedules. We did not know if any of them had classes in Norris Hall that morning.

A little while later, I walked into the hallway and one of our secretaries, Kristie Verniel, was crying hysterically.

She said, "I heard there were more than 30 people killed."

By 1:15 PM, the numbers had grown to 32 victims in all. The media also reported the gunman was dead.

What was happening here? It was just so unbelievable. It wasn't very long before someone from the university's administrative offices called to tell us to send everybody home. We told every staffer to go home to their families and we locked the offices.

It takes me about 11 minutes to drive home from the office, depending on whether I hit a green light or red light at the intersection I drive through on my way out of Blacksburg. By the time I got home and joined Cheryl in front of the TV, all the national networks were doing live reports from campus. It was all so bizarre. And for the rest of that day, we sat there watching in disbelief.

The rest of America was watching, too, but this was in our own backyard. The images I was seeing were from buildings, parking lots, and landmarks I'd walked by a thousand times over the years.

I sat there with Cheryl in front of the television from about two in the afternoon until 11:30 that night. The details were shocking. The shooter fired 174 rounds in only 11 minutes, killing 25 innocent students and five faculty members, in addition to the two students he had killed earlier at West Ambler Johnston.

It was unbelievable. I always thought if there ever was a campus where something like this could never happen, Virginia Tech was it.

Once Cheryl and I started crying, it was hard to stop. Just thinking of those innocent and defenseless kids tore me up inside. I don't think either of us got much sleep that night.

I left the house early on Tuesday and when I arrived on campus I couldn't get over the sight of all those satellite trucks. They were parked everywhere I looked. I was supposed to be on the air with NBC's Matt Lauer that morning, but their representatives called me to delay my appearance.

It didn't take long for the media to begin to criticize the university police chief, Wendell Flinchum, and our president, Charles Steger.

Katie Couric was being very tough on Chief Flinchum, complaining about a lack of information being released to her liking. She is a UVA graduate, but I don't think it had anything to do with her tenacity. Whether the campus should have been locked down at the moment they discovered the first shooting at West Ambler Johnston was the big issue for the media.

The media peppered Chief Flinchum with questions.

"You can second-guess all day," he said. "We acted on the best information we had."

I know both men personally and I felt very bad for them. Dr. Steger was in the same graduating class I was and I have always trusted that man to make the right decisions at the right time. They were both good men and I hated seeing them getting the third-degree over something nobody ever could have predicted. I know it comes with the territory of their positions, just like it does with mine, but my decisions never bring life-or-death consequences.

Dr. Steger always stood firm and said how it was, and why they did what they did that morning. At that point, with 32 people dead, there is not an answer people think will be good enough. But he was the man in charge and I think he handled it as well as he could have.

There is a backstory to the decisions he made that day. The April 16 shooting wasn't the first shooting we had on campus—and it wouldn't be the last.

On August 20, 2006, just about nine months earlier, a local man by the name of William Morva was awaiting trial for an armed robbery charge. Deputies had transported him to Montgomery Regional Hospital that day for the treatment of a sprained ankle. He used the bathroom at the hospital, ripped a toilet-paper holder off the wall and used it to knock a deputy unconscious. He grabbed his gun and shot the hospital security guard with it. He then escaped on foot.

The next morning, John was taking his daily run on the Huckleberry Trail, which is about 400 yards or so from the football offices. He came upon Minnis Ridenour, the school's vice president who was part of the decision to extend my contract following the 2–8–1 season in 1992. He was out taking a walk on the trail. John then noticed a sheriff's deputy riding a bicycle on the trail. As Minnis continued walking, Morva approached him from the other direction.

MINNIS RIDENOUR, the former Virginia Tech vice president and chief operating officer: *"I was taking my walk down the Huckleberry Trail as Morva approached me on the bike path. I recognized him right away from his picture in the newspaper. He was wearing a white sheet around him and I moved over a bit as he went by me. I knew he was armed, but I just smiled, and said, 'Good morning,' and kept my regular pace. I didn't look back. I just kept moving. I went and notified the police and then we heard the gunshots."*

Within a minute, Morva shot and killed the deputy John had just talked to. Morva escaped again and within an hour, the campus was in a panic. The Virginia Tech administration made the decision to lock down the campus. Police evacuated the Squires Student Center, because someone reported a man there who matched Morva's description. The police received information that the man had taken hostages and a SWAT team converged on the center.

But Morva was not on campus—the sighting turned out to be a false alarm. Police captured him a few hours later close to where the deputy had been killed. (He was later convicted of capital murder and received a death sentence three years later.)

Dr. Steger and the campus police came under heavy criticism in the aftermath of the Morva episode. The critics claimed they had panicked and overreacted. They took some serious heat for taking precautions.

When the first April 16 shooting at West Ambler Johnston was reported at about 7:18 AM, the campus police had every reason to believe it was a "domestic situation." They also had every reason to believe the shooter had left campus. So no lockdown order was issued.

Of course, we all know now that the shooter showed up at Norris Hall two hours later to massacre 30 innocent people. Now the critics blamed the administration, and specifically Dr. Steger, for not locking down the campus immediately after the dorm shooting.

Many of the questions asked by reporters to students that Tuesday morning and throughout the week seemed to center on the one question, "Who do you blame for this?"

Student after student answered, "We blame the shooter, of course."

I couldn't have agreed with them more.

As soon as I got to the office, I had John send an e-mail to Dr. Steger on my behalf, letting him know I was thinking about him.

I called a staff meeting.

I could see my assistants were hurting just as much as everyone else as they filed into our meeting room. Many of them had tears in their eyes. I did, too.

"Listen, we are not going to let one deranged person take away what we have here," I told them. "We will not let that person determine how Virginia Tech will be remembered for years to come. We will pull together as one community and be stronger from this. Call all of your recruits and tell them the same thing. If you need to be with your families right now, go be with them."

At about 9:50 AM, the police announced the shooter's identity. He was a 23-year-old English major from South Korea. I won't mention his name. I always believed he didn't deserve the notoriety. He was a coward to me. Obviously, he was a troubled coward. If he was in this much pain and he wanted to kill himself, why didn't he just go into a field somewhere and do it? Why kill all of these innocent kids?

That's one thing I never understood about all of these murder-suicides and mass killings. Why can't these disturbed people just take their own lives and leave other good people alone?

Details of this kid started to come out. As people looked back, they could see things about him that weren't right. What he did, what everybody else should have done, whether he should have been at Virginia Tech in the first place—it was second-guessing after we all knew the end result.

I've been there, but a football game was never the magnitude of this. I also knew the answers from the administration and the campus police wouldn't satisfy everybody.

There were details of the shooting that I couldn't stop thinking about. The saddest thing I could ever imagine was hearing about those kids' cell phones ringing and ringing and ringing as their bodies were being removed from Norris Hall on late Monday night and into Tuesday morning. That really broke my heart, knowing a parent, brother, or sister was on the other end of those phones.

We held a team meeting Tuesday and I saw raw emotion in our kids' eyes. This thing certainly devastated those families of the 32 victims, but it deeply affected everybody on campus, including our players.

I told them, "Talk to somebody if you need to. Don't keep this inside of you. We have people here to help you."

We had counselors set up to be ready at a minute's notice and our team chaplain, Johnny Shelton, was available. He had just been hired from Elon University 15 days before the shooting.

> **JOHNNY SHELTON,** Virginia Tech team chaplain: *"The harvest was ripe, as the Bible would say. Coach Beamer came to me that day and said, 'Johnny, this is why you are here. I can't do this alone.' Our players were asking the 'why' questions. 'Why did this happen?' I spoke about eternity and tried to comfort them as best I could. But they were hurting, because they were students first, football players second."*

Later that morning, I told a *USA Today* reporter, "I don't think anything will ever be the same after yesterday—or exactly the same. My mission right now is that we're not going to let one person come here and destroy what happens here every day. We absolutely will not. We cannot."

In feeling that way, I didn't really want to cancel our spring game for that Saturday. I was so bent and determined that I didn't want this guy to get the final word on anything we did at Virginia Tech. We were expecting approximately 40,000 fans for the game, but we had no choice. Canceling it was the right thing to do. I mean, how in the world could we play a football game on the same day when parents were burying their children here?

We made the announcement that afternoon, just before the convocation honoring the victims at Cassell Coliseum was to begin at 2:00.

The convocation was gut-wrenching and very emotional.

Cassell Coliseum was full by the time Cheryl and I filed in to our seats. They opened up Lane Stadium, to accommodate the overflow of people, showing the ceremony on the big screens and broadcasting it over the loud-speakers.

I took a moment to look around the crowd and I saw many students sitting there without their parents, who were miles away in their hometowns. Many of them were sobbing. I could tell they just needed a hug. When we noticed President Steger walking in, Cheryl whispered to me, "Please, please...nobody boo this man."

Fortunately, Dr. Steger received a standing ovation. It really made us feel so good. The man deserved it, after what he had been through over the past day. The response showed what kind of students we have at Virginia Tech.

President Bush, who had addressed the nation about the shooting from Washington the previous afternoon, walked in with Karl Rove. It's the only time I ever remember any president of the United States being on our campus. At that moment, I think we all realized how big this was, what a worldwide event it was.

In part of the president's speech that day, he said, "In such times as this, we look for sources of strength to sustain us. And in the moment of loss, you are finding sources everywhere around you. These sources of strength are in this community, this college community. You have a compassionate and resilient community here at Virginia Tech. One recent graduate wrote, 'I don't know most of you guys, but we're all Hokies, which means family.'

"On this terrible day of mourning, it's hard to imagine that a time will come when life at Virginia Tech will return to normal. But such a day will come. And when it does, you will always remember the friends and teachers who were lost yesterday, and the time you shared with them, and the lives they hoped to lead."

When President Bush left the stage, he looked at me, nodded, and pointed. I wanted to thank him for coming, but I never got the chance to talk to him. I am sure his words of comfort and his appearance helped convey to our students that the entire nation was with us, lending support.

Nikki Giovanni, a Virginia Tech professor and well-known poet, read a poem she had written:

> We are Virginia Tech.
>
> We are sad today, and we will be sad for quite a while. We are not moving on, we are embracing our mourning.
>
> We are Virginia Tech.
>
> We are strong enough to stand tall tearlessly, we are brave enough to bend to cry, and we are sad enough to know that we must laugh again.
>
> We are Virginia Tech.
>
> We do not understand this tragedy. We know we did nothing to deserve it, but neither does a child in Africa dying of AIDS, neither do the invisible children walking the night away to be avoid being captured by the rogue army, neither does the baby elephant watching his community being devastated for ivory, neither does the Mexican child looking for fresh water, neither does the Appalachian infant killed in the middle of the night in his crib in the home his father built with his own hands being run over by a boulder because the land was destabilized. No one deserves a tragedy.
>
> We are Virginia Tech.
>
> The Hokie Nation embraces our own and reaches out with an open heart and hands to those who offer their hearts and minds. We are strong and brave and innocent and unafraid. We are better than we think and not quite what we want to be.

We are alive to the imaginations and the possibilities. We will continue to invent the future through our blood and tears and through all of our sadness.

We are the Hokies.

We will prevail.

We will prevail.

We will prevail.

We are Virginia Tech.

The crowd stood and applauded. I thought it was perfect. She couldn't have made a better contribution.

The outpouring of support started to reach Blacksburg that night; it was overwhelming. It came from just about every corner of the globe. Many heads of state and international figures offered condolences, such as Pope Benedict XVI and Queen Elizabeth II.

The thing I noticed most were people from every sport: football, baseball, basketball, hockey, soccer, and NASCAR, paying their respects somehow. They arranged fund-raisers for the victims' families or wore Virginia Tech hats and shirts. Hours after our convocation, the Washington Nationals wore our baseball hats in a game against the Braves, and a soccer team, D.C. United, wore Virginia Tech jerseys during a match; NASCAR drivers put Virginia Tech decals on their cars for the next three weeks.

Even Niagara Falls was lit in orange and maroon, our school colors, for a night, the first time the falls were ever lit for a tragedy like this.

On Wednesday morning, I wanted to head to the hospital to see our students who had survived the shooting. We gathered a bunch of Virginia Tech hats and T-shirts to give to them. I had Mike Goforth check with the hospital administrators to make sure me stopping by would be okay with everyone.

MIKE GOFORTH: *"Coach Beamer came to me and asked what I could do to get him into the hospital to see the kids who survived. I called over there and politely asked if he could come. Right away, they said, 'Are you kidding me? We would love to have Coach Beamer over here to pick up their spirits.' We watched him go room to room that day with that 'Coach Beamer persona' we all know and he picked those kids up emotionally at the time they needed it most. Then he would stop between rooms and almost break down. He would compose himself again and then enter another room."*

I went room to room and saw every wounded student I could. I consider myself a tender-hearted guy and I had to keep from crying in front of them, but I know I failed a few times. I didn't want to bring them down or make them sad; I wanted to cheer them up.

What amazed me was their response. None of them were feeling sorry for themselves. They had tubes running in and out of their bodies and several still had bullets lodged inside them. They were smiling and so appreciative of the outpouring of support. Those were some brave kids.

A couple of them told me, "We will come out of this okay. Don't worry, nothing will keep us down. We're Hokies."

Originally, I went to the hospital to cheer them up and I walked out of the hospital feeling much better about everything. Their attitudes picked up my spirits. Their response is exactly what I planned to preach that week and for the weeks ahead. We had to stick together. If we do, we will come through this stronger than ever.

The guy who really impressed me was Kevin Sterne. The Associated Press photo of him being carried out of Norris Hall by first responders went around the world. He had the good sense to tie a tourniquet around his leg to save his life. I talked to him quite a bit and I was just fascinated that he could think so clearly under such pressure. That guy really made an impression on me. By the way, he came back to school and finished up his master's degree.

After we saw all the kids who could accept visitors, Lester Karlin and I walked down to the emergency room to thank all of those people. I can't imagine the horrors they saw each time one of these students was brought in there. I know they worked one long day and they needed to hear how everyone appreciated their work.

There were a few kids at other hospitals off campus we could not visit. I tried to call as many as I could in their rooms.

That afternoon, Governor Tim Kaine announced there would be a board appointed to lead a review of the school's handling of all the events on Monday. At the same time, he made a statement supporting Dr. Steger.

He also said, "This kind of event could happen anywhere, on any campus. There has been an innocence taken away from the students here. But the positive values and the academic tradition of this university will help the community stay strong and keep this university attracting new students."

I granted a live interview to CNN's Wolf Blitzer.

I told him, "My mission right now is that we're not going to let one person come here and destroy what happens here every day. We will not...we absolutely will not. We cannot. There are so many times I have talked to our football team about this, but we're all in this together. Talking to the alumni, the students and the faculty here, we're all in this together. And that's the way I feel right now. Our football players are hurting just like everyone else...they are no different. We grieve with the families. But we're going to come back from this thing, too. This is a very close campus. It's a very close community here. Hokie people are very close...we're going to be tighter. We're going to care about each other more. We're going to respect each other more. And mark it down: when we open that football season next fall against East Carolina, I will bet you will see togetherness—even more than you have seen in the past."

Wolf asked, "What if any of your players want to transfer after the shooting?" It was something I didn't even consider. I never for a moment thought one of our players would leave the program because of this—and not one player ever did.

I felt strongly about that. To even bring it up at a time like this seemed ludicrous to me, because that would go against what I was saying. To leave this school because of one man's actions would have been changing the course of your own life because one person with severe mental problems set out to destroy what we had around us every day—the togetherness, the caring, the great community, and the great feelings we had for each other—the things we valued most at Virginia Tech.

Just as I was finishing with Wolf, NBC was reporting about the existence of the killer's so-called manifesto, which he had mailed to the network. Then CNN and every other network followed up. The package had arrived at NBC News in New York that day. It contained a video of himself and a long, rambling note. It was sickening to see that all over the news that night.

I really believe releasing it to the public gave him the attention he craved all long. I am no media expert, but that is one thing I wouldn't have done. As all the news stations played his video, I thought, *The last thing I need to hear right now is this guy's words.* I will always believe it was wrong of the networks to publicize it, especially for the families involved. I felt strongly about this. There is always somebody out there who will want to one-up this kid.

I think investigators had proven the Columbine kids mentioned previous school shootings and tried to one-up them; and this sick guy at Virginia Tech may have mentioned Columbine. When you have a sick individual like him, this is the only way he will ever have a moment of fame, or infamy. There is no other way he would ever get a minute on national TV in his entire life unless he did something horrible like this.

We probably will never know if the kid who did the shooting at the Sandy Hook School in Connecticut ever listened to this kid's words or message.

I believed all of the focus should have been on the victims, their families and the shooting survivors. Of the 27 students killed, 14 were from Virginia and three were from New Jersey. The others were from Massachusetts, Michigan, Georgia, New York, Pennsylvania, Rhode Island, Indonesia, Egypt, Puerto Rico and India.

They each had unlimited futures and their stories should have been the focus, not any manifesto.

Ryan Clark, the second victim at West Ambler Johnston Hall, was a resident-adviser on the fourth floor. He had come to the aid of the first girl who was shot, Emily Hilscher. He was a member of our band, the Marching Virginians. I already mentioned Austin Cloyd, the daughter of Accounting Professor Bryan Cloyd, who touched everyone with his inspiring but heartbreaking e-mail. Brian Bluhm was a huge fan of the Detroit Tigers.

Matthew Gwaltney was in graduate school. He already had one Virginia Tech degree.

"He went to every women's and men's basketball game," his stepmother, Linda Gwaltney, was quoted as saying. "If there was a home football game, we knew he wasn't coming home that weekend."

Jarrett Lane ran track and played football at Narrows High School. Erin Peterson, a freshman, was 6'1" and had played basketball on her Westfield High School team. Michael Pohle would have received his degree in biological sciences a few weeks following the shooting. He had played football and lacrosse at his high school in Flemington, New Jersey. Nicole White had been a lifeguard at the YMCA in her hometown. Maxine Turner, a senior in chemical engineering, turned down Johns Hopkins because "she wanted to be a Hokie," her father said.

Matthew La Porte was a sophomore on an Air Force ROTC scholarship. He was a cadet and in uniform that day. The investigation showed that he charged the shooter from the back of his French class and took eight bullets before he was stopped just short of reaching him. That kid died a real hero.

I tried being as visible as I could during the next week. We didn't have a spring game to evaluate anyway, but coaching football and sitting around the office or in staff meetings wasn't the best use of my time at a time like this. I went to all of the baseball and softball games I could in the weeks afterward.

I felt there were students out there who needed to see a friendly face. Even though classes were canceled until the following Monday, many students stayed on campus and didn't have their parents to comfort them. As John and I walked around campus, we noticed kids just had that look on their face. They were lost. They needed comforting. Many of them needed someone to talk to.

Cheryl joined us one day when we came upon a girl sitting on a bench by herself near the math and English buildings. Her head was down and she was sobbing. I felt so bad for her because she was all alone. I sat down next to her, put my arm around her and hugged her as tight as I could. I don't even know what I said to her, but she couldn't stop crying.

Sadly, she probably represented thousands of kids on our campus who felt the same way.

14

Did We Make a Difference?

> CHERYL BEAMER: *"It was the most emotional I had ever seen Frank. I think it made him more in touch with his feelings than anything that has ever happened during his lifetime. All these years later, we can be sitting around the living room, and if the subject of April 16 comes up, or if we begin to talk about it, we both start crying all over again. It will never leave us."*

Over the next days and weeks, the outpouring of support was overwhelming and it came from every direction. Several head coaches from across the country, including Mack Brown, Jim Grobe, and Joe Paterno, called the office to see how we were holding up. So did several government leaders and politicians, such as Mark Warner.

Less than three weeks later, on May 6, I was invited to the NASCAR race at Richmond. During the pre-race introductions, drivers Jeff and Ward Burton, Elliott Sadler, and Denny Hamlin—each a Virginian—presented me with a check for $120,000 for the Hokies Spirit Memorial Fund. Richmond International Raceway President Doug Fritz, a Virginia Tech alum, presented a check for

$40,000 that was from the speedway and other tracks owned by the International Speedway Corporation.

Each car owner had placed our VT logo on their cars and would keep them there for the next three weeks. I thanked them for everything during the pre-race driver's meeting.

"I've long admired and respected what you guys do, and I come here tonight admiring and respecting and very much appreciating everything that NASCAR has done for Virginia Tech over the last few weeks," I told them.

As I spoke, I noticed Ward, Ricky Rudd, and Jimmie Johnson were among the drivers wearing Virginia Tech hats. There were a few others. It just about made me break down, realizing the support these guys were giving us.

"I want to tell you we're not going to be remembered as the place where 32 people were shot and killed," I added. "We're going to be remembered as the place where we had a terrible tragedy, and with help from people like yourselves, we will come back stronger and tighter and more caring than ever. And that's the way we're going to do it."

I finished and many of them came up to talk to me.

Jimmie Johnson, who would win the race later that day, told me, "Your words got to me—that's the exact way to go about this thing."

That meant a lot to me.

I voiced that message every chance I got over the next five months, heading into our first game of the 2007 season.

There were certain subjects stemming from the shooting that I wouldn't touch. I usually stay away from politics and I don't get involved in the issue of gun control. That's not my place. I am a football coach, not a politician.

> **DAVE BRAINE,** Virginia Tech's athletic director 1988–97: *"I still live in Blacksburg since retiring and the massacre hit us all very hard. Everybody was affected by it. While the president and the administration were busy with other things and day-to-day business running the university in the aftermath, Frank Beamer ended up being the spokesperson for Virginia Tech. He was the vocal point and he represented this school so well. He always had the right message. Nobody could have done it better."*

As we entered fall camp, we had a lot of work to do. We had canceled the final three spring practices and the spring game, which is just really another extended practice.

We knew the opener against East Carolina would be very emotional for all of us.

I looked forward to September 1, mainly because it would be the first time everybody at Virginia Tech—students, faculty, fans and alumni—would come together since April 16. There are so many elements to a college campus. During the week, people go their own way. They have their own interests, such as music, engineering, the military, math, science; students have different majors and different pursuits in life. But on Saturdays, we're all one. We all come together in Lane Stadium, rooting for the same thing.

I thought a football game was exactly what we all needed, to be in that stadium on game day.

I take a lot of pride in being the leader of our role in that. Our football program is one element which everybody on campus can turn their attention to after a difficult week of studying, learning, and going to class. I think football bonds us together as one campus. But we'd had a very difficult year since we last played a football game, December 30, 2006, at the bowl game in Atlanta.

First, we had to prepare to play well.

The one thing I worried about was our players putting that burden of lifting everyone's spirits on their shoulders. They wanted people at Virginia Tech to feel good again. They wanted to give them something to cheer about. They felt an obligation. Sometimes, we want something so much that we can't get out of our own way. I wanted us to play well and win the game, of course, but having our fans together in Lane Stadium once again was more important than the outcome of the game.

"I think people are looking forward to getting into that stadium," I told the media that week. "Sixty-some thousand will be there to show their togetherness and we're going to be tougher and tighter than ever. I think that's kind of the mood right now. There is no question people want to rally around something."

Roland Lazenby, a communications instructor at Virginia Tech, had compiled student essays about April 16. One student, Neal Turnage, wrote, "Football is the glue that holds us together. This game is our first chance to get back to our state of mind before the shootings."

I could not have said it better.

Our cheerleaders released 32 balloons before kickoff, one for each victim and there was a video tribute to the victims and a moment of silence before kickoff.

I have run out of that tunnel a lot of times over the years, first as a player and then as a head coach. There have been big games on national TV, games in which we were undefeated and needing to win to go to major bowls and rivalry games against Virginia. But I can honestly tell you, I never felt more emotion than I did on September 1, 2007. I don't think our football team and our fans ever felt more as one than that day. It just felt different. Lane Stadium seemed louder than ever.

I looked around and saw people crying, but I think many of them were crying tears of happiness that life may be returning to normal—at least for one day.

The game didn't start well: we threw an interception on the first play and then committed two more turnovers. Macho Harris picked off a pass and returned it 17 yards for a touchdown to give us a 10–7 halftime lead. We won 17–7, but we didn't play well, at least not on offense. The defense held East Carolina to 261 yards. I'm sure the emotion of the day probably had a lot to do with us not being sharp.

On that Monday, four of our players—Carlton Weatherford, Eddie Royal, Xavier Adibi, and D.J. Parker—and I walked the game ball over to the new memorial that had been constructed at the head of the Drillfield, at the heart the campus. A Hokie stone has been inscribed and placed in memory of each of the 32 victims.

In the middle of the memorial lies one larger Hokie stone with the inscription: "We Will Prevail. We Are Virginia Tech." Above it, we placed the football in a glass case. It was inscribed, "In honor of you. None of us is as good as all of us. VT 17, ECU 7—9/1/07"

We had received a request from the administration to host survivors of the shooting during a practice. I thought it was a great idea. I figured those kids needed all the support we could give them and it would go a ways toward making good memories for them.

On September 21, the day before our home game against William & Mary, we hosted 15 kids on the field. Each had been shot at least once. When they first walked out to the field, they were grouped together on the sideline. I brought all of our players over to the sidelines and they hugged and chatted with those kids as if they were lifelong friends. It was heartwarming to see.

Within minutes, those kids were smiling and having a good time. We had a few of the girls hold the football for field-goal attempts.

COLIN GODDARD, survivor of the April 16 shooting: *"It was the first time I ever stood on that field at Lane Stadium. When they all walked over to us and Coach Beamer put out his hand to say hello, I told him he had called me in the hospital. When I took the call that day, I was pretty medicated, but I remember him telling me that everybody was pulling for me. All of my buddies were in the room with me at the time and they thought it was so cool I was talking to Coach Beamer. We had a great exchange with the players at the stadium that day. Some of them wanted us to tell our stories of what had happened on April 16. I was shot four times—in each hip, above the knee and in the right shoulder—and still have three bullet fragments left in me. The only bullet which exited was through my right shoulder. I hold those football players in the highest regard, because they are just like you and me. They were there for us when we needed them most. As a shooting survivor, each of us gets access to the president's box for one game per season. I am very busy now with my work at the Brady Campaign, but my buddies and I will always return to Blacksburg for a few football games each season. To think that some people around me actually thought I would transfer after the shooting. No way! I will always be a Hokie."*

Dr. Steger has hosted several of the survivors and their families for each home game we have played since the shooting. Cheryl has done the same thing in our box, where she watches our games and has gotten to know several of the families. She still exchanges Christmas cards with some families.

One of the things I want to mention is that Dr. Steger told all of the students they did not need to make up their final exams from that spring. They could elect to receive the grade they had at that time of the shooting as their final grades. I was told more than 90 percent of them came back and took those exams.

In football, we deal with statistics. Sometimes they tell the story and sometimes they don't. Here's a statistic that tells a special story: every one of those 25 students who were wounded that day not only stayed at Virginia Tech, but eventually graduated from Virginia Tech. One-hundred percent.

Over the next few years, the shooting became a topic during our re-cruiting of prospects. Every parent we talked to knew what had taken place here, of course. The subject was unavoidable. I never waited for them to bring it up—I brought it up first because I figured it was on their minds. I told them what happened was the opposite of what our campus and our community is about. I will never know this, but I don't think we lost one recruit because of what happened on April 16.

I mentioned earlier that the April 16 shooting wasn't the last shooting we had on campus.

More than four years later, on December 8, 2011, John and I were taking our daily walk and were on Main Street when we heard sirens blasting. We heard the school's alert system going off, too. We saw a cadet on Main Street and asked him if he had heard what happened.

"There's been a shooting in your parking lot," he told us.

We rushed back up the street, thinking the worst—one of our players had been shot.

As we walked by Cassell Coliseum, John said, "Coach, there's a body lying over there."

The body was covered up by a white sheet.

A campus police officer had pulled over a car and while he was writing a traffic ticket, someone walked up to the officer's car window and shot him. His name was Deriek Crouse and he died on the scene. He was from Carroll County, where I grew up.

The gunman ran and as police closed on him, he shot and killed himself. The man had come to campus from Radford. We will never know his motives. You can understand why, when I hear a siren these days, it puts me on edge. I get worried. I just don't want to hear that noise anymore. I am on edge when I see an ambulance, too. I'm sure I'm not the only person in Blacksburg who feels this way. It is something we will have to live with and deal with as the years pass.

As the years have gone by since April 16, 2007, I think people at Virginia Tech and in Blacksburg have reacted to this thing in a positive way. They have become closer. They have more respect for one another. This always was one of the most friendly towns there is, but people have treated each other better. I have seen it.

I have taken Bryan Cloyd's message in that e-mail to heart and I have relayed it often.

"Go out of your way to make good memories. Tell each other and your parents how much you care about them."

I have tried to make good memories with everyone I have dealt with since the shooting. Cheryl has told me I don't tell people enough about how I feel about them, and she is probably right, but I have tried my best to show them.

Although we don't want Virginia Tech to be remembered for or associated with a mass shooting, the memories of this thing will never leave us.

If you were on this campus that day and went through it, it pops into your mind almost every day, one way or another. When the shooting happened at Sandy Hook Elementary in Newtown, Connecticut, in December of 2012, it took us right back to that day.

It still is very emotional for me.

I am sure it always will be.

15

Recruiting: How Many Stars? Who Cares?

You've probably heard coaches say that recruiting is a college football program's lifeblood.

There is no free agency and there is no draft in college football, as in the NFL, so recruiting is the method we use to evaluate and subsequently invite high school players to play at Virginia Tech. Meanwhile, 124 other head coaches at major college football programs are out there doing the same thing.

And the process can sometimes be an adventure.

Take our recruitment of Victor "Macho" Harris for example.

Now Macho was a big-time recruit from Highland Springs High School near Richmond. In fact, he was rated the top overall player in the state of Virginia and he had his choice of schools. He'd visited Michigan, USC, and Miami. He could do it all with the football in his hands. One night, while an assistant coach and I were standing on the sidelines during one of his high school games, he walked over to us and said, "Watch me run this one back."

Sure enough, he caught a punt and took off, ending up in the end zone. I think he scored five different ways the night we saw him. He just had perfect timing for an athlete and a real feel for the dramatic.

On December 15, 2004, Jim Cavanaugh, an assistant coach, was at the wheel of the car and I was in the passenger seat as we pulled up the driveway of Macho's house. I noticed some younger kids outside, waving their arms back and forth.

"Boy, Cav, they sure are excited to see us," I said.

But Cav had noticed something else.

"I don't think they're excited to see us at all," Cav told me. "I think their house is on fire!"

As we got closer, we could see smoke curling out from the kitchen window. Then we saw Macho running with a quilt. We burst inside and there was a large fire coming from the stove top. Macho's mom had been making fried chicken and French fries for our visit and there was too little grease in the pan. She left to go to the store and thought she turned off the stove, but there was too much play in the knob and it remained on high.

Macho grabbed that quilt to put out the fire, and all of a sudden the fire went whoosh up into his face. Cav helped clean up the mess as I watched the little kids, but when we looked at Macho, we saw some bad burns on his face and his right forearm. If anybody knows about that, it's me.

We knew we had to get him to a doctor, but there was one catch: NCAA rules.

There are very specific recruiting rules preventing us from driving prospects during off-campus visits, no matter the circumstances. But we also knew he needed treatment immediately. One of his family members drove the car and I rode with Macho and his mother to get him to VCU's hospital while Cav stayed behind to clean up the mess.

I am sure the whole thing was traumatic for Macho. I sat with him that night at the hospital and told him my story, how I was burned as a kid and what to expect in his recovery. I think it was a bonding experience for us.

VICTOR "MACHO" HARRIS: *"That night in the hospital talking to Coach Beamer, there was nobody in that room—not even anybody in my family—that could feel the pain that I felt. But Coach Beamer could because he had been through the fire. I just felt that it was a great, great, great player-and-coach bond between us. I could also tell he cared about me."*

I knew he would be fine once his pain subsided. He spent a week in the hospital, receiving some skin grafts. That is where he committed to us—from his hospital bed.

The sad thing is, on Christmas Day, 11 days following the fire, his mother collapsed and fell down the stairs. She died instantly. She had six kids. Macho was one of the biggest recruits we'd had in our first 26 years at Virginia Tech and we felt an awesome responsibility to take care of him.

Not every recruiting visit includes that kind of drama. But what is typical for us is that he was from the state of Virginia.

I get questions from our fans, boosters, and alumni all the time on my philosophy about recruiting regions of the country.

"Why aren't you recruiting more in Florida?"

"Why aren't you recruiting in Texas?"

"What about this kid in Alabama?"

And here's my answer, which we have developed, altered, and refined over the years as Virginia Tech has gone from an independent to the Big East and then to the Atlantic Coast Conference.

When we were in the Big East, and given that the ACC was right below us geographically to the south, we really wouldn't go into North Carolina for a guy because he had to pass so many schools to get to us. There were North Carolina, North Carolina State, Duke, and

Wake Forest. But we did go into Florida then. Even when we were at Murray State, I felt Florida had so many prospects and Miami, Florida, and Florida State could take only so many. There were plenty of extra players there capable of playing major college football.

With Miami being in the Big East with us, it helped us in Florida. If Miami didn't offer a scholarship, many of those players wanted to play against Miami, so we had a chance.

Now that we are in the ACC, we can go into North Carolina and take the same approach. We've been well-received there, too. We now play North Carolina, N.C. State, Duke, and Wake Forest, so those kids may not want to go to one of those four schools, but they can come with us and play against them every season.

But because of that, and a few other reasons I will get into, we don't recruit in Florida as much. Our 2012 roster included only seven kids from Florida, but we usually had many more during our Big East years.

I developed a philosophy over the years that we need to recruit most of our kids from a five-hour driving radius of Blacksburg. It's probably more like six, to be honest, depending on how long it takes someone to drive from Atlanta. The more we can recruit successfully close to home, the better.

I firmly believe we can win a national championship with the kids within that radius. If I look at our roster from 1999, we had only 10 players from Florida and 46 from Virginia.

All but 10 of our kids on the 2012 roster came from inside that six-hour radius and 60 were from Virginia. Four more were from Maryland and two from Washington, D.C.

What's important in using this philosophy is that their families can drive to our campus to watch them play on Saturdays. And when it comes to that prospect's visit, the family can come for the visit, too. If we are flying a kid in from Florida or Texas or California, chances are the parents cannot afford to fly here with their son. (The NCAA does not allow the parents' airfare to be paid for.)

If the player comes into my office that Sunday as his visit is coming to an end and I happen to offer a scholarship, it's much better if his parents are sitting in my office with him. If he tells me, "I'm coming to Virginia Tech. You have my commitment," and the parents are with him, then there is a good chance he is coming to Virginia Tech.

If they are not with him, I regard it as a "soft" commitment, sometimes a very soft commitment. When that kid goes home he may find that his decision doesn't have his parents' support. If I was NCAA president for a day, this is one change I would make to the rulebook: allow the school to pay for the parents' transportation to and from the official visit. This is one of the most important decisions the young man will ever make and the parents need to be part of that equation.

A few years ago, we were getting way too many soft commitments from the kids from Florida. We would get a commitment and then they would want to visit some other school.

I would ask, "What do you mean you are visiting another school? Let me get this straight—you are committed to us, but you are visiting where?"

"Well, I am still committed to you," they would tell me.

I would say, "No, you have a reservation with us, but not a strong commitment with us."

That just drove me nuts. I never liked that.

The same goes for recruiting a kid who has committed elsewhere. I won't do it and I have told our assistants not to do it. I am a firm believer if a kid is committed to another program we should not touch that kid…unless there is a valid reason. And by that, I mean the reason needs to be initiated from the other side, not from us. Like maybe the high school coach says the kid is unhappy with his commitment and he wants to talk to us. But the contact must be initiated from the kid or someone representing the kid for us to talk to someone who is committed elsewhere.

We took a couple of kids late in 2011 who were committed elsewhere but the coaches at their high schools told us they were not happy and they wanted to talk to us.

Some schools have offered scholarships to our commitments in the past. I just won't do the same thing to other coaches or other programs. In the big picture, there are more hard feelings that come out of it and it's just not worth it. To initiate recruiting a guy or to continue recruiting a guy after he committed somewhere else is just plain wrong in my book.

This all goes back to relationships. I am a big believer in building relationships, whether it be with the prospect's high school coach or his parents or both. That is one reason we like to recruit the same schools over and over again in the state of Virginia. We know the coaches and they know us and they can trust us to do what we say. At the same time, we can trust their evaluation of a player.

Relationships are the key to the whole process. Does that family trust me to make their son's situation here at Virginia Tech turn out the best it possibly can?

I often get asked, "Do you like recruiting?"

I have to say I like the process of recruiting, after we have identified who we want to offer a scholarship to and then face the challenge of signing that player. As coaches, the hard part is figuring out who that player is. That goes back to character, too. When we are dealing with good kids, kids with character and morals and who know right from wrong, it makes it so much easier.

The limitations they put on a head coach nowadays change everything. In the old days, coaches could stay in a kid's home the night before signing day and wake up and have him sign your letter of intent at 8:00 AM. I don't know how common it was, but it was done. Other coaches would camp outside of the top recruits' houses and get their signatures the first thing the next morning.

By the NCAA rules, we don't get the opportunity to spend much time with these recruits as we used to, which increases the chance we may misjudge his character and anything else we need to know about him. That's why I rely on kids who are already here, our assistant coaches, secretaries, and everybody who comes in contact with the prospect during his visit.

"If anybody doesn't fit in here, for any reason, let me know as soon as you can," I tell them. "Before I meet with him and before I make an offer and he accepts it."

What do I mean by "fitting in?" I am not especially fond of the superstar with the huge ego who could ruin our team chemistry. This goes back to recruiting people first and players second. I want good people as well as good players. We want people who are willing to put in the work and buy into our philosophy of team-first and me-second. We want players who will work hard to become better, on the field and off. We want people with good character, good morals, and people who respect others.

That's another reason I don't pay much attention to the "star ratings." Right now, there are many services out there that rank players on a one-to-five-star rating. I hear from fans all the time who ask me, "Why aren't we signing more five-star guys?"

Well, for one, I don't put much stock in those ratings. Most aren't based on scouts who actually watch the player play the game. Sometimes, they are even based on who is recruiting the player. If Notre Dame, Michigan, and Texas happen to be recruiting him, well then he must be a five-star player.

At Murray State, I cared more about how athletic a player was than how big he was. I never got into the size thing. Some people say "the bigger the better," but I ask, "What kind of football player is he? Does he have a nose for the football?"

That worked for me then, so I never changed my philosophy once I coached at Virginia Tech.

RON ZOOK: *"Frank is the most astute football coach I've ever been around when it comes to recruiting. I learned how to evaluate a recruit from him. I learned if that player is rated four or five stars, that doesn't mean he is a four- or five-star player."*

I could name dozens of players who have come through Virginia Tech with not many stars attached to their name and then left as all-conference or even All-Americans. We didn't beat anybody to sign Shyrone Stith. We beat only Wake Forest to sign Lee Suggs. Pierson Prioleau was a so-called two-star guy and he left here as an All-American. There were so many more.

I have always said that recruiting is not scientific. There is no magic formula. The kid you sign at 17 or 18 is not the same player you will have at 21 or 22.

We have signed a few five-star guys, however, and defensive end Cornell Brown has to rank as the most important recruit we signed in our first 10 years at Virginia Tech. We were coming off that 2–8–1 season and Cornell could have gone anywhere he wanted.

It was down to Virginia and us. And when he announced, "I am going to the University of...Virginia Tech," at his press conference, just for a split-second, we didn't think he was coming to Blacksburg.

Despite that fight he got into on campus, he became a good student, one of our leaders, and one of the most honored Virginia Tech players of all time. He was a two-time All-American, got his degree, and he coaches our outside linebackers and defensive ends today.

Guys like Cornell make it all worthwhile. He wasn't the best student when he got here, but he worked at it and we pushed him. He became great in the classroom and on the field.

I've also been asked a few times: What I would change about recruiting and the NCAA rules that go with it?

For starters, we need to get the third person out of the process. Football has become similar to AAU basketball.

When we approach any player these days, the first thing we need to know is, from where does he want approval? Is it from his father? His mother? His uncle? We always need to identify who is important to that kid. Who would help him with his decision? For years, it usually was the mother, the father, and the high school coach. Now, what we are seeing is that there is a "mentor."

This is the guy who is taking the best players to these seven-on-seven tournaments all across the country.

In the last three or four years, this part of the process has gotten a little out of hand.

These mentors are aligned with the families, and we are seeing them concentrated in areas where there is a collection of great high school talent. The mentor somewhat forces the high school coach out of the loop by taking the player to these off-season tournaments in Seattle or Texas or Oregon or wherever. The kids want to travel and receive free T-shirts and hats and other things.

The competition for these kids is great, and I don't have a problem with tournament directors making money either, as long as everything is above-board and players are not being steered to one school or another. All that would be fine if it was on the up-and-up and the mentor had no ulterior motives, but we are seeing mentors tied to certain colleges. They are getting involved in recruiting and may direct a kid, or group of kids, to a certain college. Our coaches tell me they have been seeing quite a bit of this in the Virginia Beach area.

As a head coach, I want to deal with the parent or the high school coach, or both, in discussing a player's recruitment.

This prompts a few questions: What is the mentor's incentive? Is he getting paid? And if so, who is paying him?

These are questions the NCAA or the National High School Athletic Association need to address, because it just seems the so-called mentor issue is getting worse by the year.

Another thing I won't do is participate in is negative recruiting. I have never done it and never will. I am out there selling my own school, Virginia Tech. I won't be out there talking about somebody else's school. I tell the kids only what Virginia Tech has to offer. That's how I approach it and how I want our assistants to approach it.

I will sell our football program, our people as one big family, and our academics. I will stress going to class, studying, and getting a degree more than anything. After all, that's why they are here in the first place.

> **KEION CARPENTER,** a safety from Baltimore, 1995–98, *"I was really impressed with the family atmosphere. With Coach Beamer, I got the feeling that he was like a father figure to those of us who grew up in homes with just one parent. He gave me a foundation I didn't have. My mom felt like she could call him any time and find out how I was doing in the classroom and on the football field."*

Does negative recruiting go on? Sure, it does. But I am not going to stoop to that level. It's just not right. It's not me.

We have had a decent relationship with our rival, Virginia, since I've been head coach. I have always respected how they do things. I think it is good for the state of Virginia if we both work hard at recruiting and keep the best players in their home state to play college football.

I have respected the three head coaches there whom I've dealt with: George Welsh, Al Groh, and now Mike London.

The rivalry—for the Commonwealth Cup—was always big with them, even dating back to when I played in the 1960s. But when we got into the Big East it took it up a notch: it was the Big East versus the ACC. Then we got into the ACC and we were placed in the same division. That took it up even another notch.

If you said to the majority of our alumni, "Pick one game you want us to win." The answer usually is the Virginia game. Of course, when I do my Hokie Club trips, and I happen to be in Raleigh, that answer would be North Carolina State. But more often than not, I hear the words "beat Virginia."

I learned one lesson from the very first time we played them when I got back here in 1987.

It was the second game of the season and we scored to cut the lead to 14–13. I could have kicked the extra point for the tie, but I chose to go for two points and the win. We had practiced a crossing pattern all week that was perfect for that situation, but at the last second, I changed it to a sweep, because the sweep had been working so good for us all day.

We ended up just short of the goal line, and I told myself afterward that I would never make plans for a good play again and then change my mind during the heat of battle.

We lost the first three games to Virginia and I was very frustrated about it, especially since Herman Moore was helping them beat us. He was from Danville, Virginia, and he wanted to play here, but we couldn't guarantee his acceptance academically. Virginia could. Then he had monster games to help beat us.

We finally got our first win against Virginia in 1990 at Lane Stadium. Coach Claiborne was here that day and you know how I always said he was conservative. Well, I went for it once on fourth-and-10 and we hit a post route for about a 40-yard touchdown.

Somebody asked him about it.

"I would have punted," he said.

But I just had a feeling that day. We were rolling sevens and 11s all day and we won 38–13. Virginia headed to the Sugar Bowl after that game and we finished 6–5.

The worst loss I ever experienced to them came in 1998. We were 9–2, with our only losses coming in the final seconds to Temple and Syracuse earlier that season. We jumped up 29–7 on them at the half and had the game in our control. They came back on us, scored three straight touchdowns, and then they hit a little out route, we missed the tackle and the guy ran 47 yards in the final minute to win the game 36–32.

I started 1–5 in those first six years against Virginia. But we won 16 of the next 20 meetings. Following the 2012 season, we have a 17–9 overall record against them. That is very satisfying.

As most fans know, when Al Groh got the job there in 2001, he had coached in the NFL, and when reporters asked him about playing Virginia Tech, he said something like, "We'll be playing chess while they're playing checkers."

Whether he meant to or not, he kind of offended us. I'm not sure exactly what he meant by that but maybe it just didn't come out of his mouth right. We were 8–1 against his teams, losing only the 2003 game on the road.

I told reporters, "I think we're pretty good checker players."

I like to think we have done things the right way over the years, and the fact that we have had several brother combinations here tells me I may be right. We've had four Fullers here—Kyle, Vince, Corey, and Kendall; David and Ed Wang; Chad and Cody Grimm; three Warrens—Blake, Brett, and Beau. Somebody counted recently and there were 46 families that have had fathers, sons, or brothers play here in the past 25 years.

I am as proud of that as anything, because if the first family member didn't have a good experience here, the second and third family member sure wouldn't be coming to play here. I think that makes a statement on how we do things.

That's also a big part of what I tell recruits: "The stadiums get to looking the same after all of your visits. The academics are good most everywhere. The facilities are all very nice. But we really have great people among our coaches and our athletic department personnel and we have great fans. We live in a small college town that is very hospitable. I love walking around daily and talking to people. You will find this is one big family full of great people."

I think the Internet has changed recruiting, too: it has made it tougher. These recruiting services, either the national websites or the websites affiliated with each university, can have a representative talk to a kid when we can't—and we worry about them being in somebody else's corner. The recruiting service guy may call a kid and ask, "Why wouldn't you consider so-and-so? They're a national power every year."

Which leads to the question: are coaches receiving information and giving information to that recruiting service which may somehow influence the prospect?

They have become a big factor. If a kid takes a visit, the recruiting-service guy wants to know right away how the visit went. "Who's your leader?" "What other visits do you have?" There are no regulations whatsoever on these recruiting services, because they are not governed by the NCAA.

We tell our assistant coaches, "Don't trade information with these website guys when they call you, because it's just not worth it."

Coaches are not allowed to publicly discuss a prospect, according to NCAA rules, until that prospect signs a letter of intent. So I don't do it and my assistants don't do it.

One day a few years ago, we had a prospect who we'd offered a scholarship to leave our offices during a visit. An Internet recruiting guy based in Blacksburg stood there in the hallway outside my office and asked him about his visit.

John Ballein overheard him and said, "We don't operate that way. You shouldn't be here doing this."

The guy quit his job the next day.

With all that being said, I think the illegal recruiting practices of coaches and boosters giving people things has been cleaned up, because recruiting is more public than ever. The NCAA handbook is so thick because of all the minor violations that have been committed over the course of time. And I admit, there are so many little things in that giant rule book, we sometimes don't know if we are violating them or not.

The NCAA just recently eliminated the rule allowing the head coach to visit recruits during the spring. Now that time is solely an evaluation period with no contact allowed, and I am all for that rule change.

What it evolved to during the previous spring-contact period, however, was head coaches dropping out of the sky in a helicopter to see a recruit at his school. Coaches tried to out-do the other guy and got out of hand.

Spring is the time of the year when the so-called "bump-ins" occur; a head coach will "accidentally" bump in to a recruit, which is somehow allowed. Every coach knows that is one of the most abused rules in recruiting.

The NCAA tried to pass legislation to tweak some recruiting rules in the spring of 2013, such as unlimited texting and phone calls to recruits, but coaches revolted and stopped its passage. If the NCAA had gone through with this, as well as allowing schools to expand personnel for recruiting purposes, we would have seen football coaches forming their own little "player personnel" departments like the pros have, hiring many people to handle all forms of recruiting full-time. I think that is a very dangerous precedent.

Some of these changes would have forced kids to commit earlier, just to stop all the other coaches from texting, tweeting, calling, and sending material all the time.

But I think kids are making their decisions much earlier than they used to anyway. They are making their decisions on their unofficial visits as opposed to during the five official visits they are allowed during their senior years in high school.

We pay for the official visit and we seem to be hosting kids who already have committed here. Many kids start visiting schools now as freshmen and sophomores and making their decisions by the time they are juniors. For example, every one of our 2011 recruits had already committed here before their official visits. Their official visit just becomes another trip to come here and hang out, rather than serving as a decision-making visit.

Which is fine. We love to have them. They're coming to be Hokies.

16

They Call It "Beamer Ball"

SHANE BEAMER: *"Whenever I took a job somewhere, at Georgia Tech, Tennessee, Mississippi State, or South Carolina, the first thing they wanted to talk about was what makes Virginia Tech so good on special teams. People saw that when you're blocking kicks, when you're returning kicks for touchdowns, you can win games that way. There's no bigger momentum-changer than to score a touchdown on special teams."*

On the first play of my career as head coach at Virginia Tech, Jon Jeffries returned a kickoff 92 yards for a touchdown.

As he crossed the goal line, I thought, *See, this game is not so hard—* my Virginia Tech coaching career is off to a great start. The bad thing was that we lost the game 22–10 to Clemson, and the rest of the season went downhill from there. We finished 2–9 in one long, frustrating season.

The good news: Jon's big play on special teams was a sign of things to come.

Twenty-six seasons later, we have scored 132 touchdowns on defense and special teams, which averages to about five non-offensive touchdowns per season. Our defense has scored 82 touchdowns,

197

with 54 coming on interception returns, 26 on fumble returns, and two on fumble recoveries in the end zone.

But those are only statistics.

Does it translate to winning? You be the judge: since our consecutive streak of winning seasons started in 1993, we have won 75-of-88 games in which we scored a touchdown on defense or on special teams.

We have blocked 129 kicks (64 punts, 38 field goals, and 27 extra points) over the past 26 seasons and we have usually had good, consistent kickers and punters, too.

Somewhere along the line, the media started calling our approach to winning games "Beamer Ball."

First off, I didn't pick the name, but I admit I am flattered by the term. (In fact, Beamerball.com is the name of our website, which provides fans with information on the football program.)

A lot of the writers or announcers refer to Virginia Tech's special teams as Beamer Ball, but I like the expanded definition: whatever team is on the field for us—offense, defense, or special teams—should have a chance to score points. That is what Beamer Ball means to me.

I want our coaches and especially our players to think that way, too.

Inside our program, we don't call our special teams Beamer Ball or the kicking game. We call our punt team "Pride" and our punt return team "Pride and Joy." I always tell our kids that to be a member of the Pride and Joy teams, you have to be a special player. I also coach them, so I guess they are my pride and joy.

We didn't have any name for it back then, but winning with all three phases of the game goes back to our Murray State days, when we blocked 34 kicks or punts in those six seasons I was head coach. It didn't happen by accident, even back then. I made it a point from the time I became a head coach in 1981 to emphasize special teams.

So when I got the job at Virginia Tech, I wasn't about to change.

I learned one thing very quickly as an assistant coach: being good in special teams, or the kicking game as some people call it, is the quickest way to win a football game, and having breakdowns on special teams is the quickest way to lose a football game.

It can be a momentum play.

It can be a scoring play.

And it can be a momentum and scoring play.

Basically, if we out-play the other team in special teams, we give ourselves a great chance to win the game.

There is no doubt that it helped us win nine games during the 1993 season, the turning point of the Virginia Tech program. We blocked four punts that season, including during wins over Rutgers, Syracuse, and Virginia. We scored touchdowns on a fumble return against Syracuse and a fumble return against Virginia. We also blocked a field goal against Maryland, but we saved the best for the last game of the season.

Remember those two touchdowns we scored right before the half during the Independence Bowl win over Indiana? The first was a fumble return and the second was a blocked field-goal return on the final play, turning a 14–13 lead into a 28–13 halftime lead.

The final minute of that half epitomized what I believe is the true meaning of Beamer Ball.

That game just showed how quickly scoring with defense and special teams can change momentum and turn a game around.

In our first BCS bowl win, the Sugar Bowl against Texas, Bryan Still returned a punt 60 yards for a touchdown and defensive tackle Jim Baron picked up a fumble and ran 20 yards for another score. Those two plays accounted for half of our points as we won 28–10.

Examine our 41–23 win over Clemson in 2007. We had only 219 total yards and ran 55 plays to Clemson's 90 plays. We punted eight times and still managed a 31–8 halftime lead. How did we do it? We scored three non-offensive touchdowns: an interception return, a kickoff return, and a punt return.

The best season of blocking kicks had to be 1998, when we finished 9–3. We blocked 12 kicks (eight punts, two field goals, and two PATs) that year, including two punts in the 38–7 win over Alabama in the Music City Bowl. Three of those blocked punts resulted in touchdowns. If there is anything more demoralizing for a team than to have a punt blocked, it has to be to have a punt blocked and returned for a touchdown. It's a real game-breaker. From 1987 to 2003, we scored 16 touchdowns on blocked punts.

I could tell over the years when other coaches respected our special teams. One year I think there were about four weeks in a row in which, after I studied punt protection for our upcoming opponent, the other team came out in something completely different on Saturday than what I had seen on film. That's a compliment.

There have been several schools over the years, such as Notre Dame and Ohio State, which have sent coaches here to study how we handle our special teams, and we have been very open about our methods.

The fact is that special teams comprise a third of the game, and although every coach says that, I am not sure every coach means it or believes it. How a team practices special teams goes a long way toward its importance and effectiveness on Saturdays.

A lot of schools work on special teams before practice or after practice. I think that sends the wrong message and we would never do that. What we would be telling our players is that it is not as important as offense or defense. It also punishes the kids who play on special teams, making them show up early or stay late. I like to practice our special teams right in the middle of practice. We come together in the middle of the field and make a big deal about it and that makes a statement to the players.

We also have special teams meetings daily, which help correct any mistakes made in practice as we go, rather than waiting to do it on Saturday.

I spend a lot of time on Sunday looking at special teams tape, probably at least three hours. I start with the opponents' punt protection and then on Mondays I move on to the opponents' punt rush and return. By the time I am finished studying everything, I may have spent eight hours on it.

The most obvious part, of course, is having a good kicker and a good punter. I have always stated that if we have those, we will have good special teams. It is a little bit hit-or-miss when evaluating high school punters and kickers. Some schools offer them scholarships, but we like to get them to come here as walk-ons, let them compete against each other and then put them on scholarship when they win the job.

I have heard a coach or two, like former Ohio State Coach Jim Tressel, say, "The punt is the most important play in football." And although it sounds strange, there is a lot of validity to that. I know this: if we have a key punt during the game, and we change field position with it, it is critical. Blocking or returning a kick or a punt changes field position, so there is a lot of validity to that, too.

Both go a long way toward determining the outcome of the game.

The other part that is not so obvious is that while we focus on blocking punts and kicks and scoring on defense, we cannot be sloppy in protection and allow the other team to block kicks and punts. And we can't give up long punt returns or kickoff returns. For the most part, we've been pretty good at that, too.

One day before the 2012 season, our sports information director, Dave Smith, said to me, "I don't know whether I should bring this to your attention or not, but we have the longest streak in the country of not allowing a kickoff return for a touchdown."

The streak dated back 20 seasons to the Syracuse game of 1993. By the sixth game of the season, it had reached 237 games. Then what did North Carolina do? They took a kickoff back 94 yards for a touchdown in the first quarter.

I thanked Dave for mentioning it. I wish I had never known about the streak. It's as if we jinxed the thing.

There have been times, though, when we lost at our own game.

We started the 1997 season by winning our first four games and had outscored our opponents 163–35 to jump in the rankings to No. 14. Then Miami came to Lane Stadium. It wasn't Miami of Florida, but the Mid-American Conference's Miami of Ohio. It was Jim Weaver's first game here as our new athletic director and it was homecoming, too.

Our offensive line coach, J.B. Grimes, had been having some tightness in his chest before the game and we advised him to get it checked out ASAP. I told J.B. to go up into the press box for the game, instead of coaching from the field. During a key moment in the game, J.B. was lying unnoticed on the floor of the press box as our coaches were relaying information to us. He then had bypass surgery after the game.

We lost two fumbles that night, had two punts blocked, allowed a 32-yard touchdown on a fake field goal, and lost 24–17. With all those big plays, it was a wonder the game was that close. After that game, Miami coach Randy Walker was being interviewed on the field when one of our band members marched into him.

"Damn, they hit harder than the Hokies did tonight!" he said.

Unfortunately, Coach Walker later died of a heart attack while coaching at Northwestern.

Another time we got out-produced in special teams was in the 2000 Sugar Bowl for the national championship, of course. We gave up a blocked punt for a touchdown and a 59-yard punt return for a touchdown to Peter Warrick in the loss to Florida State.

I've always wanted to put our best players on special teams, too. We had Corey Moore, the 1999 Big East Defensive Player of the Year, who was a senior, on special teams that season.

Certain guys just have a knack for blocking kicks, an instinct that is hard to teach. Keion Carpenter blocked six punts in his career while Bernard Basham blocked seven kicks from the middle of the line of scrimmage.

With all that being said, I know what the critics may be thinking about right now: where are all the blocked kicks and punts lately? What happened to "Beamer Ball?"

We blocked only 20 kicks from 2006 to 2012, compared to the 33 we blocked in the previous five seasons. Worse yet, we blocked only one kick in each of the 2011 and '12 seasons.

Let me explain what has happened in college football.

The new thing that has changed everything is the three-man shield many teams are using on punt protection. Fans ask me all the time why we haven't blocked many punts in recent seasons and that's the main reason. You can't get through that shield easily, so we basically don't waste people trying. We work on setting up a good return instead. The downside to using the shield is that the punt protection team sacrifices coverage by keeping three players back for the shield. We try to take advantage of that.

Still, we averaged 10.3 yards per punt return in 2012, good for 36th in the country, which is not where we want to be—and one of those was Kyshoen Jarrett's 94-yard return against Pittsburgh.

I think special teams play in general for the teams we face has been much better than it was 10 years ago, because I think coaches are putting more emphasis on it and they are putting their better players on it.

The fact remains that when our offense or defense struggles, that is one way we can make up some ground, and we have not been doing it lately. We have not been getting the boost and changes in momentum from special teams that we have in the past, but I really do think it's temporary.

Our punting efficiency hasn't been as consistent lately as it has been over the years, either. We've been too inconsistent. In addition to not getting to punts because of the shield, we also have been unable to block as many kicks. You just have to find the right guy, one who has the knack and timing for coming off the edge, which we haven't lately.

Despite the drop-off statistically, I don't think Beamer Ball is a thing of the past for Virginia Tech.

17

Don't Get Too High and Don't Get Too Low

JOHN BALLEIN, Virginia Tech's director of football operations: *"I handle all of our travel arrangements and I have heard the horror stories from other people in my position at other schools. Head coaches, used to getting their way, can complain about everything. The airplane was two minutes late. The beds were too hard. The meeting rooms were too cold. The food was too fattening. I know of a very prominent head coach who requires that the hotel elevator be empty when he gets on it, so he doesn't have to make small talk with fans. While working for Coach Beamer for more than 25 years, I heard him complain once. One time! We were in Tallahassee to play Florida State and we stayed at an absolutely awful Ramada Inn. I saw Coach coming down the hall the morning of the game and his hair was all matted down. He didn't even look like himself. 'New hairstyle, Coach?' I asked. 'Lousy shower heads!' he said. 'John, this place is a dump! Don't ever book us here again!' That was the one time. And he was right. The place was a dump. But other than that, he has never complained about anything. That man is so easygoing and easy to work for. He knows there is a bigger picture in life than to complain about the little things."*

One night in the summer of 2003, we returned home to the lake house in Georgia after being out to dinner with friends. I wasn't feeling well and it wasn't something I ate.

Cheryl looked at me and asked, "You okay?"

"I'm good," I told her, knowing I wasn't.

I woke up the next morning with severe chest pains.

Cheryl looked at me again and asked, "You okay?"

"Well, I think it's time to go see a doctor," I admitted.

That began what seemed like a scene from a Chevy Chase movie. Shane was a graduate assistant at Georgia Tech at the time. He got on the phone, making arrangements to have me checked out at a hospital there. We hopped in the car and began the 65-mile drive to Atlanta.

I had the angioplasty in 1989, after I felt the tightness in my chest during that game at East Carolina. I quit smoking then because I knew I couldn't continue and stay healthy. This time the chest pains were severe enough I thought I may be having a heart attack.

I was in the front seat with Shane driving while Cheryl and Casey were in the backseat. Cheryl started to get nauseous during the drive and Shane pulled over to the side of the road so we could switch places. I went into the backseat and she got into the front seat. Then we had to stop at a McDonald's so she could go inside and throw up. We were lost trying to find this hospital. She came back out, got back into the car, and got sick again, while I sat in the back seat grabbing my chest.

I wondered, *What the hell is going on here?*

We finally found the hospital and they checked me in. Cheryl, Shane, and Casey left to check into a hotel, where Cheryl happened to get sick again. Doctors ended up performing a heart catheterization on me. I was in the hospital recovering when Jim Weaver, our athletic director, called to say, "We are being accepted into the ACC!"

Wow. What great news. Matter of fact, it was the biggest news ever for us at Virginia Tech. I always thought Virginia Tech was a perfect fit for the ACC and now it would become a reality.

My chest pains disappeared, too.

When the ACC news was announced, Bill Brill, the columnist who welcomed me back to Blacksburg with the "sweater" comment during Christmas in 1986, wrote a column the next day, stating, "Virginia Tech won't win an ACC championship in my lifetime."

How's that for motivation?

Well, we didn't wait long to prove Brill wrong. We won the ACC title our first year in the conference in 2004. We won it again in '07, '08, and '10. We won four conference championships in our first seven seasons. Two other times, in '05 and '11, we won the ACC's Coastal Division but lost the conference championship games to Florida State and Clemson, respectively.

But back to that Chevy Chase–like adventure. First I was having heart problems, Cheryl was throwing up, and we got lost. Then we received the best news possible for our program.

This goes back to one of my general philosophies in life and in football: no matter what happens, don't get too high and don't get too low. Everything will work itself out in the long run if you remain calm and steady.

And somewhere in the middle is reality.

It has gotten to the point with some fans that every loss is just devastating to them—the bottom has fallen out of the program and the sky is falling.

I would be the first to tell you we haven't played as well in the BCS bowl games and some other big games as we needed in recent years. But we did get to those games in the first place, and that is a tough thing to do. I think people forget that.

Some coaches say that dealing with the criticism, as well as the losses, gets easier as they grow older. I wouldn't be one of them. I think it bothers me now more than it used to. Back when we weren't that good and I knew we weren't that good, we were coaching and playing our hearts out and maybe I accepted losses better.

I don't want to disappoint our people, our Virginia Tech fans. We have such loyal fans. They care. They care whether we win or lose and that is one reason I have a harder time dealing with a loss now. I do have sleepless nights after a loss and those nights are worse than they ever were.

I also believe the age of the Internet and the so-called instant-news cycle these days contributes to a lot of negativism.

It just seems that people can throw out criticism on these websites and comment on any story on the Internet without having any real facts to back them up. Then that comment or criticism gets repeated, just as if it were a fact.

When I played, I knew there were sportswriters who did not want to write anything to hurt you. They did their job and I felt like they wanted you to succeed. I feel like it has gotten to the point that in order to make it in that business they have to be controversial or somewhat negative to get attention. I am sure newspaper people, competing with the Internet people, feel some pressure. I think most of the writers may like me fine, but they still have to sell their product. I do understand that. And I have to understand that to understand them. I like to help them do their jobs and I think everybody in our program treats them fairly.

I remember there was one writer who covered Virginia Tech a while ago and he told me he was up for a big writing job somewhere in the Midwest.

"If you want me to, I will write a nice letter of recommendation," I told him.

"You would be the *last* person I would want to write a letter of recommendation for me," he told me.

I was taken aback by his comment.

There are not many coaches in the game today who have not been criticized at one time or another. That's part of the deal. Nick Saban has won three national titles in four years, and if he has a few 8–4 seasons, the media will be asking him why he has trouble winning games. That just comes with the territory and most of us accept it.

I really don't read the coverage anymore and I certainly don't listen to talk radio. It's really a better way to go. Why get all worked up about people talking about the way we do things if they really don't know what they are talking about? It's a waste of time and energy.

That doesn't mean I can keep Cheryl from listening to it, though.

CHERYL BEAMER: "*I learned my lesson a long time ago not to get into the football business with Frank. One day I was listening to the local ESPN radio guys argue about which quarterback should be playing between Sean Glennon and Tyrod Taylor. So when Frank got home from work, I went on and on about what they had said. All of a sudden, he snapped, 'You know what, Cheryl? If I want to know that stuff, I will listen to that stuff. Otherwise, don't tell me about any of it!' And since then, I haven't.*"

What coaches really don't like is when the instant coverage that comes via the Internet affects a player in a negative way.

Mack Brown once told me that he had a prominent player injured during practice, and before he could get into his office to call that player's parents, the news of his injury was already on the Internet. Can you imagine those parents sitting somewhere, reading about their son being injured before receiving a call from anyone at Texas?

That would probably make me mad, too.

Mack's story reminds me of something that happened to me.

I attended a Brad Paisley concert in February of 2011 at the Roanoke Civic Center. Beforehand, I was talking to Brad's dad. He told me that Brad had never had a drink in his life, but one of his big hit songs is called "Alcohol." When Brad started to sing that song that night, he motioned for me to get up on stage. Now Brad is a huge West Virginia fan. I didn't exactly know what was happening at the time, but he stuck a West Virginia hat on my head. I heard the crowd react, so I took the hat off and noticed that blue and gold 'WV' logo. When Brad turned around, I threw the hat to the ground and stomped on it. The crowd went wild.

The next day, the Virginia Tech football coach wearing a West Virginia hat was all over the Internet.

It was a funny deal, really. Brad was just having a good time with me. Anybody who knows me will tell you I like to have fun and I am not beyond poking fun at myself. I mean, why else would I agree to do a Harlem Shake video like the one that hit the Internet in the spring of 2013? I have never been known for my dance moves, but I do think I have a pretty good sense of humor.

BRUCE GARNES, Virginia Tech's deputy director of football operations: *"Coach has a great sense of humor, but sort of a dry sense of humor. A few of the coaches were flying back from a basketball tournament in Washington, D.C., one time and the plane got to bouncing around up there. It was foggy and raining sideways and there was bad turbulence. I was nervous as ever. Coach Beamer was reading his newspaper, as calm as could be. He's always calm, no matter the situation. He must have heard us talking about the weather and noticed we were nervous.*

He turned around and said, 'You know…this is exactly how JFK Junior died, don't you?' Then he just smiled and went back to reading his paper."

Yeah, but Bruce didn't think that was too funny when we were bouncing around at 20,000 feet.

Bruce started here as a student manager when he was a sophomore in 1989. There was a fight on campus in which one of our baseball players had been injured. Somebody cut him over the eye and I was told that Bruce was involved in the fight. I couldn't believe it: one of our student managers causing trouble like this. I called him in and really let him have it.

"I'm sending you home! Your life is about to change!" I told him.

Bruce was adamant that he was in his dorm studying for a math exam at the time of the fight. Sure enough, I'd received bad information. He had nothing to do with it. When I heard that, I picked up the phone.

"Bruce, I am so sorry, I got some wrong information on this deal," I said.

"You don't have to apologize to me," he told me. "Just know that I will never do anything that will make you send me back home. I am the first one from my family to go to college and I won't do anything to mess that up."

Bruce became the first in his family to graduate from college, too. After he worked a few years as an intern with the Dallas Cowboys, I hired him for a full-time position just like I told him I would. And there isn't anything he won't do. He is a great team player. Anybody who knows me well knows there are a few things I hate to do, such as waiting in traffic or pumping gas. I absolutely hate having to pull into a gas station. If I notice my tank is low when I drive to work, I'll throw my keys to him when I get to the office and ask Bruce, "You busy right now?"

One time, I was driving home from the office and the red light on the gas gauge came on, so I had no choice. I stopped, filled up the tank, and headed home.

It wasn't too long until there was a knock at the front door. I looked out the window to see a police officer.

I opened the door and asked, "Oh no, what did one of my players do now?"

"Your players are fine," the policeman told me, "but would you mind coming back to the gas station to pay for your gas?"

That officer must have thought, *If he can't remember to pay for his gas, how does he run an entire football program?*

I am sure my mind was on something else when I left that service station.

It takes a lot to make me angry. Cheryl will tell you she has probably never seen me blow my stack. There may have been a few times over the years, but it certainly had nothing to do with a football game or a bad call. Our players getting into trouble off the field certainly has led me to raise my voice a few times over the years. Nothing makes me madder than our kids doing dumb things and getting their names in the newspaper for all of the wrong reasons.

I never really had to yell much at our two kids, but maybe that was because they were always pretty good kids.

Shane will tell you the maddest I probably got at him was when he got a speeding ticket in high school. I found out about it while he was at school. Cheryl and I just happened to be leaving on vacation. As we left the house and drove down our street, I happened to see Shane driving home. I stuck it in reverse and backed up next to his car and really gave it to him good. I went on and on as our cars sat side-by-side.

"Yes sir, yes sir, it will never happen again," he told me.

We got to the airport and Cheryl had that look on her face.

"Now Frank, if our plane goes down, that will be the last conversation you ever had with your only son," she said. "Do you want him to remember that for the rest of his life?"

You know, she was right. I called him from the airport and smoothed things over, but I am sure he understood where I was coming from.

I think I take the same approach with our players as I did with my own children. We have certain expectations from them and if they keep up with those expectations—always go to class, work hard in practice every play of every day, stay out of trouble, just to name a few—they never hear a cross word from me or any of our coaches.

And we do push them hard, on the field and in the classroom.

That reminds me of a funny story involving John Engelberger, one of our great defensive ends from the late '90s, although it wasn't very funny when it happened.

It was during a Monday practice when our defensive line coach, Charley Wiles, was pushing John real hard. They were going back and forth about something that had happened, and Charley happened to say, "Well, if you don't like it, hit the tunnel!"

John started to walk up the tunnel toward the locker room. Somebody motioned for me and I ran after him. Now here was one of our best players, who had a great NFL future ahead of him—and he was quitting the team.

I caught up to John in the tunnel and started to plead my case, "Now John, let's just calm down. You don't want to do this. What would you do if you left here and you didn't play football?"

"I would join the Army," he said, without hesitating.

He was dead serious.

"But John..." I started before he interrupted.

"Yeah, I'll join the Army."

"John, now let's come on back here and finish this drill and you'll be okay," I pleaded.

John walked back to the practice field, made up with Coach Wiles and my heart rate returned to normal. He went on to have a dominant senior season, became a second-round pick of the San Francisco 49ers, played nine seasons in the NFL, made a lot of money, and is doing well today. In fact, he donated $100,000 to the program to pay for every inch of carpet in our football facility.

But I'll tell you, I may have cost our country one fine enlisted man.

I learned from that halftime tirade at Tulane that first season: yelling and screaming doesn't always get results. They know when I'm not happy, because I may call them a certain name, but don't get the wrong idea—it's not a swear word or anything like that.

JIM CAVANAUGH, former Virginia Tech assistant coach: "*He has a way of keeping you in line if he's pissed off at you: He calls you 'pal-sie.' As in 'pal,' but he adds an ending to it. So when you hear 'pal-sie' you know he's mad at somebody. The first time I heard it, it was shortly after I was hired and we were recruiting somewhere near Newport News. We had stayed at a Hampton Inn, woke up and checked out and hit the road. I had my Diet Coke and just assumed he grabbed a cup of coffee in the lobby. Everybody knows that Coach likes his coffee in the morning. So we jumped into the car and I was anxious to get to this recruit's house. He asked me, 'Hey, how about pulling over to the next 7-Eleven, so I can get some coffee.' I said, 'Okay' and continued driving. I must have passed one and didn't see it. He didn't say anything. I guess I passed a second one and he still said nothing. So there must have been a third 7-Eleven and suddenly, I hear, 'Hey, pal-sie! Pull your ass into that*

Our family in the backyard in Blacksburg. We never take the view for granted.

I was not cut out to race a stock car. But after doing so a few times at those celebrity events, I have a ton of respect for those NASCAR guys.

In my only visit to Huntington, West Virginia, before we played Marshall in 2010, I had to see the memorial of the Marshall airplane tragedy of November 14, 1970. It was very emotional for me, thinking of my good friend and teammate Frankie Loria.

Wounded Warrior and Virginia Tech graduate Ben Keirnan addresses our team after practice in 2012. We love to have these American heroes talk to our players.

With my family during a ceremony celebrating my 25 years as Virginia Tech's head coach. That portrait hangs in the entrance to my office.

Addressing the media before the 2012 Sugar Bowl: It appears I like the question. The ensuing loss to Michigan I didn't like—we should have won that game.

Bud Foster and I were happy with this big win. In my opinion, Bud has been the best defensive coordinator in college football and his loyalty to Virginia Tech is unmatched.

My family has known me to get emotional often over the years, like when I was about to give Casey away.

Our family at Casey's big day in the summer of 2012.

Cheryl and I love being grandparents to Shane's daughters, Olivia and Sutton.

Here I am with (left to right) my director of football operations and good friend, John Ballein, and longtime friends Wayland "Street" Overstreet and Greg Roberts at our annual Myrtle Beach golf outing in May 2013.

My favorite moment each week: waiting to lead the team onto the field at Lane Stadium.

I have learned to savor every win, like this one against Georgia Tech to open the 2012 season. And it never gets old when we can enjoy a win at Lane Stadium, along with more than 66,000 of my closest friends and family members.

7-Eleven. I need a cup of coffee!' The second time, we were on the prac-
tice field and I was working with him on punt protection. I must have
said something to the punter and all of a sudden he comes across the
line of scrimmage and I hear 'Hey, palsie!' and he proceeded to tell me
off. I shouldn't have messed with his punter. That's his territory. Another
time, I was in the press box during a game and I was always on the
defensive headset. Coach would go back and forth on the headset,
depending on whether we had the ball or we were on defense. Our of-
fense was on the field at the time, but he didn't switch over to offense
on his headset, because he was out there arguing with the officials. He
was getting farther and farther from the sideline as he argued. He got
out to the numbers [and] I said over the headset, 'Somebody better
get out there and grab his ass. He's about to cost us 15 yards.' All of a
sudden, it was like a voice from God. 'Hey pal-sie! You worry about the
damn defense and I'll worry about dealing with the officials!' I didn't
even know he was listening. I just said, 'Yes sir' and I shut the hell up.
So when the game was over—fortunately we won—he was standing at
the entrance to the locker room greeting all the players like he always
does. 'Who was giving you hell about the officials?' I asked him. He just
laughed and slapped me on the back. That's another great thing about
him—nothing like that ever carries over. But I am probably the only guy
who ever got three 'pal-sies' and didn't end up getting fired."

I really don't know where I got that term, but I guess it goes way
back to Murray State. I have been using that word for a long time.

My family will tell you I can get emotional at times. I may not always say what I am feeling and I know I need to get better at that, but
sometimes they know how I feel by looking at me. Cheryl and I had
a hard time trying to stop crying on and after April 16. I cried like a

baby while giving Casey away at her wedding recently and there have been several other times, I am sure.

When I looked at the 2011 schedule, I knew I would be emotional during our game at Marshall on September 24. I had not been to Huntington since the plane crash some 31 years earlier, but I thought of Frankie Loria often over the years.

I've been asked many times: "If Frank Loria was alive, would he be coaching for you?"

I always answer, "No, I would be coaching for him."

That's how I have always felt about Frankie, because he was ahead of his time. He would have become one of the top coaches in college football.

FRANK LORIA, JR., who was born one month after his father's 1970 death: "I was told that Frank Beamer was asked if Frank Loria were still alive today, did he think my dad would be working for him? Coach Beamer said he thought he would be working for my dad. I think that answer is Coach Beamer being the classy guy he is. He's one of the good guys. I appreciate him saying that."

I would not go see the movie *We Are Marshall* at the theater when it was released, but when it played on our team bus ride from Blacksburg to Huntington, West Virginia, the day before the game, I had no choice. As I watched it, I couldn't help but think of Frankie. It was one of the saddest movies I have ever seen, because I lived through that horrible time. It wasn't just a fictional movie to me—it took me back to one of the saddest times of my life.

When we arrived at the stadium that day, a police officer met us and told John and me to get into the back of his squad car. John brought a Hokie stone we inscribed to honor both Frankie and Rick Tolley, who was the Marshall head coach in 1970 and a Virginia Tech graduate.

"We don't have a whole lot of time," John told the officer.

The policeman must have taken John's words to heart because those next four minutes were the most scared I've ever been in a car. He was weaving in and out of traffic and I thought we would crash about three or four times. But he got us to the monument honoring all the victims of the crash. I placed the Hokie stone down in front of it, and as I thought of Frankie I know I had tears in my eyes.

That day, Frank Jr. flipped the coin before the game. It was great to talk to him. We had a close game for a while, but we pulled away late to win 30–10. Like the game at Rutgers after September 11, 2001, and the home-opener against East Carolina after the shooting in 2007, it was one of the most emotional days I've had in coaching.

Before you start thinking I am just a big softy, they tell me I do have a competitive side to balance that. I admit I don't like to lose at anything. Never have.

We've had some knock-down, drag-out racquetball games during the lunch hour at Virginia Tech over the years. Racquetball is a great game to work out the stress and have some fun, but I want to win it when I play.

BOBBY ROSS: *"Let me tell you when I really learned how competitive Frank Beamer is. We had an outdoor racquetball court at The Citadel and it seemed like it was always hot and humid down there. So Frank and I would go out to play a 'friendly' game and he used to wear me out on that racquetball court. I thought with me being the head coach that he might let up on me or take it easy once in a while. He never did. Not one time. He would dive for points. And he used that racquetball court to reach kids, too. We had a defensive back who struggled in school and struggled on the field. Frank said to me, 'Why don't I get him on the racquetball court and get to know him a little better and maybe I can reach him and get him turned around.' Sure enough, he got to playing racquetball with this kid and the kid changed almost instantly. He got better in school and on the field and then he got his degree. Frank not only was one of our best coaches, he was one of our best tutors. We couldn't afford tutors, so he would tutor them in his apartment. There was no stone left unturned by Frank Beamer."*

One time, my buddy Street and I lost a golf match to Greg Roberts and John, a match we should have won, and there was an exchange of two one-dollar bills to pay off our bet. John took a picture of those two George Washingtons changing hands and still brings that picture out now and then when I am not around. It's not funny to me. I didn't like him rubbing our noses in that loss.

When coaches say something like the tough losses hurt more than the big wins feel good, they probably are right. I also think I am having a tougher time getting over losses than I ever used to. Maybe that's because we are expected to win every game since we turned the program around. I don't know. I just know I hate letting our fans down.

Speaking of emotional highs and lows, John and I were sitting around the office just recently trying to compile a list of our top-five wins and our top-five losses at Virginia Tech. This is highly subjective, but here goes:

Our top-five wins:

1. 22–20 over West Virginia in 1999—They had us pinned back deep and Michael Vick made the great run to set up Shayne Graham's winning field goal on the final play. That got us to the Sugar Bowl to play for the national championship.

2. 45–24 over Syracuse in 1993—This win secured the Independence Bowl bid, our first bowl during my time at Virginia Tech. It also got me off the so-called "hot seat."

3. 28–10 over Texas in 1995 Sugar Bowl—It was our first major bowl, and it came against a prominent program.

4. 38–14 over Boston College in 1999—This game at Lane Stadium officially secured the national championship berth; we celebrated for a while that night.

5. 36–29 over Virginia in 1995—I think it was the best game in our rivalry with Virginia. We hit a pass to Jermaine Holmes to take a one-point lead late in the final minute and then Antonio Banks sealed it with an interception return for a touchdown on the final play. There's nothing better than beating our state rival to earn the right to go to a major bowl.

An honorable mention has to be the 2010 ACC Championship Game. We beat Florida State 44–33. First, it was for the ACC championship and it came against a team we had played several times over the years, but we hadn't had much success. What also made the game special is that it was played in Charlotte, where I feel the ACC Championship Game should be played, rather than in Jacksonville. And it also came against a quarterback who left our state to go to Florida State—E.J. Manuel, who was filling in for Christian Ponder.

Our top-five losses:

1. 46–29 to Florida State in the 2000 Sugar Bowl—Need I say more?

2. 41–21 to Miami in 2000—We had an 8–0 record and a chance to play in two straight championship games, but we were playing

without Michael at full strength and André Davis missed the game with an ankle injury.

3. The 1998 season brought us three heartbreakers and I can't separate them: 28–24 to Temple—We were 5–0 and 29-point favorites at Lane Stadium, but we dropped what would have been a winning touchdown pass on the second-to-last play of the game. 28–26 to Syracuse—We had them beat and Donovan McNabb rolled out and threw back to the tight end coming across for a touchdown on the final play; there probably never was a loss which we should have won more than this one. And 36–32 to Virginia—Which we should have won but lost when we failed to tackle their receiver late in the final minute of the game.

4. 23–20 in overtime to Michigan in the 2012 Sugar Bowl—This one still hurts. We needed a BCS win and the replay officials overturned what I still think was a great touchdown catch by Danny Coale.

5. 27–24 to Cincinnati in 2012—We took the lead in the final two minutes and then let them throw one over our heads for a 39-yard touchdown with only 13 seconds remaining.

Unfortunately, I can probably remember more tough losses that could be added to this list, such as the 24–21 loss to Kansas in the 2008 Orange Bowl, or any of the losses to East Carolina, Louisville, Rutgers, or Virginia in that 2–8–1 season in 1992; or the last-minute losses to Boise State and James Madison to open the 2010 season. We needed one more yard to get a first down and run out the clock to beat Boise but we didn't get it. Then Boise quarterback Kellen Moore hit a touchdown pass in the back of the end zone with only 1:09 remaining to win the game 33–30. Only five days later, we fumbled in the red zone at the end of the game and James Madison upset us 21–16 at Lane Stadium.

After that loss, I said, "We're having no more Monday night games on the road and then follow it with a Saturday game."

We got home at five in the morning that Tuesday from Washington, D.C., after the Boise State game and then we had to get ready to play a game on about three days' preparation. (We scheduled the same way to open the 2012 season, beating Georgia Tech on a Monday and then Austin Peay on a Saturday, but both were home games with no travel involved.)

We've always hosted a reception at my house following a home game each season for the sponsors of our website, beamerball.com. Well that season, the reception just happened to be scheduled right after the game against James Madison. We had just lost another heartbreaker, we had an 0–2 record after losing two games we probably shouldn't have lost and we had an entire season in front of us.

I didn't feel much like partying when I arrived. But I believe you've got to do what you've got to do. So if I said I was coming, I was coming. I showed up and talked to people and had a relatively good time, because that is what was required, no matter the outcome of a football game. I would never want to be one of those guys who hides somewhere after a loss or doesn't fulfill an obligation.

I went back to work the next day and told our staff: "It is what it is. We're 0 and 2. Don't get down. Be positive when you deal with the kids. Believe in each other and stay the course. Let's get to work to fix it, starting today."

That's the only way I know how to approach a so-called crisis. We went on to win the next 11 games and the ACC championship game over Florida State before Stanford beat us 40–12 in the Orange Bowl.

SHANE BEAMER: *"Dad never gets too high or too low. I've been at other schools and on a Sunday after a loss, you come into the building and you have to ask, 'How is he today?' meaning, what kind of mood is the head coach in? You don't have to do that with Dad. He's the same every day, after a loss or after a win. And he's the same now as he was during that 2–8–1 season in 1992. There was never any kicking the dog or screaming at the kids."*

If I think about all the ups and downs we've experienced at Virginia Tech since I was hired in December of 1986, a roller-coaster ride wouldn't come close as a comparison. But it was important to keep my emotions somewhere in the middle or we never would have made it through those first six years.

It all started when Dutch Baughman took some severe heat for hiring me, but he stood behind the decision and I will always be thankful to him.

"Some people have questioned this decision because he is not a big name," Dutch was quoted saying at the time. "But it's a sound decision, and I'm standing by it."

Then he resigned.

I am sure that Dave Braine received some criticism for keeping me around after 2–8–1 in 1992, the same season in which poor little Casey got berated on the phone by an angry fan.

I never took any of it personally. I never got too low during that horrible season because I would not have been able to see the way to fix it, knowing better days were ahead. And I never got too high when we won the Independence Bowl the following season or the Sugar Bowl two years later. I knew we had plenty of work in front of us to build and then maintain one of the country's top programs.

I had to keep my emotions somewhere in the middle, plow through it all, and stay the course.

We came out of the other side of those troubled years in pretty good shape, too. So to answer that original Bill Brill column written when my hiring was announced, I like to think I've been a pretty comfortable sweater for my alma mater all these years.

18

Surround Yourself with Good People

The title of this chapter could be the key to either being successful as a head coach or someday getting fired. If you hire good people, you can be successful. If you don't, you could fail to win enough games and get fired.

It doesn't matter how much you know or how good you think you are as a head coach, if you don't have good, solid assistant coaches, or the right assistant coaches at the right time, you will fail.

I imagine this philosophy extends to just about any profession, whether you are a CEO, a president, or a boss of any kind. You have to make sure you have good people around you. And when you need to make a change for the betterment of the cause, you have to clench your teeth and do it—no matter how painful it is.

Making the changes in the coaching staff when things were not going as planned, such as after the 2–8–1 season, as Dave Braine suggested, was unavoidable if I wanted to continue to coach at Virginia Tech. Sometimes, a head coach just has to let people go, no matter how difficult it is. It's not personal; it's business. And it's something very common in this business.

Sometimes, we just need to find new energy, and often new assistants bring it with them.

Since 1993, I think we have done a good job of hiring good people, making sure they were paid well, and doing our best to keep them happy. The consistency and continuity of the staff, I believe, are main reasons we have had the successful run we have had.

I hate terminating someone's employment and affecting his life in a negative way. He usually has a family, and sometimes getting let go means the family will be getting uprooted.

And the other side of that is to recognize coaching talent when you see it.

When I left The Citadel to become Murray State's defensive coordinator in 1979 for Mike Gottfried, I didn't know anyone but Ron Zook. I certainly didn't know what type of defensive players I would inherit at Murray, but there was one guy who was a coach's dream. He was a guy who always gave full-out effort every day in practice and on Saturdays.

His name was Bud Foster.

Bud has been on my team ever since.

When his playing days were finished at Murray, I hired him as a graduate assistant in 1981 and then promoted him to outside linebackers coach in '83. He added special teams coordinator in '86 and when I got the job at Virginia Tech, I brought him with me as an inside linebackers coach. He has never left and has been our defensive coordinator since '95.

After all the years he's been on my staff, he knows me well and knows what I want from him. We are to the point now that I just let him do his job. He's always had a real good feel for the game and now he matches that instinct with knowledge and experience. There isn't a better defensive coordinator in the game of college football.

Bud has seen just about everything there is to see from offenses over the years. Offenses will do things differently now than they did the week before, or the week before that, but Bud has the experience to adjust as well as anybody.

There have been so many examples of this over the years, I wouldn't know where to start, but I will give you a quick example. We played East Carolina at home a few years ago and we had been blitzing some. East Carolina continued to complete passes to a wide receiver right beyond the line of scrimmage where our blitzing linebacker was coming from. They were killing us with that play and they were leading us at the half.

At halftime, Bud said he wanted to continue to blitz, but he wanted to drop our ends right into that spot where they were hitting the pass. That put an end to their offense's effectiveness and we came back to win 49–27.

Bud brings more than his X-and-O expertise; he's as intense as any coach you will find anywhere, and he hates to lose as much as I do.

When Syracuse's Donovan McNabb hit a pass to beat us 28–26 on the final play of the game in 1998, the players told me they saw Bud run full-steam into the locker room at the Carrier Dome and crash face-first into a locker. He didn't even slow down! I think part of his frustration that day was the fact he had just told the defense what Syracuse would do on that final play. Sure enough, Syracuse ran that exact play. McNabb rolled one way and threw back the other way to the tight end. But our guys missed their assignments. That's frustrating for any coach. Bud once broke a grease board at Georgia Tech and John stuck that in our trophy case.

There will be times when I'll say over the headphones, "Okay, Bud, we need to calm down here. It's okay."

"I'm good, Coach, I'm good," he always responds.

I know one thing: the kids love to play for him. They know he will put them in the right defense and they have confidence in him because he knows what he's doing. At the same time, he is demanding of them during practice and that keeps them sharp. As each season progresses and we get into November, his defenses usually get better and better and that is a sure sign of good coaching.

The bottom line is that I trust him and there is nobody I would rather have running our defense.

Look at the numbers: our defenses have been ranked in the top five of a major defensive category 35 times from 1995 through 2012. In his first season as defensive coordinator in 1995, we led the country in rush defense, allowing only 77.3 yards per game. Ever since, we've usually been in the top 10 in scoring defense and total defense. Bud won the Frank Broyles Award as the nation's top assistant coach in 2006, when our defense was No. 1 in total defense (219 yards), pass defense (128 yards), and scoring defense (11 points).

What really tells me something about Bud as a coach is when I look at our defense after it loses several starters. We lost seven starters on defense after the 2007 season, all of whom were signed by NFL teams. You'd think we would struggle the following season, but the 2008 defense finished No. 7 in the country in total defense (279 yards per game).

That "lunch-pail" defense he and Rod Sharpless came up with back in the 1990s symbolizes Bud's work ethic perfectly. He always has his players ready to work and our players love that tradition, which has grown over the years. It's a perfect theme for what Bud does each day and for what he teaches our defensive players to do. He wants hard workers who never quit, who put in a full day's work.

I admire him for his loyalty, too. Bud has had chances to move on to become defensive coordinator at top programs such as Georgia, Florida, and Florida State, but he stayed with us. He's had his chances for a few head-coaching jobs, too, but he stayed with us. I talk about staff loyalty all the time and nobody exemplifies that better than Bud.

He's been picky about his opportunities, but I'm sure he will be a head coach someday. He just needs the right opportunity.

I realized we needed to properly compensate Bud for his loyalty, too. A few years ago, the school added a clause to his contract: he will receive an $800,000 annuity payment if he stays through the 2014 season. And I see what some other defensive coordinators are making at places like Texas, Michigan, and Clemson, so Bud deserves it.

BUD FOSTER: "I've had plenty of opportunities to leave, but it's gotten to the point now that I don't even tell Coach Beamer the job offers I get. What's the use? I know I will be staying here in the end anyway. Kevin Sumlin just offered me a job when he was named head coach at Texas A&M after the 2011 season and I didn't tell Coach Beamer about it. But probably the closest I ever came to leaving was to Florida to work for Steve Spurrier after the '98 season, when Bob Stoops left to go to Oklahoma. I interviewed for the Pittsburgh head-coaching job a few years ago, but my wife and I decided Pittsburgh was not for us. Coach Beamer trusts me to do my job well and believe me, I don't take advantage of him. I respect and admire him way too much for that. I'm very happy here and now that I've been here this long, I figure I will hang in here until Coach Beamer retires and then go looking for work somewhere."

Before the 2011 season, I made some changes again and brought my son, Shane, in from South Carolina. Since playing for us from 1996 to 1999, he coached at Georgia Tech, Tennessee, Mississippi State, and South Carolina, and I really thought the time was right for him to come back.

Some family members asked me several times over the years, "Why don't you bring Shane back?"

I always told them the timing had to be right. We had talked at least once per week when he was at South Carolina, and he gave us a lot of good ideas when it came to special teams. I know how bright Shane is and I knew he was ready, too. I've seen way too many father-son combinations that didn't turn out right, but we had gotten to the point where we had lost some kids during recruiting who we shouldn't have lost. I knew Shane would help us recruiting-wise. And Billy Hite was ready to give up coaching, but I really wanted to keep him on the staff.

So we hired Shane as the running backs coach. He is really, really good at recruiting because he stays on top of it and he is young enough that he can talk to these kids on their level. At the same time, his opinion is important to me. He has great enthusiasm, ideas, and a knack for coaching the game. He knows many people on other staffs—way more people than I do—and he makes an attempt to know more and more coaches every season. That always helps when it comes to swapping information and trading ideas.

I really think he has a great future ahead of him.

I am old enough now that I don't particularly think of myself as a friend to a kid when I am recruiting him. I am more of a father-figure who wants to lead that kid in the best direction. At the same time, I need younger assistants like Shane who know what is happening with kids these days. He can talk to them and relate to them.

As far as these latest staff changes following the 2012 season, when we finished 7–6, it was just something that had to be done.

Looking back to August before the season kicked off, I was concerned from the get-go. We would be playing a freshman tailback and that was a big worry. We would be playing with three new offensive linemen. We would also be playing with two new receivers. With that combination, I just didn't know how consistent we would be. I didn't like how our schedule worked out either, playing at Clemson, at Miami, then Florida State at home, and at Boston College in a four-week span in early November.

We started 2–0 with wins over Georgia Tech and Austin Peay, but we were really lucky to get by Georgia Tech in overtime on Labor Day night. We went to Pitt and the Panthers were coming off losses to Youngstown State and Cincinnati. I know some of our guys may have thought they were not very good. They had an up-and-down quarterback coming into the game. We turned it over four times, they played great, and their quarterback was up that day. That's how we got beat 35–17 when we were big favorites to win the game. We beat Bowling Green 37–0 in one of our best games, because as it turned out, Bowling Green turned into a pretty good team and went to a bowl game.

I think the season changed on one play. We scored in the last minute to take a 24–20 lead on Cincinnati at FedEx Field in Washington. We were just moments from being 4–1. Then we misplayed a pass when we were in three-deep in the final seconds, letting a receiver run right by us for the winning touchdown. That loss really hurt.

After a terrible loss at Miami in which we stalled in the red zone all night and a tough one at home against Florida State in which we gave up the lead in the final minute again—games played on consecutive Thursday nights on ESPN—we had a 4–6 record, wondering how it all went wrong.

We went to Boston College knowing we had to win. If we did, we knew we had to come home and beat Virginia just to get to 6–6 and keep our bowl streak alive.

I was very nervous about going to BC. I knew if we lost the game, we would have our first losing season in 20 years. All the things being written in the newspapers and on the Internet were bad enough, but I thought, *If we lose this game, it's about to get much worse.*

We somehow pulled it out 30–23 in overtime.

We came into the Virginia game having beaten them eight straight years, but I never take that game for granted no matter what our records are. Virginia could be 0–10 and I would be apprehensive about taking them lightly. It's a rivalry game, so throw out the records. We were tied 14–14 when cornerback Antone Exum got a big interception for us.

We worked our way into scoring position in the final minutes. We just had to score points and not leave them much time on the clock to come back to beat us. I think we got lucky, because they didn't use their remaining timeouts very well in those final two minutes, allowing Cody Journell to kick the game-winning field goal with only four seconds remaining.

As the football cleared the uprights, our bowl streak was extended to 20 seasons.

In some ways, I was more proud of that team than I was of some of our 10-win teams. These guys didn't give up or get down on themselves when they were 4–6. They just kept fighting through the adversity and hung in there to win those final three games.

I know it was a disappointing season for our quarterback, Logan Thomas, but it wasn't all his fault. He had some inconsistent throws, but a lot of it went to his supporting cast. In the past we could always count on David Wilson breaking some tackles. He had rushed for 1,709 yards a season earlier, but he was not there. Our two leading receivers from a year earlier, Danny Coale and Jarrett Boykin, were gone. They had combined to catch 121 passes the season earlier.

It takes time to develop timing with new receivers. I think we also threw too much at them, coaching-wise, for some games. We couldn't get any running game going to establish our play-action. Our best lineman, center Andrew Miller, went down with a broken leg in the seventh game, against Duke. He was the leader of that offense, the glue that held it all together.

And to boot, our special teams have not been near as consistent as we want in recent years.

We had escaped Boston College and Virginia to keep our bowl streak alive, but that didn't mean I was happy with where we were as a football team.

On the Friday before the Virginia game, I met with our athletic director, Jim Weaver, and told him I planned to make some staff changes following the season. Jim has been very supportive of me and we have a great working relationship. He played football at Penn State in the 1960s and he knows the game, so I asked for his opinion. He had a good evaluation of our staff and we agreed on everything I was about to do.

On that Monday after we beat Virginia, I called the offensive staff in for a meeting and told them I needed to make some changes. There was a perception out there that was not positive and I couldn't make it go away without doing something.

I met privately with Bryan Stinespring, who had been our offensive coordinator since 2002 and on our staff for 20 years, and told him I had to make a change. One of the things Jim had brought up, and I agreed with him on this, was to try to keep Bryan here somehow. I wanted to keep him on the staff, because he is a good coach and a good recruiter, so I asked him to stay as our recruiting coordinator. He wanted to take a day to think about his options. Bryan and his family have lived in Blacksburg for a long time. He is a very loyal guy and I hated to lose him. It takes the right kind of guy to do what I was asking of him and he had to be comfortable with the move.

The next day, he told me he would accept the new position and stay on our staff.

Bryan and Shane knew their status as we headed to the bowl in Orlando to play Rutgers, but no one else on our offensive staff was sure about their future. I had told the staff I wasn't sure who I would dismiss or who I would keep, but much of it would be up to the new offensive coordinator I would hire after the bowl. I did not know who that coordinator would want to bring in with them.

Our receivers coach, Kevin Sherman, asked me if he would be one of the coaches let go and I couldn't answer him right away. He had an opportunity at Purdue and I am not sure he wanted to wait around to see if he had a future with us.

"If you want to make a decision to leave now, that would be okay, because I do not want to see you left out of a job," I told him.

> JIM WEAVER, Virginia Tech athletic director: *"Frank has said he doesn't like change—he likes continuity, but at the same time, he is a realist. He was very professional about how he went about letting people go after the 2012 season. He was very concerned for those people. He wanted to try and wait until after the bowl game, because he thought it would be easier for them to get other jobs if they were still employed here. That's how much he cares."*

I knew by the end of the season that we needed to get more physical up front and run the ball more effectively. I told the media before our bowl game in Orlando, "I think improving our running ability is going to be our first priority. Being able to run the football is always something that is important to us. When we do that, our play-action passes are always a lot better, so that is the first thing we've got to attack."

I wanted to keep a pro-set offense and improve the running game. There was no way I wanted to change to the spread like a lot of teams were doing. I just don't think a team develops the toughness on offense—or defense for that matter, since they have to play against it in practice—by running the spread all the time.

After we rallied to beat Rutgers 13–10 in overtime in the bowl in Orlando, I went to the coaches' convention in Nashville with a primary mission of finding a new offensive coordinator and filling my offensive openings.

In between meetings and interviews, I must have talked to more than 20 coaches around the country, doing my research and asking for referrals. The list of people I called or talked to in person in Nashville was a who's who in the coaching business: Florida's Will Muschamp; Georgia's Mark Richt; Bobby Bowden; Ohio State's Urban Meyer; Alabama's Nick Saban; the Seattle Seahawks' Pete Carroll; Temple's Steve Addazio; Bruce Arians, whom I've known for years and who coached the Colts while Chuck Pagano was battling cancer (Bruce then got the Arizona Cardinals' head-coaching job after our discussions); Lloyd Carr, the retired Michigan coach; and both Harbaughs—Jim and John.

Jim Harbaugh just raved about Pep Hamilton, who had worked for him at Stanford before Jim left to take the 49ers head-coaching job in 2011. Pep had worked closely with Andrew Luck and I could never forget that Stanford just kicked our butt 40–12 in the Orange Bowl a few years earlier. I was impressed by everything they did that week and in the game.

I remember during the introductory press conference that week in Miami, Jim had slipped and mentioned his team was honored to play "Georgia" Tech. When the press conference finished, I whispered to him jokingly, "I am going back to tell my team that you called them "Georgia" Tech.

He smiled and responded, "Go ahead, and I am going to go back to California and tell my team you called them 'Samford'—the small school in Alabama."

We laughed about it, but I thought then, *Now this guy is sharp.*

On Jim's recommendation, I met with Pep and he was a very impressive guy. We had a good talk, but he made it clear that he thought he had a chance at a head-coaching job somewhere, and if he didn't get one, he had some NFL opportunities ahead of him. Weeks later, he was hired as the Colts' offensive coordinator, replacing Bruce. When I heard the news, I thought, *This guy really was close to Andrew Luck.*

I talked to Urban Meyer and Lloyd Carr about Scot Loeffler, who had played at Michigan and was the offensive coordinator at Florida during Tim Tebow's senior year (2009).

Urban told me, "He is a great coach, but if you are looking for a spread guy, he's not your man. If you want to run the ball in a pro-style offense, this is your guy."

That was a good recommendation for what I wanted to do, and Lloyd couldn't have been more complimentary about Scot. He loves him. That was good enough for me. In the end, we hired Scot as offensive coordinator and quarterbacks coach and he recommended Jeff Grimes as an offensive line coach. They had worked together at Auburn and had developed a good working relationship.

I told Mike O'Cain, our quarterbacks coach, he would not be retained. Now Mike and I go back a long way, to The Citadel days. He understood it completely. He was a head coach once and he knows it is a business and sometimes you have to let people go. I also let go Curt Newsome, who had coached our offensive line since 2006.

Again, just like in earlier years, it was not easy for me. I know my decisions affect people's lives. I try to make the right decisions at the right time for the entire program.

Kevin Sherman had decided to take the job at Purdue and I had to fill the receivers' position to complete the staff. Pep had brought up Aaron Moorehead's name as a receivers coach during our interview. He had been on that staff at Stanford and everybody gave him glowing recommendations, so we hired him, too.

Those were three impressive new coaches and I was very happy with our new staff. I will turn the offense over to Scot and let him do his job, just like I did with Bryan and I have done with Bud for almost 20 years. I don't get too involved, although there were times I met with Bryan and made suggestions, such as, "We can do a little more of this, or a little less of that…."

I want our offense to look more like Alabama's and Stanford's offenses. I want to run the ball effectively and get the play-action passes working. I am optimistic about the future of this offense.

Of the new guys on staff, all of them are young and have families.

So the other thing we will do is bring back our family dinners on Tuesday nights during the season with the coaches, their wives and all their kids. We used to do it years ago but got away from it. It's just a fun thing, given how much time coaches spend away from their families during the football season.

We also will have our recruiting lunches on Saturdays where our coaches' wives and kids can be present. I think we have always promoted a family atmosphere in this program and I want it to continue.

Again, I want the Virginia Tech staff to feel like one big family. Most of all, I want this family to be successful.

19

Hitting the Links

SHANE BEAMER: "*This story may tell you more about his competitiveness than his golf game, but one day I showed up at the Georgia lake house and we played a round of golf and I beat him. I made the mistake of coming back to the house and bragging to Mom, 'Yeah Mom, I just got here from being on the road all day and I went out and whipped Dad at golf!' Well, it really ticked him off. I spent three weeks down there and he beat me 10 straight times after that first day—and he never said a word about it. It got to the point where I wished he would have just told me, 'Never rub it in again!' But he never said a word. He just hit it down the middle, never got in trouble, never made mistakes, made every putt he needed to, and beat me day after day.*"

Every major college coach in this day and age should have a hobby to relieve the pressure we face almost year-round from our jobs, or at least something to take our minds off of football for a few hours. Some coaches hunt. Some coaches fish. Some coaches hunt *and* fish.

I love to watch golf.

I love to talk about golf.

I love to read about golf.

I love to practice golf.

And I love—and I mean *love*—to play golf.

As far as my other interests, there really aren't many. I am not much of a movie guy. I think I will catch up on movies when I retire. I haven't read many books. Cheryl is the big reader in the house; she reads a book or two about every month.

I watch only snippets of NFL games, mostly because we are at the office working on Sundays, so I may see some of the Sunday night game or maybe *Monday Night Football*. I don't watch much NBA or baseball. I will watch Wimbledon and I do enjoy watching NASCAR on Sundays, mostly because I know a few of those drivers and car owners. And when we have an off weekend during the fall, there is nothing better for me than sitting down and watching all of the college games on a Saturday.

But my best days in front of the TV are watching the Masters final round on Sunday at Augusta—or watching any other major, for that matter. Heck, I even enjoy watching the LPGA, because distance-wise I am closer to their game. I am amazed at the swings I see on the LPGA Tour and I try to pick things up from them. You won't see a funky swing on the LPGA; they all have beautiful swings.

My love of golf didn't start until after college, because I didn't play much before the age of 22 or 23. I just picked up some clubs and started hitting them, really the opposite of how you should learn the game and develop fundamentals. So when I did become serious about the game later, I had to break all of my bad habits. You could say I took the long way in learning to play golf.

But once the game got into my blood, I had it for good.

I even put off—in fact, canceled—an important surgery because of my love of golf.

I appeared at a Hokie Club meeting somewhere one night and I flew home on our school airplane. I was carrying my little bag I always carry with me. As I got off the plane—the exit steps of the plane have ropes, not rails, to hold onto—the strap of my bag got caught and it turned me sideways. I reached for a rope, but it didn't hold me and I fell onto the pavement on my shoulder. The next day it turned blue as all get out. So I went to see our trainer, Mike Goforth, who looked at it and said, "Well, you sure did bruise the heck out of it."

I had our annual golfing trip to Myrtle Beach planned the next day, with John and my buddies Greg Roberts and Street. Then my arm started to turn a deeper blue and I went to get it checked further. Doctors told me I had torn the bicep loose.

"You can get this surgery to re-attach it, but you have to do it now," the doctor told me. "If you wait, we will have to use a cadaver's ligament to re-attach it, or you can choose not to have surgery at all but you will lose about 15 percent of your strength and have a deformed arm."

If I had it performed immediately, I would have to miss my golf trip.

I asked the doctor, "If I go with the surgery later, can we make sure that cadaver belonged to somebody who used to be a good golfer?"

In the end, I decided not to do anything, to go with the deformed arm and the loss of 15 percent of my strength. I was not going to miss our annual golfing trip. I would play a round, then I would ice it down. Play a round then ice it down for the entire trip. To this day, that bicep still just flops around on my arm.

I know I am fortunate that I get to play some courses other people don't get access to, such as Augusta and Pebble Beach. I have probably played each course five or six times. There is so much history on each of those courses. Every time I play them, I think about all the big shots that have been made there by all the legendary golfers.

Augusta is just all green with those beautiful white traps. You couldn't find a weed if you wanted to. Everything is so perfect there, from the food to the housing to the course. Then there is Pebble Beach, right on the Pacific Ocean.

If I had one more round of golf to play in my life, it would be a tough choice between those two courses.

For years, I always said I would like to go to Scotland to play some of the British Open courses such as Saint Andrews, just for the history and all that. But why would I want to go over there and take an average golf game and test it in the wind, the rain, and the cold and act like I'm enjoying it?

I figured it would probably never happen. And I really had no desire ever to go to Europe, other than to play golf. I never wanted to see Paris or Rome or any of those places.

Then we were at an auction for charity one night recently when my friend John McConnell, a Virginia Tech graduate, was bidding on a golfing trip for four people to Scotland.

He asked me, "If I win this trip, I want to take my son. Will you and Shane go with us?"

I thought of my game in that wind and rain on those courses, wanting to tell John thanks but no thanks. But in my moment of weakness, a "yes" came out of my mouth. Sure enough, he won the trip that night and we played a beautiful course at Crail, then the Old Course at Saint Andrews and also Carnoustie in May of 2013.

Another great thing about living in Virginia: I don't need to travel far to play a great golf course. Within a two-hour radius of Blacksburg are several of the best courses in the country. The Virginian and the Olde Farm in Bristol are great courses. The Homestead in Hot Springs has three courses and the Greenbrier has three courses. Just off the Blue Ridge Parkway is Primland, built on a mountain which overlooks North Carolina. Ballyhack in Roanoke is a destination course and Roanoke Country Club is a very nice course. And my friend John McConnell owns about eight beautiful country club courses throughout North Carolina and South Carolina.

When I am home, I love to play the Blacksburg Country Club, which I can reach in a minute by driving the golf cart out of my garage.

Somebody once asked me when I am happiest on a golf course. That's easy—on the first hole. When I examine my scorecard coming off the 18th, I'm not always so happy.

How's my game? I guess you would call me steady.

I've been to Jim McLean's Golf School at Doral Country Club in Florida, and I take plenty of lessons here with the pro at the Blacksburg Country Club, Brad Ewing. I pick up all the golf magazines and read the tips that supposedly can make my game better. Despite all that, there is not much I can do about how far I hit the ball. I don't hit it a mile like the younger guys. I just try to be consistent and steady. I can generally keep the ball in play and not beat myself with double-bogies. I can usually shoot in the low-to-mid 80s and I have had a few rounds in the 70s.

In 2007, they started a two-man scramble tournament in Atlanta sponsored by Chick-fil-A for college head coaches. We were allowed to partner up with a past athlete from our respective universities. John told me right away to get Dell Curry, who was a great basketball player at Tech in the 1980s. I had never played with Dell before, but John said, "Do you want to win the thing? Then get Dell Curry."

So I did. And we won the inaugural tournament. Dell just crushed the ball all day and he was fun to play with. We donated the $100,000 prize to the Hokie fund to benefit victims of the April 16 shooting.

Steve Spurrier had played with the singer Darius Rucker, who's a South Carolina grad, in that first tournament. The next year, Spurrier showed up with Sterling Sharpe, the great receiver who I can still see in those silky, black warm-ups back in 1987, and they won the tournament. Then they won it again in 2009.

Later, I played a round with Darius at Ballyhack and he told me, "Yeah, I had a good time in that tournament, but I will never see that thing again because Steve found Sterling Sharpe."

Darius is a great guy. We had him sing the national anthem before one of our games at Lane Stadium in 2012.

The tournament became such a big deal, now every coach has his horse. Paul Johnson at Georgia Tech got Jon Barry, the former NBA basketball player who just hits it a mile. They have won the last few tournaments.

When I spoke at one of those Success seminars, I met Donald Trump in the green room. He was speaking that day, too. We got to talking about golf and he told me, "You should come on down and play my course in Palm Beach, Florida…."

I thought, *Now, did he say that in passing or did he really mean it?*

He probably didn't know what a golf addict I was when he made the offer, but the golf bug in me told me to call him on it. So when my buddies and I happened to be in South Florida the next time, I called him.

"Come on over," he said. "You'll love this course."

And we did. It was beautiful. Mr. Trump greeted us at the course and we had a great time.

I do practice and work on my game, so I don't embarrass myself because I do get to play in front of a gallery once in a while. In the summer of 2012, I played in the pro-am at the Greenbrier Classic up the road from us in White Sulphur Springs, West Virginia. It was one of the best days I ever had on the golf course, because I was paired with Phil Mickelson, the governor of Kentucky, and the manager of the Greenbrier.

I always followed Phil on the PGA Tour and I could tell right away he is one of the nice guys. There was a big gallery following us and Tiger played right behind us, so there were two massive galleries on back-to-back holes as we worked our way around the course. Phil couldn't have been nicer to everybody he came in contact with. He went out of his way to be cordial to us and he was great with the galleries.

The one thing I've never been real good at is chipping and on about the seventh hole, he showed me this technique where he keeps the club close to his body and hits the ball with the toe of the club. Soon after that lesson, my ball was just off the green a little and Phil told me, "Now this is the perfect time to try it."

I knocked it up there within about two feet and got a good round of applause. Then I missed the putt and got a large groan. I saved my best for last. On our ninth hole, which is really the 18th hole of the course since we had a shotgun start, a par-3 where there was a huge gallery, I hit it on the green and two-putted for par.

Playing with the pros like Phil, I really noticed just how much farther they hit it. I would walk to my ball and then watch them keep on walking to their ball down the fairway. They usually get up and down and they putt so well. Seeing it up close really drove it home more than watching it on TV.

Recently, I was at the LPGA tournament in Williamsburg when Natalie Gulbis' caddy approached me.

"I went to Virginia Tech and I love the Hokies," he told me. "Would you like to meet Natalie?"

Now Natalie always has been one of my favorite golfers to watch, so I jumped at the chance. She was somewhere else getting ready for her round, and as I waited, I saw that Annika Sorenstam was about to tee off so I walked down to watch her. Then a TV guy from Richmond grabbed me to do a short interview, just as Natalie walked up to introduce herself. She signed a picture and gave it to me and couldn't have been nicer.

When I turned around, I noticed the TV guy was still filming me, so I looked into the camera and said, "Happens to me all the time... good-lookin' women always come over to me."

Another one of my special moments in golf was playing one hole with Gary Player, Jack Nicklaus, and Arnold Palmer at the "Big 3 for Mountain Mission Kids" in the summer of 2010. It turned into the single largest fundraising day in PGA Tour history, raising more than $15.1 million at the Olde Farm club.

I talked with Nicklaus during that hole, because he had a grandson who was a tight end who was being recruited at the time. (Nick O'Leary signed with Florida State the following year.) Jack really loves college football. We played a par-3—the 16th—and that experience was over pretty quickly.

I've had my share of fun on the golf course over the years, getting away from the pressure of football, but it wasn't always that way.

I remember one day when Ralph Friedgen and I coached at The Citadel back in the '70s, we played a round with our equipment manager, a guy by the name of Paul Martin. Paul was a wise, older retired military man.

Ralph and I were having a miserable day, throwing our clubs and cussing.

We got to the 16th hole and Paul said to us, "I don't mean to tell you guys how to act, but you already take one game very seriously. You ought to come out here and have some fun no matter how you are playing."

The more I thought about what he said, the more I knew he was right. That made sense to me. From that moment on, I don't think I've thrown a club once or swore much at all, at least not loud enough for my partners to hear me. I think Ralph changed his behavior that day, too.

One thing that might get me to grumbling is slow play. All of my golfing buddies hate slow play. It just drives me nuts to hit and wait, hit and wait. So one day at Myrtle Beach, we were all getting frustrated with the pace of play. We drove our carts up to a tee-box at a par-3 hole and saw three groups waiting to tee off and another group near the green. We were just about to quit and head back to the beach when the marshal drove up in his cart.

"Sorry, guys, a bear and her cubs are holding up play," he said.

Sure enough, there was a big bear meandering across the green, playing through.

We played a few more holes before we spotted a rattlesnake.

Street and I sat in the cart a safe distance away, while Greg was over there messing with the rattlesnake with one of his clubs. We saw these groundskeepers working in a sand trap and they were dangerously close to this rattlesnake, so we tried to warn them. When we teed off, we noticed the workers hiding behind trees, trying not to get hit by our tee-shots. Our Spanish must not have been too good, because they figured we were trying to warn them to take cover.

Not that our group hits it down the middle each time.

We were on the second hole at Rivers Edge at Shallotte, North Carolina, one time and the course pro, Bruce Harper, drove up in his cart.

"Can I play one hole with you guys?" he asked.

Street hit his tee-shot into the left bunker. I knocked mine into the woods to the right. John hit his way to the left. Then Greg dribbled one off the tee. John headed up to locate his ball just as Greg hit his second shot. Greg hit a low liner right at John, who jumped up to try to avoid it. The ball hit him squarely in the bottom of the foot and broke a bone. (He finished that round riding with his foot in an ice bucket.)

We were just all over the place on that hole. We finally got up to the green and I think we each three-putted to finish the hole. I turned to Bruce and asked him, "How do you like our game so far?"

We all broke up laughing.

We were down at Jim McLean's in Miami one time when we spent one entire day with nothing but golf. We took lessons for about four hours in the morning, then we played a round at Doral that afternoon. It was in the middle of the summer and as hot and humid as you can imagine. We were soaked through our shirts and I think Greg's hands were bleeding by the end of the round. He was tired. John was tired. Everybody was tired…except me.

I told John, "Come on, I'm going to teach you how to draw the ball."

He didn't want any part of it, but we headed to the range anyway, where they have those covered tee-boxes. We stood elevated from the range a little bit. I took my shaving kit and placed it down just outside his ball. I wanted to prove to him that he could hit a draw.

"Don't worry, you won't hit it," I told him. "Just swing inside out and you'll get a nice draw out of the ball."

He reared back and swung and there went my shaving kit, flying into the air. At that very moment, I realized I had placed my eyeglasses in it.

"My glasses!" I screamed.

"I told you I would hit it!" John yelled.

The guys get a little perturbed at me at times because I hate to miss a round of golf. If we have the opportunity, I want to play. John loves to tell the story of all of us sitting in golf carts in the middle of a round at Myrtle Beach one day, while it is lightning and pouring rain. He tells the story as if the water was flooding the golf carts and they are lifting their feet up to keep their spikes dry while Noah's Ark is on its way.

As the story goes, I look at the sky and say…

"I think it's clearing up."

And all three of them fall out of their golf carts laughing at me. At least that's the way John always tells the story and he swears it's true, but I don't remember it. I probably did say it though.

They also know I will play through injury. My left knee had just been killing me for a few years and I can pinpoint exactly when I hurt it, too.

In my junior year during the '67 season, we were in a punt return and Frankie Loria was deep. I was one of the two guys aligned about 10 yards in front of him, to the side, along with Ron Davidson. The other team kicked a punt short and I blocked a guy, but got twisted up in the pile and couldn't get my leg out of there to free my knee. I got up and started walking toward the sideline and I knew it wasn't right. I figured I tore it a little bit, and over the next 40 years or so, it continued to get worse.

It never stopped me from playing golf, though. I just limped around the courses as it got worse. We were down at Myrtle Beach one time and as I hit a bucket of balls on the range, which was full of other golfers doing the same thing, I would limp back and forth to my golf bag to change clubs. John and Greg sat in a golf cart watching me, when some guy pulled up in his cart and asked, "I hear the Virginia Tech football coach is out here. Which one is he?"

Greg smartly replied, "He's the one up there with the bad gait!"

They both got a kick out of that one.

Cheryl and I were down at the lake house in Georgia just for a few days after recruiting season in 2008 and we decided to walk nine holes one day. I almost didn't make it back to the clubhouse. The pain was terrible and I told her, *Enough is enough. I need surgery.*

A month later, I got my knee replaced. I always heard people say that if I got my knee replaced, I would wonder why you didn't do it sooner. The first week I couldn't say that and the second week I couldn't say that. The rehab was terrible and I couldn't get around much. It took about eight weeks for it to start feeling better.

That is when I was stuck at home on pain pills and we held conference calls with the assistant coaches in the office. One day, they called me and put me on the speakerphone, just as I was feeling pretty good.

I told them, "Guys, you will have to call back later—*The Price Is Right* is on TV right now!"

And I hung up the phone. I don't remember it, but they have reminded me about it ever since, so it must have happened. I was stuck at home and couldn't walk, so I was becoming addicted to TV game shows.

Now that I have my new knee and I have managed to deal with my right bicep flopping around and deformed, I can play a round mostly pain-free.

One thing left on my golf bucket list: I would like a hole-in-one. I've never had one.

Right after I was hired at Virginia Tech, I played in a tournament at Ford's Colony in Williamsburg. They were offering a new green BMW to anyone who had a hole-in-one on this certain par-3.

I hit my tee-shot and I knew it was right on line. Then I saw these ladies next to the green jumping up and down. For a brief moment, I could picture myself driving that green BMW home from the tournament. I walked up to the green and to my disappointment my ball had stopped about two feet behind the cup. I looked over to the ladies and one of them held her fingers about an inch apart. That was the distance by which my ball missed rolling into the hole.

I know one thing: if it had rolled in, I would still be driving that green BMW today, all these years later.

There is another reason I love the game of golf and this may be the most important one. I always claimed I could tell a person's character by the way he conducted himself on the golf course. Is he honest?

Does he have the right temperament? Does he throw his clubs or cheat? How does he handle disappointment? How does he handle success? All of these things come out on the golf course.

It really is a game of honor, the only game in which you call a penalty on yourself if you break a rule.

Can you imagine doing that in the game of football?

"Ah, ref, I think our guy held the defensive end on that play. Could you penalize us 10 yards?"

It doesn't work that way, of course, but it does in golf—if a man is honest.

In January of 2013, NASCAR's Rick Hendrick, owner of Hendrick Motorsports, asked me to address his team operation in Concord, North Carolina. I was honored to do it and here is what I told his employees that day, and much of it related to the game of golf:

> *There are certain qualities I look for in a coach, a player, and a friend. It is my belief that every successful program must have a group of individuals with certain characteristics and with a common goal in order to have success. Before I get into those characteristics of the individuals, I want you to leave here today with at least one thought on your mind. If you do not take anything away from listening to me today, I want you to take this with you: one-point-six.*
>
> *Whether it is in ounces or whether it is in inches, 1.6 can define each of us. I want you to remember 1.6. I have been fortunate to surround myself with some outstanding individuals over the years both on and off the field. Each of them has taught me a little something about myself as well as given me the opportunity to find success. I have determined that there are seven qualities I look for in individuals which can make a program*

successful. With each of these, I have been fortunate to have a person impact me in a way that defines these qualities.

The seven characteristics are: loyalty, patience, concentration, handle adversity, handle success, competitiveness, and honesty.

Although I will talk about what each of these mean to me, do not forget the 1.6.

1. Loyalty: I begin each season with a staff meeting of our entire organization. The first item I cover is loyalty. This is what I tell my staff: "I hold loyalty in the highest regard, especially between staff members. Loyalty is a quality that is hard to find. It is earned and can be destroyed with one conversation, one email, one tweet, one Facebook post."

How many of you know the name Jack "Chappie" Blackburn? Not many I bet. But Chappie was one loyal man. He was a corner man for probably the greatest boxer of all time, Joe Louis. In boxing, when things go bad, where do they look? To the corner. Now we know the name Joe Louis and probably have never heard of Chappie Blackburn. My point is this: you need to have a corner man or woman in your life. The most important quality: loyalty. I have been blessed to have a corner woman for over 30 years. Someone I can go to and lay it on the line. Spill my guts to. Cry when I am sad, laugh when I am happy, and get advice whether I need it or not. But, the one thing I can count on is her loyalty. Find yourself a corner man. Find yourself a Chappie Blackburn, or find yourself a Cheryl Beamer.

I promise you, my wife shoots it straight and we all need that. Before I went on this recent diet, we were headed to some function and we were getting dressed. I jumped out of the shower and she was putting on her makeup. I stood in front of the mirror, drying off, and I had been putting on some weight. I didn't like it. So I told her, "Wow…I look old, I am ugly and I am fat." There was a pause and I said, "Cheryl, I really need you to pay me a compliment right now…and she says, "Well, your eyesight's damn-near perfect!"

2. Patience: We live in a society of instant gratification. Our ever-changing world of Twitter, email, texting, and so forth is causing all of us to become less patient. How many of you can go the next 30 minutes without checking your phone? And if you do go the next 30 minutes without checking, I am betting it will be the first thing you check as you head off to the restroom. Whether we are on our smartphones, computers, or at casinos, we are a culture that is driven for our need of instant gratification. We want—no, we demand everything right now. Once a virtue, patience has become as rare as handwritten letters.

With that in mind, I had our team write thank-you letters throughout the season to someone who has helped them throughout their career. Just the few minutes to sit down and think about it and write it down on a piece of paper was not only for them to show thoughtfulness, but to show patience as well.

Your profession and my profession are very similar: They are performance based. People do not want to be patient. They want results and they want them now. I can honestly tell you that I would not be the head coach at Virginia Tech today if the results of my first few years had happened in today's world. But what I learned is that those around me showed patience and now we are only one of three teams in college football to go to 20 straight bowls since that time.

I was severely burned at my home when I was seven years old. I had over 30 surgeries in three years. Each summer while others my age were out playing baseball, I was in the hospital. There was one person I could count on to be there and she was patient all the time during the time of my injury. My mother was a school teacher and took control of every situation. In her classroom, you knew who was in charge. She was demanding, yet she was patient. The time she took to help me through my surgeries as well as take care of my brother and sisters showed not only love, but patience. When I did start feeling sorry for myself, my mother would make me walk the halls of the hospital and visit those who were less fortunate than me. She would tell me to be thankful for what I have and show patience. I encourage each of you to be demanding, but show patience.

3. Concentration: I want to tell you a story about concentration. I had an opportunity to drive a stock car at Bristol. Let me tell you, I was dialed in with total concentration. Probably the best athlete I had that exemplifies concentration was Michael Vick. No matter how big the stage, Michael was always able to concentrate on the next play. He never looked at the end result. He looked at what would get him there: the next play. No matter how big the game, the only thing you can control is the next play. That is what I tell my players. No matter how big it is, the only thing you can control is the next play. The bigger things get, make them seem small.

4. Handle Adversity: Our team chaplain says the following: You are either getting into a storm, you are in a storm, or you are getting out of a storm. I tell people to prepare each day for something bad to happen, because it is going to happen. The question is: How will you react? We will all face adversity in our lives, so prepare for it. It is going to happen, but how we respond is what makes us.

5. Handle Success: Cornell Brown is an assistant coach on my staff. He has won the following awards as both a player and a coach: national Defensive Player of the Year, a Big East Championship, an ACC Championship, an NFL Europe

Championship, a Grey Cup Championship, and a Super Bowl as a member of the 2000 Baltimore Ravens. I can tell you Cornell knows how to handle success. Following his senior season, Cornell went to play for the Ravens. After a few years with the team he became a free agent and signed with the Oakland Raiders, but the Raiders soon cut Cornell.

What did he do? He returned to Tech, earned his master's degree, and the general manager of the Ravens re-signed him because of his academic efforts. From there, he went on to win the Super Bowl. Last week Cornell was inducted into the Virginia Sports Hall of Fame. Upon his induction, Cornell said, "Being able to play in the NFL was a dream come true, but the biggest thing is to see the success and where we are today at Virginia Tech." Cornell knows how to handle success.

6. Competitiveness: On September 9, 1991, we were getting ready to play a junior-varsity game. Most of our players had no interest in lining up against Fork Union Military Academy. We had one player who was not scheduled to play and was not even on the JV roster for that game. In an effort to get a look at him, we encouraged him to play in the game. He played and we noticed. He had six catches for more than 200 yards and two touchdowns that day. Following that JV game, he was quickly promoted to varsity where he became one of our all-time great receivers. Then he went on to the NFL, where he was the main target of Brett Favre with the Green Bay Packers. Of course, I'm talking about Antonio Freeman. He went on to win a Super Bowl, and that competitive desire that we saw on that day with about 15 people in the stands is the same desire that drove him to all that success.

You never know when or where it is going to happen, but a person with the competitive spirit is going to show up—whether it's a JV game, the Super Bowl, or in the Daytona 500. I like to have people around me who compete. I know there are a lot of talented, competitive people in this room, so be prepared, you never know when your opportunity will come. Take advantage of it when it does, just like Antonio Freeman did.

7. Honesty: I really enjoy the opportunity to play golf. In my free time it is probably one of the most enjoyable things I am able to do. With that in mind, it brings me to Blayne Barber. Recently, Barber was competing in qualifying school in order to make the PGA Tour. "Q school" is a series of tournaments which golfers compete in order to gain a PGA card. During the tournament in Pine Mountain, Georgia, his ball was in a sand trap on the 13th hole and he played it out. Barber was not sure if he'd brushed a leaf in the trap. His caddy had insisted there was no movement. But to be on the safe side, he penalized himself a stroke. Problem was, the penalty for such an infraction is two strokes—not one. Because his caddy insisted that there was no movement, he continued playing the final two rounds. But his conscience would not let it go. Six days after the tournament ended, Barber called the PGA tour and submitted his disqualification, because he had signed an incorrect scorecard. There is one sad irony: Barber was five strokes ahead of the cut line so even if he had added the penalty, it would not have hurt him. He would have qualified for the PGA Tour.

"I feel peace about it," Barber said. "Doing the right thing and doing what I know is right in my heart and in my conscience is more important than short-term success."

How about that? Would you like somebody like Blayne Barber on your team? You are doggone right you would. What I would say is do not let short-term success affect decisions you *make. Something tells me we'll never see Blayne on Oprah's couch coming clean after years of lies.*

You heard me mention 1.6 today. Blayne Barber knows what 1.6 is. It's the weight of a golf ball in ounces and its size in diameter. That little golf ball—and how we act when we're around it—tells us so much. How will you handle adversity? Will you cheat? Will you lie? Are you trustworthy? Will you maintain character in defeat? Will you be a gracious and respectful winner?

I look around this room, and it feels just like my team. We all have a role. You wouldn't be here if you weren't talented. Take pride in what you do, every time—every time!—when you do it. You never know who's watching, and I promise you, somebody is always watching. And it just might change your life, like it did in that JV game for Antonio Freeman. But more importantly, it's critical to the overall success of this team.

I am serious about the ethics issue when playing golf. I always believed that guys who used the so-called "foot wedge" to improve their lie, or purposely marked their ball incorrectly for an advantage, would get paid back by bad karma by the time their round was finished. You can't cheat the gods of golf.

I guess I'm a little superstitious about it, too. That's no different to how I approach the game of football, either. Baseball players are the guys known for their superstitions, but I have my share.

For years, our equipment manager, Lester Karlin, has placed two packs of gum inside my left shoe at my locker before I get dressed for every game we play. It must be spearmint, too. I really don't know remember how it started, but I've gone along with it and I'm not going to tell him to stop now. I never liked the way coaches looked chomping their gum on the sidelines, so I keep those two packs to chew during the week.

And if we are on a winning streak, I stick to the same routine during the week. We eat the same food at training table and sit in the same spot before games. I will wear the same suit when we travel, if it becomes a winning suit.

It was fun to talk to the Hendrick guys, because I admire them so much, and after a few of my driving exploits at those celebrity events, I really respect what they do. They are among the toughest and strongest guys in sports these days with the demands put on them in a race car. I think there were about 600 people in the audience and I hope my little speech made sense to them. I believe a racing team is much like a football team. It takes so many people to do their jobs the right way to give the entire team a chance at success.

> **KASEY KAHNE:** *"It was great to listen to Coach Beamer because of what he has done in football. I have been to some Tech games and watched them on TV plenty of times as well. It's impressive what he has done, and to listen to someone like that who brings a lot of experience and things to the table, everybody was pretty motivated and excited when it was all over."*

My admiration for Rick goes back years. Jeff Motley, a Virginia Tech graduate who is the communications director at Las Vegas Motor Speedway, invited me to a race back in 2001, and I brought Shane, John, and Greg with me. They flew a helicopter to the Luxor to pick us up. I remember it was just a few weeks after Dale Earnhardt lost his life at Daytona. We listened from the back of the room that day during the drivers' pre-race meeting as Teresa Earnhardt thanked all the drivers for their support.

Brian Whitesell, another Virginia Tech alum, was Jeff Gordon's crew chief at the time and we happened to talk to his wife, Mary, down in the pits before the race. She told us, "We have a good car today, so if we win the race, y'all come down to victory lane and celebrate with us."

We rode in the pace car before the race and then headed upstairs to a suite to watch it.

With 20 laps remaining, Jeff was winning the race, when Shane asked me, "Are you going to the pits?"

"No, I'll just stay up here and relax," I told him.

I had my bad knee back then and I didn't want to fight that mob scene running down there after the race.

Ten laps later, Jeff still was in the lead.

"You sure?" Shane asked again.

I told him no again, but he and Greg left the suite to head down there anyway.

I got to thinking about it. How many chances do you get to celebrate in victory lane with a NASCAR winner? So John and I headed down to the pits. Sure enough, Jeff won the race. The four of us took off running along pit lane, well, I was hobbling, and we arrived just as Jeff pulled the car into victory lane. Greg leaned in Jeff's car, taking pictures of him with this little portable camera, blocking the Fox Sports camera guy who was trying to show Jeff inside the car to a live national television audience.

The guys were having their pictures taken with these Las Vegas showgirls and high-fiving members of Jeff's crew. I also had my picture taken with Jeff on the podium.

It was just about the perfect day. When the excitement died down, we sat there exhausted.

I looked at the guys and asked, "Well boys, what more can we do today?"

We climbed into a courtesy van for our ride to the helicopter pad. Before we could get there, a Coors delivery truck had stopped in front of us. All of a sudden, the back doors flew open and the truck driver dumped ice and cans of Coors beer onto the ground. The guys grabbed a few cold ones, got back into the van just as a car pulled up next to us. It was filled with the Las Vegas showgirls, who smiled and waved to us.

I smiled and said, "This is as good as it gets."

It was as if we were living in one of those beer commercials on TV.

Anybody can play golf and relate to the professional golfers on some level, but few people ever get the chance to race a heavy stock car around a track like Charlotte or Bristol or Talladega. I've been in a few of those celebrity events and let me tell you, that is one of the toughest things I ever tried to do.

A few years ago, they convinced me to drive in this 15-lap celebrity race at Bristol, Tennessee. That's a smaller oval, a little over half a mile in length, where drivers are always turning and fighting the car. They invited Lane Kiffin, then the coach at Tennessee, and they had built this thing up as "Virginia Tech versus Tennessee." Others in the field were Mike Compton, who played for West Virginia and then for the Detroit Lions; Terry Bowden, who was coaching North Alabama at the time; and David Akers, the kicker who played with the 49ers in a recent Super Bowl.

As I walked through the pits wearing my firesuit, Jimmie Johnson noticed me.

"What are you doing?" he asked. "You are not getting in a race car, are you?"

We were using those Richard Petty School cars and I couldn't move the seat up or back in those cars. I took about 15 practice laps real slow, because I couldn't reach the clutch with my short legs. I told them, "Hey, I am really uncomfortable in here. I can't even reach the clutch."

"Don't worry about it," the race organizer told me, "When you come back from lunch, we'll have a piece of wood there, so you'll be able to reach the clutch."

We went to lunch and came back and there was no piece of wood. Right then I should have backed out. I looked around and didn't see Terry Bowden.

"Where's Terry?" I asked.

"Well," they told me, "we had a lot of trouble getting him through that driver's side window this morning. Then he went and had lunch and now we really can't get him in the car."

I said, "Is that the truth, or is he like me, and wants the hell out of this race?"

I couldn't get out of it, so I thought of the next best thing: I went around to all the drivers before the race, pleading for them to take it easy once the race started.

"Look guys," I said, "we don't want to be out there running into each other, so let's all stay at the bottom of the track and if you want to pass, go around on the outside. That way we won't wreck."

They all basically said the heck with that, they wanted to race.

"Okay, but I will tell you where I am going to be—right at the bottom of the track," I said. "Don't run over me."

Right before the race, the race organizers told me Lane's wife wouldn't let him in the car, because it was too dangerous. The strange thing for me was that Cheryl was pushing me to do it.

I started right behind Akers. I was trying my best not to run into a wall, and I was in my own little world, focusing on staying low, but I noticed cars going by me on the outside. That was real work on a little track like Bristol. The cars were close to me and I was constantly working the steering wheel. Anyway, I survived the race and climbed out of the car just as my daughter, Casey, walked up to me.

"Casey, did they all pass me?" I asked.

"I don't know if everybody passed you, but that Akers guy passed you *twice!*" she answered.

Akers won the race easily. I always liked watching NASCAR anyway, but once I got to drive like that, I had a newfound respect for those guys. And I've gotten to know Jimmie, Dale Earnhardt Jr., Jeff Gordon, Elliott Sadler, Denny Hamlin, Ward, and Jeff Burton. Denny's crew chief, Darian Grubb, is also a Hokie. They are all good guys and we have hosted many of them with sideline passes during our games.

There was another time where I actually did jump out of the race car and refuse to race. Steve Johnson, who played here for us in the 1980s and who employed Casey at the time, owned a Porsche that he drove in those sports-car races such as the 24 Hours of Daytona. One time he invited us come down to Danville to have some fun racing his Porsche.

It was July and hot as heck. This was when I weighed more than I do now and I had some trouble getting through that window, just like Terry Bowden did. We ran a few laps in the morning and then Steve hosted us for a nice lunch. I put my helmet on and I climbed back in that car, when suddenly, something came over me. I was out of breath.

I screamed, "Get me out of here! I can't breathe!"

The guy helping me said, "No, no. You get going down that straight-away and you will get your breath back."

"To hell with that!" I told him. "I am getting out of this car!"

And I did.

I soon got my breath—and my courage—back and climbed back in the car to go racing again.

I guess I wasn't cut out to be a race-car driver.

But golf?

No fear there.

Give me a sunny day, or even a drizzly one, a good golf course, and a few of my buddies, and I am good to go.

20

College Football: The Game I Love

Almost everyone who has a job enjoys a certain special moment each week, or at least should have one.

For some, it may be the moment they punch the time clock on a Friday afternoon and head home to their families. For others, it's the moment the airplane lifts its wheels off the ground to begin a business trip. Or the moment that paycheck touches their hands.

For me, it comes when I leave our locker room on a Saturday afternoon or evening, exactly seven minutes before kickoff for a home game in Lane Stadium.

I then walk the 300 feet to the tunnel that enters the stadium, with my team close behind me. The clatter of the players' cleats tapping the pavement with each step is a one-of-a-kind sound. It has a rhythm that doesn't end, until we reach the exit of the tunnel. We all reach up and touch the Hokie Stone. To the left, it reads: "For those who have passed, for those to come…reach for excellence."

That is where we stop and pause for a moment, listening to Metallica's "Enter Sandman" blasting through the air. We can see the sellout crowd of 66,233 fans—I am proud to say we've had 93 consecutive sellouts through the 2012 season—jumping up and down, anticipating our entrance. Behind me, one player is holding an American flag, another holds a state of Virginia flag and a third carries our Hokie spirit flag.

This is *my* special moment.

At that moment, with a football game about to kick off and an entire university and community coming together at one point in time, my life couldn't get any better. And it never gets old. In fact, our team entrance at Lane Stadium recently was voted the best in college football by *Bleacher Report*.

It would definitely get my vote, but I am sure many other coaches feel the same way. That's the way it is all across the country on any given Saturday.

From Bevo leading my friend Mack and his Texas team onto the field, to Clemson touching its rock and running down a hill, to Florida State and that giant horse I am so familiar with, to Colorado and its buffalo storming the field, there are dozens of traditions that make our game so great.

I've always said that college football is the best game going. The tradition makes it that way. The alumni and students come together for one day each week, pulling for the same cause. I wouldn't attend an NFL game these days even if I had the time, unless it was to watch one of our former players, but I can sit around and watch college football all day on a Saturday whenever we have an off weekend.

That being said, I want to address all the issues our game faces. There are always issues, some serious and some not-so serious, in amateur athletics. College football is no different.

Such as the salaries head coaches are paid today. I have read and heard all the criticism as they have escalated since the early 1990s with the increase in TV and bowl revenue—and I am one of the many guys benefiting from it.

I have always joked that Cheryl could tell you all of my starting salaries from my past jobs.

To think that I started out making $150 per month at Maryland and now make something north of $2.4 million per year, that sometimes boggles my mind. There are a lot of coaches who make less than me, and at last count, about 30 Football Bowl Subdivision coaches who make more annually. Some coaches in college football are now making more than $5 million. I would never complain about the money I make and I won't do it here.

I realize how fortunate I am.

I can honestly say that our lifestyle hasn't changed a whole lot. I know the value of a dollar. As a kid, I milked cows and sold the milk for money. I baled hay in the hot sun. I started my career making $10,600 as a teacher and coach at Radford and left that job to take that large pay cut to become a graduate assistant at Maryland.

Now, some people would think I was crazy for making that move.

That goes back to a philosophy I had from the beginning, with the help of Coach Claiborne's advice. When I started out, he told me to never let money be the determining factor of whether I would take a job or not take a job. And I haven't. I always thought that the money would take care of itself if I did a good job.

That being said, I always have had an appreciation of Virginia Tech for staying with me after we went 2–8–1 in 1992. I never wanted to hold the school up for more money during contract negotiations, because they could have fired me way back then and they didn't. They also have given me a contract now which states that for eight years after I retire, I will be a consultant to the athletic director for $250,000 annually. I will do some fund-raising and give speeches and things like that. Right there's an extra $2 million they will pay me after I retire.

People say, "But Frank, you're the longest-tenured coach in college and you have more career wins than so-and-so…."

But when I consider the big picture and all the things that have happened and how they have been good to me over the years, I don't really care if 25 coaches, or 30 coaches, or 50 coaches for that matter, make more money than I do.

The way I look at it, I know I make good money and Jim Weaver and President Steger have always treated me fairly. Part of that, too, is the fact that I have always wanted to have a competitive staff and make sure their salaries were competitive with the schools we are competing against. If that means me sacrificing money so the assistants can be compensated fairly, I am all for that.

Following the 2010 season in which I hired Shane, I also hired Cornell Brown, who had been a graduate assistant here and also coached in the Canadian league. He was about to interview at North Carolina for a full-time position. I didn't want our All-American, one of the most important recruits and players we ever had here, to be coaching at North Carolina, so we hired him.

With Shane and Cornell on staff, I also wanted to find a way to keep longtime assistants Billy Hite and Jim Cavanaugh around. They are two veteran coaches and I trust their judgment and knowledge.

I didn't want their salaries to be cut either, so to make it work I volunteered some of my salary to compensate theirs. That way, they wouldn't sustain a drop in income, because they were being re-assigned.

The bottom line is this: I realize where I came from and how fortunate I am now. I want to value my relationships with people over the almighty dollar.

It's funny, because I believe how you grow up goes a long way toward how you act as you grow older. There were times when I finished eating in a restaurant with my mom and I may have left a $10 tip. By the time we got back to the car, she would be handing me $5, saying I tipped too much. Let me tell you, Mom knew the value of a dollar. But since I've had some money, I have always believed that people who work hard and do a nice job deserve it. I will tip waitresses who do a good job and hotel maids who don't make much money very well.

There are two sides to these so-called big salaries that coaches make nowadays.

We all know that the more they pay a coach, the quicker they expect results.

College football is not like the NFL, where everybody has good players and there is a small difference between the good teams and the bad teams. In the NFL, you can make a coaching change and add a couple of free agents and a few good draft picks and all of a sudden, you have a much better team.

In college football, it doesn't change as quickly.

It takes longer to rebuild a program the right way. And let's be honest, the market drives these coaching salaries. Texas probably wouldn't pay Mack Brown $5 million per year if there wasn't another school that would hire him and would pay him that much.

I've heard coaches ask, "Is all the stuff we put up with worth the money we make?"

As I stated earlier, the criticism is instant nowadays with the Internet. People talk about you on the Internet, whether it is fact-based or not. Then if one person says it, it is taken as fact and repeated. I really believe the business is tougher on coaches than it ever used to be. I can still picture little Casey answering the phone at home when she was 11 after the loss at Louisville in 1992.

If a plumber or electrician did a poor job at work that day, people are not calling him to cuss out his kids.

And I think there have been some unjust firings, too. My buddy Ralph Friedgen should not have been fired from Maryland after the 2010 season. I know they needed to sell more tickets to home games, but Ralph did a good job there and won a lot of ballgames. His dismissal after being named ACC Coach of the Year and a 9–4 season shows just how brutal this business is. That was his alma mater and he won 75 games there in 10 seasons.

The critics of college athletics will tell you coaches aren't worth the money they are paid, but those numbers are being driven by the money coming from television.

When it comes to this issue of whether to pay money to college football players, most college football coaches have to be for it, on the record. The reality of it is, players get a college education and there is a certain amount of value to that. They get tutoring and there is more value in that. They get benefits from the university. They get access to a training table with good food and nutrition. They also can apply for and receive Pell Grants, based on their family's income.

I think we have a very good system, but I hear the arguments from people who point to the millions of dollars being made from TV and the bowls. I realize all of that and those are good arguments, but there is more to it than that. If that money potentially paid to college football players would come from the athletic department, which it would, then how do they pay all of the men's athletes and women's athletes in other sports? There are non-revenue sports which are not on TV, nor do they produce bowl money. How would it be funded?

The issue of bowls versus playoffs has been a hot-button topic for several years, but it has really heated up in recent years. I think the Bowl Championship Series, despite its critics, has been wonderful for college football. Now we are headed to a four-team playoff, beginning in 2014. I have to admit I am looking forward to seeing if it works. I think it will—and I am hoping we will be a part of it someday soon.

I have always been a big bowl guy. Bowls are unique in the landscape of all sports. It is a great thing to take our team to a city for a week and our fans can spend three or four days with us. Everybody seems to have a good time and it is certainly a reward for our players for a long, grueling season of hard work. I have learned that we had better win that bowl, too, because it is a long off-season when we don't. We always have a lot of alumni functions during the off-season and it is much easier facing my own fan base coming off a bowl win.

That being said, what changed my thinking about a playoff system a little was our meeting with Auburn in the Sugar Bowl following the 2004 season. Auburn was undefeated at 12–0 and ranked No. 3, behind No. 1 USC and No. 2 Oklahoma, who also were undefeated and meeting in the Orange Bowl for the BCS national championship.

After losing to Auburn 16–13, I knew they were good enough to play for the national championship, but they never got the chance. So this four-team playoff system could be a good thing and I think it is the right number of teams involved. I really don't think a 16-team playoff is feasible. It's not like basketball, where you can play a game every other day.

No matter what system we use, I want all of the BCS bowls (Sugar, Rose, Orange, and Fiesta) to remain relevant to college football.

Since I mentioned the Sugar Bowl, that loss to Michigan following the 2011 season still bothers me, and it is a good place to go over my views on officiating.

That wasn't a game that was officiated—or replayed—very well. I still think Danny Coale laid out and made an amazing touchdown catch, one that likely would have won the game for us in overtime.

I didn't know right after the play if he had caught it or not, but Danny was not one to lie to me. When he came to the sideline, I asked him if he caught it.

"Yeah, I think I had it," he said.

The reason I trusted him was I remembered back to the game against Duke in a similar situation when he said the same thing. The replay showed he caught it then. Then when I saw the replay of his

Sugar Bowl catch, it was a good catch to me. When I saw the film later, I knew it really was a great catch.

So how did a replay official overturn it? Well, I still don't have an answer. I never heard an explanation from the Pac-12 crew that had officiated the game.

Remember me getting on the officials before halftime of the 1993 Independence Bowl?

As the years have passed, I have tried not to make a habit of it. But sometimes, I just can't help myself.

To start the 2004 season, we played Southern Cal at FedEx Field in Washington, D.C., and the game was being called by an SEC crew. We were down by three points and completed a pass down to about the 5-yard line. The official on our side of the field called offensive pass interference. I had a good view of the play, which as a coach is not always the case. I was convinced it was an awful call and it wasn't that official's call in the first place. The guy who was in position to make the call didn't call anything.

As the guilty party walked up the sideline, I was standing right next to him and I let him have it for about the next three plays.

"How can you make that call?" I screamed at him. "I can't believe you made that call!"

Finally, he turned to me and in this big, deep Southern drawl, said, "Cooooach, if I were you, I would go back to cooooaching."

I told him, "Hey, the way you are calling the game, the way I coach isn't going to make one damn bit of difference!"

I quickly turned my back and walked away before he could throw the flag on me.

But the fact is, I don't get on them like I did when I was younger. In the old days, they had those split-crews; half of the officiating crew would be from our conference and the other half from the conference of the team we were playing. So they would try to out-do each other and I would be screaming at all of them, whether they were ours or theirs.

For the record, I will take this opportunity to apologize to all of them.

I think for the most part, they work very hard and they are honest, but they are going to make mistakes now and then. When they do, I realize they are not intentional mistakes. I do think TV and replay helps keep them honest, even though that Sugar Bowl experience still leaves a sour taste in my mouth.

As far as my colleagues, I can honestly say I respect most all of them and get along with them very well. I think most every man in the coaching profession is honorable and has the student-athlete's best interests in mind.

I am probably closest to Mack and Wake Forest's Jim Grobe. I think we share a lot of the same values, such as how we treat people. They coach their teams to play within the rules and do a good job teaching discipline. I have a tremendous amount of respect for both of them.

Mack will call me when he is checking the background on a potential new assistant coach and I will do the same. A few years ago, he was changing offensive coordinators and wanted to know about Bryan Harsin over at Boise State, because we had played them in the 2010 opener. I gave him high marks and he ended up hiring the guy.

I respect his opinion and he respects mine. When the North Carolina situation was happening with me in 2000, I called to get his opinion, since he had coached there for 10 years before getting the Texas job. He was very flattering toward North Carolina.

Another coach I really liked was West Virginia's Don Nehlen, who retired a while ago. We always got along well, despite the intense nature of that rivalry among our fans. Jimmye Laycock and I have been buddies a long, long time. I've always admired what he has done at

William & Mary, and of course, Ralph and I have been close friends dating back to our days as GAs at Maryland in 1972.

There really aren't many bad coaches these days. I know if you are not a good coach, you won't last very long. There are no 2–8–1 survivors anymore. Really though, 15 years ago, I thought we could out-coach certain people, but not much anymore.

As far as other coaches I don't know well, but I admire, I really think Butch Jones, now at Tennessee, has the right stuff. As far as the NFL, Pittsburgh's Mike Tomlin is impressive to me. I love his demeanor and how he handles people. Both Harbaugh brothers—Jim and John—obviously are great coaches. So is Bruce Arians, a friend who recently got the Arizona Cardinals job.

You know who else impresses me? Virginia basketball coach Tony Bennett. I am a Hokie through and through, but I like the way he handles himself and how he coaches his team. When it comes to hoops, my buddy Mike Brey has done a remarkable job resurrecting the Notre Dame program.

No matter what happens on or off the field, I really try to go out of my way not to say anything about another coach that may come off as sour grapes, or complain about the way another coach coaches his team. I did break that rule a few years ago, however.

In a 28–23 loss to Georgia Tech in 2009, I made a public statement about what I thought was an illegal block on their final touchdown. I think a few of our guys had been getting chop-blocked—an illegal play where one blocker engages a defender and then a second blocker hits that defender low at the same time. The NCAA and the NFL have made this block illegal because it leads to injury.

Well, Georgia Tech had gotten away with a few during that game and I said something to the media after the game. Their slot receivers were also cutting our defensive backs low from the blind side and that can always lead to injury. They did it to Kam Chancellor, a guy who now has a nice pro career going; fortunately he didn't get hurt on the play.

I have no problem with blocking below the waist as long as the defender can see it coming. It is very dangerous when the defensive back is looking somewhere else and he gets cut from the blind side and can't protect himself.

My comments didn't sit too well with Georgia Tech coach Paul Johnson, who told the media, "They got out-schemed. So it's illegal to out-scheme them, I guess. We blocked them the same way we blocked them a year ago and they weren't complaining when they won."

Paul and I talked it over that week and I admitted I was mistaken on their final touchdown. I looked at the tape and saw that was a good block, but the illegal blocks had occurred earlier in the game. He said they didn't coach it or intentionally do it. His argument to me was that the offensive guard, who was engaged with the defensive tackle, was trying to get through to get to the linebacker but he was being held up by our defensive tackle. Then the center would cut the defensive tackle at the same time since that was his assignment. It was happening because they were playing within their offensive scheme.

Anyway, Paul and I have been good since that disagreement and I also think our ACC officials do a good job of calling it.

I really can't name many in our profession whom I dislike. I get to see another side of most of the coaches during the annual Nike trip. For many years, Nike CEO Phil Knight has sponsored an annual trip for all of the head coaches whose schools use his brand of shoes and equipment. He hosts it in February in Hawaii, the Caribbean, Mexico, or some other exotic place.

The coaches and their wives get a chance to mingle and know each other, without the competitive aspect of trying to out-recruit or out-coach the other guy. When we start hanging around each other on the golf course or at the beach or over dinner, it's just natural that our associations grow much stronger.

Anyway, the first one we ever attended was in Cabo San Lucas, Mexico, many years ago. As Cheryl and I changed airplanes in San Diego, we bumped into Joe and Sue Paterno. Now, I have to be honest right here: what I knew about Joe was what I always heard from the Maryland coaches back in 1972. They thought he was a used-car salesman. Of course, he was beating them pretty good every year— on the field and in recruiting. He had that Brooklyn accent and the rolled-up pants and I just didn't know him personally.

Beginning with that meeting in the airport that day, Joe and Sue couldn't have been nicer to us. They took us under their wing and treated us great during that whole trip. I remember coming back from that trip, we sat at the airport with Joe and Sue and Bobby Bowden and his wife, Ann. It really hit me that I was sitting with two guys who have won their share of ballgames.

After I spent a little time around Joe, I thought he had a lot of common sense. He wasn't a used-car salesman at all and I had him all wrong. He had a comical side about him and he was very funny at times. The one thing about Joe—he never played golf. So when all the other coaches would head off to the golf course, Joe would sit back at the pool or beach and hang around all the ladies, or be off somewhere quiet reading one of his history books.

One day, we headed off to golf and I saw Joe relaxing on the beach. He would have his toes in the sand while we would be grinding over four-foot putts.

I told one of the other coaches, "He's probably a lot smarter than all of us."

Everybody has an opinion of the Jerry Sandusky scandal that hit Penn State, something that has dominated the headlines in recent years. I didn't know Sandusky when he coached, so all I can go by is my first-hand experience with Joe.

I can understand Joe, at his age and from his generation, not quite understanding the severity of what was happening there with Sandusky. I really can. To men of his age, that is not a common thing. Now, if he covered anything up as the Freeh Report suggested—and we may never know that—that is a different story.

The only thing I could not understand was letting Sandusky back into their football facility, if he supposedly did those things. He should have been turned in, but I don't have any answers for that. I like to think I would know how to respond and do the right thing. But I know that making the right decision in hindsight is always easy. "What we should have done is…." Everybody can get that one right.

Even today, there seem to be two sides to that story as far as Joe's actions or lack of action. The Paterno family issued a new report in February 2013 and it gave another side of the story.

Following the 2010 season, the Maxwell Club presented me with the inaugural Joseph V. Paterno Award. It was intended to be given to the head coach "who best exemplified Coach Paterno's dedication to the development of student-athletes and the advancement of the university beyond just athletics."

I sat with Joe that night at the banquet in Atlantic City and I thought he was aging. Within a year, the scandal hit and Penn State fired him. Then the Maxwell Club took his name off the trophy, before it was even awarded the second year, meaning I have the only one they ever issued.

I removed that award from my office and placed it in storage later, thinking then that was just the proper thing to do. The media asked me about it the day at the ACC meetings, and I admitted that it was no longer on display. I am still not sure removing it was the right thing to do, either. This thing was so complicated and I don't know all the facts, so I felt like I was between a rock and a hard place. If I supported Joe and his legacy, it wasn't the politically correct thing to do as far as the media and public were concerned. And yet, I do not know if he knew about this and covered it up. Maybe we'll never know definitely one way or the other. The bottom line was that I considered him a friend.

One of my lasting memories of him, and they brought this up at his funeral, was the time he got up on stage at a Nike convention and sang "Wild Thing." I will always remember that night with a smile.

The whole thing at Penn State just really made me sad. It hurt me. But no matter what, you will never hear Frank Beamer say a bad thing about Joe Paterno. Never. He meant a lot to me and I will miss him.

Cheryl wrote a letter to Sue and we sent flowers when he died in January of 2012. I know Cheryl called her later and talked a bit. Then in January the following year, I picked up the phone at home one day—and I never answer the phone at home—and it was Sue, asking me to consider hiring Bill Kenney, a coach who had been on Joe's staff for years. I told her I was working on my staff openings, but eventually I went in another direction.

Anyway, it was great hearing her voice again.

The NCAA stepped in and hit Penn State's football program with historic sanctions, including a four-year bowl ban and a $60 million fine. They also took away 112 of Joe's wins from 1998 through 2011, dropping him in the record book from first on the all-time wins list to fourth.

I thought that the punishment was very harsh. The NCAA kind of got into a different category than what it was used to overseeing. I think it is somewhat questionable they went in that direction, and I think it's not wrong to question their jurisdiction in this. Maybe they could have penalized Penn State with a fine, but those sanctions will penalize players and coaches who came to the school after these incidents occurred for years to come. I can speak of that from first-hand knowledge.

I guess people just have to choose which side of that mess to believe.

That being said, I agree with what NCAA president Mark Emmert is doing otherwise. If a rule is broken, we need a system where the punishment is handed out quicker and more severe than it has been in past years. That could eliminate some of the cheating. I am totally in line with that.

And that appears to be where we are headed.

It appears to me the slaps on the wrist for NCAA violations are a thing of the past.

I do want to say this: there are plenty of reasons college football is the best game going. It is more popular than ever. Many of the stadiums, like ours, are filled every Saturday and TV ratings are increasing each year.

What everybody else needs to do now is find a way to catch up to the SEC. We are all behind them and we know that. That area in the southeastern United States is just perfect for football. There are a lot of great recruits close by and I think they have a big advantage geographically. They all have big and rabid fan bases to go with it. It is the perfect mix in which to build a dynasty.

Now that I've said that, I never thought I would see one school win championships in three out of four years as Alabama has done recently. That is pretty impressive in the age of 85-scholarship limits.

When it comes to conference realignment, it has been a very fluid situation in recent years. I hated to see Maryland leave the ACC for the Big Ten. It didn't make sense to me. I really don't think it will have a great impact on the ACC. I am sure the financials were one reason for Maryland. Of course, we left the Big East for the ACC years ago, but I just believe geography should have a lot to do with conference affiliation. And we fit geographically with the ACC.

As far as the ACC, I think this conference is strong—very strong. I think the additions that we made have helped us. Notre Dame certainly will help us. Louisville has strong basketball and football programs.

I just wish we would start playing a little better in those big non-conference games and in bowls.

Facility-wise and recruiting-wise, the ACC improves every year. I know we have a pretty remarkable record of putting guys in the NFL, and having first-round picks, but we just haven't won enough outside of our league. Everybody is chasing the SEC and Alabama right now.

There has been talk in recent years of Florida State leaving for the SEC, but I think it is in FSU's best interests to stay put. People in our league may sometimes grumble about North Carolina having too much power, but I tell them, "Hey, go talk to the Big 12 people and see what they think about Texas."

And I say that knowing Mack Brown is one of my good friends.

We still don't know when this conference expansion is going to end and it's tough to keep track of it all.

I admit I liked it the way things were.

But then again, I am an old-school guy.

21

What's Next?

When we left New Orleans on the morning of January 4, 2012, I felt terrible.

Downright miserable.

We had lost the Sugar Bowl to Michigan 23–20 in overtime the previous night in a game we never should have lost. What would have been a winning touchdown catch by Danny Coale had been overturned by replay officials for some reason. We had a third-and-1 and jumped offside at a crucial moment. There was no doubt in my mind we were about to score a touchdown in a play or two if we hadn't committed that penalty. In the first possession of overtime, if our running back makes the right read, he hits his head on the goal post and we probably win the game. We had out-gained Michigan. And I am the first to admit that we had made some coaching mistakes, too.

278

I also felt that we let the Atlantic Coast Conference down. The conference really needed to win a Bowl Championship Series bowl. We left town with a 1–5 record in BCS games and were being reminded of it daily. When I thought of all those things, I can't think of a loss that was tougher to swallow—other than the 2000 Sugar Bowl, of course.

Add all that up and you know why I was feeling so down.

And on top of that, I was fat.

After that game, I was not feeling good at all. That reversal of Danny's remarkable, should-have-been-touchdown catch wasn't the only reason. I was simply overweight. I was up to almost 210 pounds and when I bent over to tie my shoes, I almost could not catch my breath.

I had let my health go and I had to do something about it. In the past, I think I always did what was needed. When I had some heart problems, I had stopped smoking.

Casey's wedding was coming up that summer. I didn't want to be some fat guy standing there at the head of the aisle, giving away my daughter on the biggest day of her life.

I decided to cut out the bread, pasta, snacks, and sugars (I am not a big dessert guy anyway, so that was fine with me) and the weight just started dropping off.

I used to be a guy who could get into a bowl of potato chips at night and eat the whole bag. No more. Now I eat fruit and vegetables and very few snacks. I still may have a glass of Johnny Walker Black once in a while, but I factor in those calories and eliminate something else to accommodate for it.

Now I am down to about 180 pounds and feeling so much better. I feel healthy again. I get my cholesterol checked regularly. I also have been walking around campus for exercise almost daily and I can honestly say, "I will never be fat again."

Even though I lost weight and was feeling much better, I encountered another serious problem the day before camp started for the 2012 season. I always underwent a full physical in Georgia at Dr. Bob Cowles' clinic, usually during the first week we are down there each summer.

Well during my checkup in 2009, the doctor noticed something on the left side of my neck while he was testing my arteries. He said, "There's something there and we need to keep an eye on it."

I had forgotten about it over those three years. I'd been having some congestion in my chest in the summer of 2012 and my doctor, as well as our team doctor, Gunnar Brolinson, sent me to an ear, nose, and throat doctor to get it checked out. He immediately noticed something in that artery of my neck and told me, "We really need to get this checked out further."

Dr. Brolinson had connections at the Cleveland Clinic, so he sent me there.

I left Blacksburg thinking this was no big deal, but when I got to Cleveland, the doctor there said, "You have some major blockage in your carotid artery. It's a good thing you got in here when you did."

When they told me that, and then they made me sign all those papers such as a living will, I knew it was serious. They told me I could have had a major stroke if they hadn't caught this problem in time, and they really caught it just by chance.

Doctor Sunita D. Srivastava performed the surgery, which lasted several hours, on July 26, just a few days before our summer camp was to begin, and I spent the night in the hospital. They discharged me the next day, but wouldn't let me fly home, so Cheryl and I spent the next night in a hotel. Then they also hit me with the news that I shouldn't return to work for six weeks. Well, that would have interfered with the start of training camp, so I wasn't going to follow those doctor's orders. I couldn't miss any practices, so John got me a stool to sit on in the tower during practice.

I never mentioned anything about it publicly.

The weird thing is that they used part of a cow testicle as a bonding agent inside my neck.

When I got back to the office following the surgery, I made the mistake of mentioning that fact to John.

"You're not going to start mooing, are you?" he asked.

Now I have a small scar down the left side of my neck. Sunita did such a great job with the surgery that I sent her a signed football. "We award footballs for 'outstanding performance.' This football is for your outstanding performance—Frank Beamer."

When I went back for my checkup a month later, she told me that football made her the envy of all the doctors there.

If only the 2012 season had gone as well. Seven-and-six is nothing like 2–8–1, but it made for many sleepless nights.

Ralph, who lives in Charleston now, called me after the season and asked, "You know what the problem was this season, don't you?"

"What?" I asked seriously, thinking Ralph had some good coaching insight for me.

"You lost all that weight!" he joked. "You were much better as a fat coach!"

Losing is never funny, but I had to laugh at that one.

Despite our hiccup in 2012, I believe the future is very bright with our program. Jim Weaver came to me a few years ago with the idea of upgrading our future schedules and I agreed with what he wanted to do: schedule one big-time BCS program per season for our fans' sake.

Now our future schedules will be a much more attractive, albeit a bit tougher. We will play Alabama, Ohio State twice, and Wisconsin twice, before Notre Dame comes onto the schedule in ACC conference play in the coming years. I always said that you have to be careful not to over-schedule, like what the administration did those first few years I was here. But it is always more exciting for our players and fans when we playing big-time opponents like this, as opposed to those teams our fans think we should beat easily.

And if our players didn't want to play in these big games, I would worry about them.

There's no question having these games on the schedule will help us in recruiting, too, because every kid wants to play in those games. If we have success against these teams, we have done something significant. We would hate to be undefeated at the end of the year and have the critics pointing out that we didn't play one team with much name recognition.

Besides, nothing great occurs without opportunity.

Playing the Alabamas, Ohio States, Wisconsins, and Notre Dames is great for Virginia Tech's profile and our fans, but it will make it a bit tougher to accomplish what every Hokie fan dreams of....

If you walked into our football building, you would see top-notch facilities and a beautiful new locker room and a gigantic weight room that is among the best in the country. We have spent millions to upgrade our facilities and I really believe Virginia Tech is thought of differently than it was 20 years ago. When I think of other top programs, Notre Dame has always been Notre Dame. Same goes for Alabama and Michigan. But Virginia Tech is not the same Virginia Tech it was 25 years ago. We've improved everything, including the facilities, the stadium, and the size of our alumni and fan base.

If you walked straight ahead from the lobby, you would see our trophy room. Along the walls are hundreds of trophies, from wins in the Sugar Bowl, Gator Bowl and Orange Bowl as well as our ACC Championship trophies. There are tributes and jerseys from past players such as Frankie Loria, Bruce Smith, Jim Pyne, Jake Grove, Cornell Brown, Michael Vick, and Corey Moore.

You would see an empty glass case in the middle of the trophy room, with an inscription that reads: "Future spot of the national championship trophy. Go Hokies!"

When my blinds are open, I can see that empty case from my office.

I have no problem with that case being there, because it is a goal we don't want to run from. But I am reminded often by some critics that it is empty. When we fill it, the picture here will be complete.

We have to be really good and really fortunate in the same season to win it. The year we played for it and lost, we were good and fortunate, such as kicking that field goal to beat West Virginia when we were behind and at our own 15-yard line with under a minute remaining.

Maybe if we ever win one, it would be easier for me to watch the one we lost. But things have to fall into place perfectly. How we schedule and who we schedule plays a part. We've been right up there. We've gone to BCS bowls in four of the last six years and we have gone to 20 straight bowls overall, as of the end of the 2012 season.

I've always felt if we stay up there knocking on the door enough times, eventually we will get a chance to knock the door down.

I would like to do it just for our fans. We have devoted, caring fans who know the game and know when to be loud. We've had several years of consecutive sellouts at Lane Stadium, which is as loud as any place I've been. To be here during the stadium expansion and having our new practice fields here, I take a sense of pride in that. When they start the first note of "Enter Sandman" and everybody is jumping up and down, I can't help but have a smile on my face.

As I look back on my time here, there is no better word to describe this university than "family." From the first time I saw a game at the old Miles Stadium with my Uncle Sharrell, who was an alumnus, the university became a large part of my own family. I guess that's the overriding reason I never left here.

Not only did my brother Barnett and I graduate from here, so did both of my kids. So did more than 30 of my cousins. It's just a special place for me and for all of my family.

That's why we were all hurting so badly on April 16, 2007.

Maybe this football team and this program played a small part in a healing process for a community and a university that suffered a terrible tragedy. Maybe we made them smile and laugh and celebrate that next fall at a time when they needed it most. I know that nothing we did could ever bring back the people we lost, but maybe we helped the survivors, the victims' families, and the entire community. I don't know if I am the person to answer that question, but I hope it is true.

Cheryl and I not only love Virginia Tech, we have always loved living in the town of Blacksburg. I haven't spent much time in too many other college towns, other than flying in and out to play a football game, but I can't imagine a better place than Blacksburg. I think *USA Today* recently had a poll and it was named "the number one college football town in America."

I would agree.

Most important, it is home.

I've always known how fortunate I am to do this for a living and make the money I make. To live this life I have, I never take it for granted for one second. I do get asked when I might retire from coaching. I usually joke, "As long as I have a good quarterback and my health is okay, I am good to go."

Seriously, all I can say is that as long as I feel good and feel capable, then I hope to coach at Virginia Tech. I can tell you one thing: I never get bored with this job. In so many other jobs, you do the same thing Monday, Tuesday, Wednesday, or whatever day it is. In the football business, not only is each day of the week completely different, but so are the seasons of the year. And by the time August rolls around,

I put away the golf clubs and get my motor going. I am focused and I am ready for another season.

Each season is a new challenge. Can we get the chemistry right on this team? Can we get everybody playing together for one goal? That challenge gets me going. And I like being around our kids. They keep me young in a lot of ways.

I admit I do take losses harder than ever. I have a hard time getting over them and I don't like that part of it. I don't like the Internet and talk shows and hearing people's opinions how we're doing things all wrong, not that I ever did. That part has worn on me over the years.

Somebody prominent recently asked me about potentially running for office some day and I politely told him that wouldn't interest me. I get all the problems I want to solve with this job. At one time I thought that politics might interest me, but I don't see much progress being made in Washington no matter how good some politicians are. And I would want to feel like I could make a difference.

Even if Virginia Tech never wins a national championship while I am its coach, I like to think we accomplished something even more important in the big scope of life. We made a difference here. We helped develop hundreds of young boys into men and helped them get a college education so they could better their lives. I think we did it the right way too, teaching them how to treat people and respect everyone along the way.

We never took short cuts or cheated the rules or played unfair, on or off the field.

So when it is all said and done, I believe that how other people feel about how we ran the program and how they feel about us as coaches and players will be more important than how many national titles we won or didn't win.

The wins and all that have always been nice, but the biggest question for me was, "How did we affect people's lives?"

And, "What did they think of us as people, not just as football coaches?"

Kids like Waverly Jackson make it all worthwhile. He came here from a small school in southeast Virginia and had a learning disability. He never missed class. He always sat in the front row. He got his degree and now he's a high school football coach in Florida. He never would have gone to college without the game of football.

There are many more like him, kids who entered this football program when they otherwise wouldn't have gone to college. They come out the other side four or five years later with a degree and a bright future and that trumps any satisfaction of winning football games. We didn't develop only good football players. We developed great people.

Those cases prove what I always tell our coaches: "These kids aren't here for us; we're here for them."

Several years ago, we had a girls basketball player at Virginia Tech by the name of Rayna DuBose. She came down with meningitis and they had to amputate all of her limbs. She came back to school and this is what she told the media: "It may be hard for other people to understand, but being an amputee is a great thing, because it has presented me with so many new opportunities in my new life. I always thought I would be a professional basketball player, but my priorities have changed. I could never say that I actually loved something before, so I wanted to find something I love. Now I love to talk. I love kids. I love to travel. I love other people. I love life, basically, and I really believe my life was meant to help others."

I would never compare my childhood burns to what Rayna has gone through, but I can relate to her words and her attitude. My getting burned and having all of those surgeries taught me a lifelong lesson, because I discovered there were people in the hospital a lot worse off than I was. That stuck with me. Not only did it help me later when we were struggling those first six years to win games, but maybe I was meant to teach kids something about football and the game of life.

Not that all of our players needed us to guide them through life.

I have seen so many kids come through here and do the right things from the moment they stepped on campus until the day they were handed a college diploma. Take Cody Grimm, for example. Cody was a walk-on without one scholarship offer. He became a great linebacker who led the team in tackles in 2009 and was named to a few All-American teams. He loved to play the game, he was a good student, he had fun, he was a leader, the guys looked up to him, and he never had a bad day. He was a Virginia Tech–type of guy.

Guys like Cody, and many others like him, have made my job fun and rewarding.

I am not one to point to how many wins we've had and all that, but our record on the football field makes me very proud. It's a tough business to stay in as long as I have and to now be at the head of the active group in career wins. It's certainly something I never thought of when I started out coaching as a graduate assistant at Maryland five decades ago.

Bryan Stinespring told me the other day, "You're the same guy when we played for the national championship as you were when we were 2–8–1."

That matters to me more. It matters that I treat people the same way today as I did back then. It matters that my players feel the same way about me.

What I think is important is that it's not awkward at the end of my career here, whenever the end is. I think I'll know exactly the right time for me to finish up at Virginia Tech. I think so much of this place, this university, and this community that has been so good to me. I will know when the time is right. I am well aware that it is possible to stay around too long.

When that time comes, when I decide to retire, it also will be Jim Weaver's decision and the president's decision. We'll take care of it together when the time gets here.

A few years ago, we went back to Murray, Kentucky, to attend a wedding and I said, "Cheryl, it's been 25 years since we lived here. Twenty-five years!"

Now even a few more have gone by.

I guess it's true what they say: "When you're enjoying life, time really does fly by."

Being in this business, I really don't take the time on a daily basis to reflect on my life and I guess that's probably true for most people. Who has the time? We go from training camp to the season to recruiting to planning our recruiting for the following year. Then we take a little time off and August is upon us again. In fact, recruiting is pretty much a 365-day-a-year job, even with the dead periods the NCAA mandates. If we are not meeting with a recruit, we may be evaluating recruits on watching film or in meetings. So there is little time to sit around and smell the roses, as they say. Maybe someday when I am through coaching....

If I did take the time to reflect, I know how lucky I've been. I grew up down the road in Fancy Gap with wonderful, caring parents and a great brother and sisters, came here as a player and got to play, had great teammates who became lifelong friends and then was named team captain for my senior year, got married to a wonderful girl, had two wonderful kids, and then it worked out that every move I made in my career—and more importantly the ones I didn't make—worked out just right and led me back home, where I've been for more than 25 years.

Just to think that when I was a boy I used to come over to Blacksburg with my uncle and see guys like Bobby Schweickert and Carroll Dale out there on the field and then to get a scholarship to come back here for college. And to sit on that hill over there at Blacksburg High after that first freshman game in which I didn't play, wondering if I was good enough to play here and thinking maybe I should go somewhere else. Then to leave teaching math behind to get into coaching and eventually get the chance to come back here and be the head coach, and watching this program turn around, seeing the facilities that we've built, enjoying every sold-out Saturday in Lane Stadium....

Now I sit in my office overlooking the stadium almost 50 years later. And I know I'm a fortunate guy. I think the story of my life also says something about working hard and treating people right. Not a coach in the world would survive a 2–8–1 record today, but I had good people working around me and above me who could see the big picture and knew I was doing the best I could. I am thankful for that every day, too.

Things sure have worked out for me. I'm very thankful for everything I've received. Nobody knows what the future will be. I surely don't. But I just hope it will be as good as the past has been. It's been a wonderful ride so far.

I've accomplished some things and fallen short on others. I hope I have made an impact. I hope I have affected people's lives in a positive way. I've seen my share of pain and heartache and I've also experienced joy and happiness.

My brother, Barnett, once told a reporter that I dreamed bigger dreams than the others. I really don't know if that's true.

I do know this: The youngest son of Raymond and Herma Beamer couldn't have dreamed of a better life.

Acknowledgments

I want to thank all of the assistant coaches, administrators, and support personnel of the Virginia Tech football program, past and present, who aided me with their time, thoughtful contributions and consistent generosity. In writing this book with the patriarch of the program, Frank Beamer, I developed a deeper understanding of how an entire major college athletic program should be regarded as one large family.

I would especially like to thank Dr. John Ballein, the Hokies' director of football operations. John approaches his position not as a job, rather as a passion. He handles his duties with the utmost attention to detail and thoughtfulness and he was extremely invaluable in providing us with the resources to write this book. Many thanks go to Coach Beamer's executive secretary, Diana Clark, and to Gary Long, who can edit copy with the best of them.

Also, I want to thank Bob Knight, a basketball coaching legend, who graciously wanted to write the foreword for the autobiography of a football coach.

That may tell you something about Frank Beamer.

In writing about football for more than 30 years, I've worked with dozens of coaches across the country, including some legends of the game past and present. Thus, I like to think I can offer some perspective on a highly pressurized profession where wins and championships are the bottom line.

To that, I can say no coach has been as unaffected by success as the Virginia Tech head coach.

He is not only a winner in the game of football, but a champion in the game of life. He is not only a good football coach, but a great person, father, grandfather, and husband. Simply put, you will not find a nicer man in any profession. It has often been said that good things happen to good people. Accordingly, Coach Beamer is now the longest-tenured and winningest head coach in major college football. And if the gods of this great game owe anyone a national championship season in exchange for a lifetime of good deeds, then they owe one to him.

Someday when he retires from coaching football, giving him more time for his beloved hobby, it would only be appropriate if he had to remove a gaudy national title ring to slip on his golf glove.

Show me a living legend who balances the competitiveness it takes to succeed with a non-existent ego and a heart made of gold, and I will show you Frank Beamer.

Coach Beamer, those unique qualities, as well as the countless hours you offered reliving your life, made participating in this project with you a privilege.

—Jeff Snook

About the Authors

Frank Beamer, who received a bachelor's degree from Virginia Tech in 1969 and a master's degree from Radford University in 1972, is the winningest and longest-tenured head coach in major college football. During 32 seasons as a head coach, including 26 seasons at Virginia Tech, he has a 258–127–4 record. Beamer has coached the Hokies to wins in the Independence, Music City, Gator, Sugar, and Orange Bowls. He and his wife, Cheryl, reside in Blacksburg, Virginia, and are the parents of Shane Beamer and Casey Prater.

Jeff Snook, a 1982 graduate of The Ohio State University School of Journalism, is a freelance writer who has written 11 books on college football. A native of Ashland, Ohio, he resides in Boynton Beach, Florida, with his wife, Amy, and children, Savanna and Dillon.